Making and Breaking States in Africa

...Making and Breaking States in Africa..........

THE SOMALI EXPERIENCE

I.M.Lewis

The Red Sea Press, Inc.
Publishers & Distributors of Third World Books

P. O. Box 1892   P. O. Box 48
Trenton, NJ 08607   Asmara, ERITREA

The Red Sea Press, Inc.
Publishers & Distributors of Third World Books

P. O. Box 1892  P. O. Box 48
Trenton, NJ 08607 Asmara, ERITREA

Book design: Saverance Publishing Services
Cover design: Ashraful Haque

Library of Congress Cataloging-in-Publication Data

Lewis, I. M.
  Making and breaking states in Africa : the Somali experience / I.M. Lewis.
    p. cm.
  Includes index.
  ISBN 1-56902-289-5 (hard cover) -- ISBN 1-56902-290-9 (pbk.)
  1. Somalia--Politics and government--1960-1991. 2. Somalia--Politics and government--1991- 3. Nation-building--Somalia. 4. Failed states--Somalia. I. Title.
  DT407.L48 2010
  967.7305--dc22

                                        2010019436

Table of Contents

Acknowledgements

Chapter One was originally published as "Integration in the Somali Republic" reprinted from A. Hazlewood (ed.) African Integration and Disintegration, Oxford: University Press, 1967/pp.251-284.

Chapter Two is a lightly edited version of "The Politics of the 1969 Somali coup", Journal of Modern African Studies, 1972, pp.383-408.

Chapter Three is based on "Kim Il-Sung in Somalia: The End of Tribalism?" originally published in W.A. Shack and P.S. Cohen (eds.), Politics in Leadership Oxford: Oxford University Press, 1979.

Chapter Four "A Controversial Conference: Mengistu and His Friends in Europe", is from Les Orientalists sont des aventuries: Guirlande offerte a Joseph Tubiana, reunis Paris Alain Rouaud Sepia, 1999, pp.199-202.

Chapter Five is based on "Clan Conflict and Ethnicity in Somalia: Humanitarian Intervention in a Stateless Society", published in D. Turton (ed.), War and Ethnicity, Global connections and Local Violence. San Marino, University of Rochester Press, 1997, pp.179-201.

Chapter Six is an edited version of "Making Peace in Somaliland", Cahiers d'Etudes africaines, 146, XXXVII-2, 1997, pp.349-377 written jointly with my colleague and friend the late Ahmed Yusuf Farah. He carried out the pioneering field research on which it is based.

Chapter Seven is drawn from "Recycling Somalia from the Scrap Merchants of Mogadishu", Ms. Rome, Ministry of foreign Affairs, 2000.

Chapter Eight is a revised version of "Visible and Invisible Differences: The Somali Paradox" Africa, 2001 vol. 74 No 4.

Chapter Nine is an edited Personal Interview with Professor Charles Geshekter, originally published in BILHAAN, International Journal of Somali Studies, vol. 1, 2001, pp.53-86.

Dedication

This book is dedicated to the memory of my colleague Dr Ahmed Yusuf Farah, a young Somali social anthropologist who was a brilliant field worker and researcher. Ahmed died tragically of cancer in 2002 in Kenya. His brief career included the publication of the first professional monograph on the Somali production of myrrh and frankincense and numerous studies of Somali peace-making and the sociology of Somali refugee camps. All his work was marked by a high caliber of direct observation and analysis rarely equaled in the research of his contemporaries. As can be seen in Chapter Six below (of which he was the primary author), his death represents a major loss to Horn of Africa scholarship where he was destined to be a major figure. Ahmed's self-effacing modesty makes his loss all the more bitter.

Note on Somali Orthography

The orthography followed in this book follows standard Somali usage, without, however indicating long vowels or the Arabic letter *áyn* written as 'c' in the current Somali script. Somalis will have no difficulty reading and understanding our text and will know how to pronounce it correctly. For English speakers generally, the presentation here will not greatly distort the spoken sound and should avoid unnecessary linguistic puzzles.

Introduction

✦

In the Horn of Africa, the most striking feature of the political landscape at the start of the twenty-first century was the parallel existence of a dysfunctional lapsed state, "Somalia", still internationally recognized, side by side with an unrecognized but fully functional state, "Somaliland". The latter, a former British Protectorate, had reasserted its independence after the collapse in 1990 of Somalia's last functioning government, the despotic regime of the military dictator General Mohamed Siyad Barre. The rest of Somalia then became effectively a war zone without government.

The consequent threat to order in this inflammable Muslim area on the edge of Christian Ethiopia, with potential repercussions in Kenya, prompted a string of high-profile and extremely expensive international peace conferences. Although these stretched over a period of more than fifteen years, the results were unimpressive. At best, they only managed to produce an ill-assorted succession of short-lived dysfunctional 'transitional' administrations, governments in name only—all persistently virtual rather than real. Real politics remained a monopoly of the anarchic warlords of rival lineages, fighting for power and resources in the increasingly derelict city of Mogadishu. This disjunction between fiction and reality, however, did not deter organizations such as the United Nations (UN), African Union (AU), Arab League, and most recently the European Union (EU) (egged on by Italy, Somalia's former colonial ruler) from hastening to bestow formal diplomatic status on the successive ephemeral outcomes of the long-drawn-out peace process—as it was so inaccurately and misleadingly presented.

Phantom Polities

The latest of these phantom polities was the so-called transitional federal government (TFG), cobbled together at great expense, over a period of two years in Kenya under the aegis of the Kenyan authorities and with strong involvement of EU and UN bureaucrats (see Chapter Seven). With rampant corruption, massive vote-buying, and exaggerated claims concerning the representative capacity of the various candidates—many of whom could not safely go back to the places from which they claimed to originate (and to represent)—a transitional assembly was eventually formed. This fractious body, notable for its colorful fist-fights, chose a provisional president in the shape of the Ethiopian favorite, Colonel Abdillahi Yusuf (formerly head of the semi autonomous north eastern Somali region of Puntland, based on the Mijerteyn and related Darod clans).

Having experienced their custodial hospitality during the years in which he fought as a guerrilla leader (or also known as a terrorist) against Siyad Barre, Abdillahi was no stranger to Ethiopia. Thanks to the largesse of his current Ethiopian backers, of all the candidates he was reputed to have been the most richly endowed with disposable electoral expenses. The resulting administration, with its cabinet of a prime minister and other ministers, moved back to Somalia in 2005 but not to the former capital, Mogadishu, which was considered too dangerous. Instead it settled first at Jowhar, on the Shebelle River about a hundred miles from Mogadishu, under the protection of a prominent local warlord; and when President Abdullahi fell out with him, moved to the provincial town of Baidoa, among the Digil Mirifle (Rahanwin) cultivators. The TFG, though now back on Somali soil, had marginalized itself geographically as well as politically.

Meanwhile, an unexpected force had entered the political scene in southern Somalia. This was the Union of Islamic Courts, an expanding association of puritanical, fundamentalist sheikhs and jurists. These religious leaders were mainly of the Habar Ghiddir (Hawiye) clan, linked doctrinally to the Saudi Wahabis. In a matter of months, they had extended their control over most of southern Somalia. In each locality they chased out the resident warlords, and with the support of local ulema, (religious leaders) set up Shariah courts from which their influence quickly spread to the neighboring regions. Moving steadily forward from district to district, in the course of a few months they had gained an impressively widespread following among the general public, which was exhausted by mistreatment at the hands of the warlords, who had made no contribution whatsoever to public well-being.

The so-called transitional federal government, existing mainly on handouts from EU and other sources, had likewise made no positive contribution to Somalia's governance and served largely as a loose cover for the continuing criminal activities of its warlord members who, although they might hold ministerial posts, remained largely independent. Other totally free-range warlords roamed at large outside Baidoa, preying on those who were too weak to defend themselves. They now enjoyed the clandestine support of the Central Intelligence Agency (CIA) and other sinister U.S. agencies, and were employed to search for terrorists whom the Americans believed to be hiding in the safe anonymity provided by the failed Somali state. The main activity of the TFG president was to attend international meetings where he sought publicity in the name of Somalia and further alms and arms. Like the warlords who dominated it, the key objective of the transitional regime was survival. There was, consequently, a striking contrast between the legitimacy bestowed outside Somalia on this ramshackle enterprise by the EU, UN, African Union and latterly the United States and the contemptuous disregard displayed toward it by the majority of the Somali population. This was a government for outsiders only, and not for those it purported to represent.

Here, as usual, in the treatment of Somali issues by out-siders, the latter's ill-informed assumptions and interpreta-tions of local events were remote from realities on the ground. These omnipotent foreign makers and shakers behaved, in a word, as though they were quite ignorant of, and totally indifferent to, what Somalis actually though and desired.

A Short-lived Islamic Revolution

The new Islamic authorities thus moved into a power vacuum in southern Somalia where, although not every-one welcomed their puritanical policies, they were seen, as indeed they were, the first organization to seize control from the warlords, instituting law and order, reestablishing basic social services, as well as repairing the shattered economy. For the first time in over fifteen years, ordinary men and women could move safely about in the streets of the capital, which had been cleaned up and repaired. Traders were no longer subject to unpredictable attack by thieves and other marauders; women were equally safe and no longer subject to casual rape. Mogadishu's airport and the main seaport, out of action for more than a decade, were restored in remarkably short order, and traffic returned to both very quickly. Prices of vital everyday foodstuffs began to fall. Attempts were made to force illegal occupants of properties to restore them to their original owners. Most audaciously of all, chewing the favorite Somali stimulant *qat* was banned. No Somali government had ever attempted to do this, and the proscrip-tion was generally extremely unpopular, especially because it was enforced with stringent Shariah penalties. Its positive effect, however, was to reduce the proportion of the family budget used by husbands to pay for their *qat* supplies, releas-ing much-needed cash to spend on food.

Overall, it seems that these positive reforms were gen-erally appreciated, although this could not be said of the puritanical measures taken to ban popular songs, television entertainment, and even watching football soccer matches on television. There was clearly not tolerance of Western secular tendencies and all this contrasted markedly with the traditionally relaxed attitudes of most Somali Muslims. Of course, this was not the first time puritanical currents associated with nationalism had developed in Somali Islam, and their recurrence at this time coincided with external reactions to the Union of Islamic Courts, seen as a branch of Al-Qaeda. It has to be said in this context that, before the emergence of the Union, several of its leading figures were suspected of being involved in the murder and attempted murder of European aid workers in Somaliland. Indeed, the head of the Courts Supreme Council, regarded in the United States as a terrorist, was in October 2006 on trial in absentia in Somaliland on suspicion of participating in these crimes. Other figures in the movement had similar reputations, although the majority espoused a less fiery style of Islam. These allusions to the wider struggle between Islam and its Western enemies strengthened the atmosphere of *jihad* that was being whipped up against America and Ethiopia (regarded as its local representative).

America's Proxy War— Ethiopian Intervention

By the end of 2006, Ethiopia had sent troops across the border into Somalia to defend Abdillahi Yusuf and the TFG in Baidoa and to prevent the ragtag Islamist forces from advancing further. Actually both sides had by then massed their forces ground Abdillahi's base at Baidoa and war seemed inevitable. The outcome, after a brief series of bitter battles in which there were heavy civilian as well as military casualties, was the defeat of the Islamists at the beginning of 2007, and their retreat southward through Kismayu into the Kenya borderlands. By this time they had shed thousands of *mujahidin*, most of whom appeared to have resumed their civilian roles and clothes, retaining as many of the weapons as they could carry on foot or by light truck. This unexpectedly rapid reconquest of southern Somalia essentially by regular

Ethiopian forces, in alliance with the nominal transitional president, Abdillahi Yusuf and his few-hundred-strong clan militia, demonstrated the vastly superior firepower of the Ethiopian military who were equipped with tanks, heavy artillery, and air cover. It also illustrated how excessively the jihadists had overvalued their own military capability—and their trust in God. Encouraged by the chaos and anarchy gripping the country under the ineffective authority of the transitional federal government, the Islamists had intervened to reestablish law and order. Now in a period of two weeks, they had been ousted (at least for the present) by the Ethiopians (who held some of their leaders responsible for earlier terrorist attacks in Addis Ababa). To the bewilderment of many observers, the transitional government, which had never governed and even feared to enter Mogadishu, was now faced with the challenge of actually ruling. Would it succeed?

The omens were not propitious: The TFG had previously shown no capacity for joint action and in the two and a half years since its formation had done nothing to consolidate its position. Apart from the ineptitude of senior ministers and the absence of administrative support, the TFG entered the world with a major structural fault. Its main figures were warlords, with well-established and profitable rackets, implemented by militias who owed their masters loyalty for a mixture of economic and kinship considerations (see Chapter Seven). Their recruitment had been directly encouraged and assisted by development officers and other officials of EU governments—including the United Kingdom. These amateur social engineers seem to have optimistically assumed that once the warlords had joined the Somali government, they would change their character and become patriotic citizens. There were, of course, no empirical grounds at all for supposing that participation in governance would transform these felons into devoted public servants.

What was perhaps most remarkable of all was the persistent belief of EU ministers and officials that their misguided enthusiasm for Abdillahi and his ministers would somehow modify the striking skepticism of the Somali public. European arrogance in these matters is, of course, well-known and seems to flourish in direct proportion to factual ignorance. Having spent so much public money on this highly dubious project, it would also presumably be difficult to admit defeat. It is likely, too, that part of the motivation of European governments reflected the hope that the reestablishment of the state of Somalia would reduce the flow of Somali refugees to Europe. The rise of the Islamists, in opposition to the transitionals, provided further European eagerness to support their failing brainchild and, from their point of view, brought the welcome addition of U.S. assistance to this project. Whether any of this was to the benefit of the ordinary Somali population was another matter and one that these and other external parties evidently found of little concern.

A Neglected Somali Democracy

In contrast, in the north, following their contribution to the overthrow of the dictator Siyad, the peoples of the former British Somaliland had slowly and painfully achieved a viable self-governing democracy, with regular elections and civil institutions. These achievements, so rare in Africa generally, are today the envy of the beleaguered southern Somalis, some of whom treat independent Somaliland like a phantom limb, as though it was still organically attached to their body politic. Somaliland is however indeed a separate real-life state, not a magical entity, and as such a sore thorn in the flesh of southerners who bitterly resent its success. But, in contrast to political realities, the northern state remains, at the time of writing, without formal diplomatic recognition.

Traditionally, Somali society is extremely uncentralized and individualistic to a point verging on anarchy. Effective political cohesion at the wider level cannot be taken for granted. It requires to be tenderly cradled and, above all, built up from the bottom. This is the slow peacemaking recipe, employing traditional methods, which has been applied so successfully in Somaliland, working upward gradually from small to larger local units, until finally embracing the whole state. It is undeniable that the obstacles posed by ruthless gangsters in the south are more formidable and deeply entrenched, but this slow, painstaking method has never been tried there and, alas, is probably now too late. The largely externally driven peace and reconstruction initiatives in the south have not seriously considered this home-grown model, being far more interested in high-profile theatrical displays, and in far too great a hurry to proceed intelligently from a slow and careful analysis of local Somali political realities. Those agencies involved did not have an appropriate technology of peacemaking for Somali conditions. It was sufficient to pour in money, and blindly repeat the mistakes and errors of preceding initiatives—even literally ten times over! This was short-termism gone mad.

This sad tale with its tragic outcome is of course all too familiar to those who objectively evaluate Third World development projects where blithely ignoring local knowledge, developers routinely make it a point of honor to disregard previous work, sparing no effort to achieve a fresh start, untrammeled by their predecessors. It also has to be said that as people whose traditional political culture is acutely uncentralized, Somalis have an unusually wide-ranging tolerance of the absence of centralized government. From a traditional perspective indeed, they could be said to need states less than states need them!

Of course, this does not excuse the warlords, who are the leading local protagonists of destruction, and whose rival petty ambitions sabotage all efforts to secure rational collaboration. Their main achievement has in many cases been the enslavement of local peoples belonging to weak groups without militias to protect them. Those fortunate enough to escape swell the tide of refugees desperately fleeing the country. Driven by narrow selfish interests and the total lack of anything approaching patriotism (or even often clan solidarity), these southern Somali warlords thus appeared incapable of combining to rescue the country they struggle to dominate, even when, as in April 2006, it was ravaged on an appalling scale by drought and famine.

This collection of essays is concerned with the sociopolitical background to this bizarre situation of an unrecognized state in the north with a recognized ex-state in the south. Whereas in Africa generally, national unity is usually threatened by ethnic divisions as well as by external neocolonial interest, in Somalia and Somaliland ethnic divisions are largely replaced by clan rivalries. Unlike those who belong to competing ethnic groups and usually speak different languages, the members of different Somali clans are not generally distinguished by obvious external markers or, save in a minority of cases, by linguistic and cultural distinctions. In the few instances where such ethnic differences do occur, they are usually assimilated to clan distinctions and so absorbed into the overriding genealogical idiom of Somali political culture. These invisible identities based on clans and clan segments are nevertheless extremely important in Somali politics and social life generally. This whole system has been imported lock, stock, and barrel and applied indiscriminately by respective European governments to asylum seekers, with the creation even in some cases of new clans.

As I reflect in Chapter Eight especially, the Somali concept of kinship (genealogically)-based identity is in fact similar to the European concept of race, although in the Somali case there are not systematic physical differences between clans (as are assumed in the European concept of race). As the following chapters seek to document in a variety of situations, the pervasive and enduring power of these remarkably adaptable loyalties is truly astonishing.

This is not to argue that Somali politics are actually biologically determined. What we are describing and analyzing is folk political biology, not real scientific biology. I Insist on this distinction between Somali folk biology and real biology because those who do not read my writings carefully often criticize me for claiming (as Somalis themselves believe) that Somali politics is actually biologically determined, and so treat Somalis as automatons, impelled by their genetic endowment to think and act as they do. Nothing could be further from my intentions. These, on the contrary, stress the impressive skills individual Somalis display in manipulating kinship to their own ends and, at the same time, utilizing whatever other levers come to hand.

With these issues in mind, this book brings together nine previous publications (here reedited to varying degrees). The chapters are arranged in historical order, and while all deal with political dynamics, their publication in this format seeks to highlight different phases in the wayward saga of modern Somali politics—pre and post-independence. I was able to observe most of these at first hand, and became more engaged in Somali affairs than is usual for a social anthropologist. This involvement is considered in Charles Geshekter's interview with me in 1999 which focuses upon the circumstances of my fieldwork (Chapter Nine).

In putting this material together I have revisited (intellectually) my own as well as Somalis' pasts, and this perhaps further justifies the inclusion of Geshekter's interview. At least it seems to me to help to complete the record. Like other anthropologists, what I have consistently sought is to record as accurately as I could determine what Somalis thought and how they acted. In the process in the late 1950s, when the nationalist movements were under way, I was not unaffected, and was flattered to be counted a supporter of Somali aspirations. At present it seems clear to me that these aspirations are again being fulfilled in Somaliland, so that the accusation of partiality that is sometimes leveled at me I take as a compliment, and only feel disheartened that the oppressed southern Somalis have still to regain their freedom—from internal and external interference and oppression.

One

A LOP-SIDED ALLIANCE: SOMALILAND AND SOMALIA FROM COLONIAL RULE TO SELF-GOVERNMENT

✦

Before their colonization in the second half of the nine-teenth century the Muslim Somali people formed a distinctive ethnic group, predominantly pastoralist in occupation and ethos. The majority spoke Somali, with a large enclave of cultivators and agropastoralists in the fertile land between the Shebelle and Juba Rivers watering southern Somalia, speaking the related Af May, more a separate language than a dialect. Both tongues belong to the Cushitic family, with other related languages spoken in the Horn of Africa (e.g, Afar [or Danakil], and Oromo). Scattered along the rivers and in some coastal towns, there were small groups of Swahili-speakers, mostly ex-slaves. However, the main non-Somali population, in the coastal trading towns (known collectively as Benadir, i.e, coastal region), were settler communities of largely Arab origin. Over the centuries, many of these were progressively Somalized and spoke locally distinct dialects. Typical were the Reer Hamar citizens of the oldest quarter of the capital, Mogadishu (Hamar in Somali), speaking what is known as Af Hamar. This dialect which is quite distinctive, shades into the standard southern Somali spoken more generally in the Benadir region, which extends south of Mogadishu to Kismayu, where the local fishing community known as Bajuni is related to and extends into northern coastal Swahili. The speech of the Bajuni is indeed very close to Swahili, of which it is usually regarded as a branch.

Despite these distinct cultural traditions, the powerful pastoralist cultural identity, to which the smaller agricultural and trading groups tended to assimilate, dominated and formed the basis of an overarching framework that I call "cultural nationalism". This, however, did not provide a centralized political organization that could appropriately be labeled a state. Although there were some small coastal sultanates, the dominant mode of local Somali politics was uncentralized and democratic in the extreme. Centralized states, in the full sense, only came later as a consequence of colonization and decolonization. Nevertheless, this ancient sense of ethnic identify, among a people speaking the same language, was enhanced by a long-standing and strong attachment to Islam, which with Arabic, offered another and international language enabling Somalis to participate in the wider Muslim world. This, indeed, was the first language to be taught and written: at this stage Somali remained oral.

Partition by Britain, France, Italy, and Ethiopia led not only—as so often elsewhere—to the dismemberment of a single people among a number of arbitrarily constituted colonies, each an ethnic patchwork, but also very significantly for the future to the formation of two self-contained and almost exclusively Somali territories. These were the British Somaliland Protectorate established in 1884-89 (following a round of Anglo-Somali treaties with individual clans), and, in the same year, the larger and more agriculturally promising Italian Somalia. At the same time, the more common African colonial situation was represented by the incorporation of other segments of the Somali nation in eastern Ethiopia (where the Ogaden region was named after the principal local Somali clan), and in Kenya, where the northeastern region was mainly populated by Somalis. French Somaliland (the *Cote des Somalis*, established effectively in 1889) actually also included the equally Cushitic Afar (or Danakil) pastoralists (both populations extending into Ethiopia) and competing for grazing and water in this extremely barren region of the Horn of Africa. Although both are Sunni Muslims and sometimes intermarry conflict has inevitably dominated their relations. At independence in 1977, they nevertheless adopted the neutral name of their capital and principal port and called the new state the Republic of Djibouti.

This multiple experience of alien rule, by non-Muslim people regarded by Somalis as heathen (*gaal*), served to quicken and intensify the deeply engrained Somali consciousness of cultural exclusiveness and identity, and helped to promote its gradual transformation into a vigorous political force. While in other parts of the continent newly independent states with polyglot and heterogeneous tribal populations strove to achieve national integration and, in effect, sought to transform themselves into nations, the pan-Somali movement aspired to extend the national boundaries to encompass the whole Somali nation. The union of British Somaliland with ex-Italian Somalia at independence in 1960 to form the Somali Republic (population c. 2,250,000 in 1960) was seen as a step in this direction. It left outside those Somali communities in the contiguous areas of French Somaliland, Ethiopia (with a Somali population of about 1 million), and northern Kenya (then about 200,000 Somalis) who, in the pan-Somali view, desired to join their kinsmen in the Republic. The Somali Republic was thus from its formation set at loggerheads to its powerful neighbors, with irredentist Somalis in the surrounding countries regarded there as dangerous separatists.

The great wedge of territory occupied by the Somali lying to the east of the Ethiopian escarpment—from halfway through French Somaliland in the Somaliland northwest, along the Gulf of Aden coast and down the Indian Ocean littoral to the Tana River in northern Kenya— consists for the most part of dry savanna plains and semi desert scrub with occasional patches of true desert. In this area north of the Tana River there are only two permanent watercourses of any consequence—the Juba and Shebelle Rivers, both flowing through the central and southern part of the Somali Republic; and of these only the Juba actually reaches the sea near the port of Kismayu.

The region between these rivers is the most fertile part of Somalia; the annual rainfall here is often twelve inches or more, and a wide variety of crops are grown, ranging from bananas (Somalia's principal export crop) to sorghum, Indian corn, sesame, beans, and squashes. The only other significant area of cultivation lies in the northwest, between Hargeisa the former capital of British Somaliland, the Ethiopian border post of Tug Wajale (where, during the 1970s, inspired by "scientific socialism", a state farm produced wheat and sorghum), and the administrative centre of Borama. On this high ground the rainfall is sometimes as much as twenty inches, and considerable areas of country are cultivated by ox-drawn plows (in the south the traditional means of cultivation is by hand hoe). Elsewhere, and especially on the torrid coastal strip along the Gulf of Aden coast, where the principal ports are Berbera and Djibouti, the rainfall is often no more than four inches annually and varies greatly in quantity and distribution from year to year. There are many small trading centers scattered around wells and water points throughout the region. The largest towns in the south are along the Benadir Coast, where Mogadishu (the old capital of Somalia) had in 2005 an estimated population of between 1.5 and 2 million—but little more than one million in 2009 when so many people had fled the city's endemic conflict seeking refuge abroad.

In this often arid and generally harsh environment the population is distributed widely and sparsely with an overall density of about one person per square mile. The prevailing economic response is that of pastoral nomadism based on the herding of camels, cattle, sheep, and goats. Within this animal husbandry complex, the balance varies with ecological circumstances. Cattle tend to replace camels in the better-watered areas of the south and northwest in association with cultivation. Elsewhere, camels and sheep and goats constitute the nomad's principal wealth and his primary means of support.[1] The milk grazing camels are usually separated from the sheep and goats or cattle, especially in the dry seasons, and move over great tracts of country in the care of young herders. This pattern of husbandry reflects their greater powers of endurance and their less demanding water requirements. In the dry seasons camels can go for up to twenty days without water and can thus be taken to regions of lush grazing far from the wells around which the sheep and goats have to cluster, returning only periodically for watering. The sheep and goats are attached to the primary domestic unit, a group of closely related families moving from pasture to pasture, but never far from water, in search of good grazing.

Although corporate and individual rights to deep wells are asserted and maintained, if necessary by force (but not where water is freely abundant), pastureland is not subject to such rights of ownership. This distinction follows from the scattered and uncertain distribution of rain from season to season and year to year. The nomads have achieved an accommodation to their environment in which grazing land is not viewed as parceled out among different groups. Consequently, nomadic movements are wide-ranging and primarily dictated by the presence and relative abundance of grazing. Nevertheless, especially in relation to those wells customarily frequented by camels in the dry seasons, some degree of consistency is apparent in grazing movements from year to year. And at least these home-wells and trading posts, where some nomads often live semipermanently, limit any complete and free-ranging nomadism on the pattern of the grand nomads of North Africa or Arabia.

This mode of life is still followed today, wholly or in part, by what is probably a majority of the total Somali population, and consequently exerts great influence in all spheres of modern life and politics. Apart from those who live permanently in towns in employment in business or trade, the rest of the population are mainly cultivators. These grow sorghum and Indian corn as their staple crops and live in permanent village settlements where the land is traditionally vested in clans and clan sections. Individual farmers derive their title to land from membership of the landholding group and participation in its affairs. Since the collapse of Somalia in 1990, this traditional pattern of land use has been brutally disturbed, especially in the Benadir and surrounding areas, by the invasion of marauding militia gangs. This usurpation by people of the Hawiye clan-family has radically changed the clan composition of southern Somalia.

But the economic division between cultivation and nomadism, and between town and country in general, is not as wide or as significant as at first appears. Many cultivators are also pastoralists or part-time nomads, or have nomadic kin, and the fields of cultivators are regularly traversed by nomads in their quest for grazing and water. Frequently cultivating groups have contractual relations with adjacent nomadic groups for the exchange of stubble-grazing rights and watering in return for dung, milk, or money. The social structure of the numerically dominant nomadic population, though modified in agricultural and urban conditions, tends to embrace the whole nation. It provides the dominant *weltanschauung*. This became even more evident after the collapse of the state when survival depended increasingly on how well-armed groups were, and political dominance was directly a matter of relative firepower. Here the pastoralist clans with their long history of conflict and feud were at a tremendous advantage compared to the less belligerent cultivators and political status was directly a consequence of military power.

The basic organizing principle upon which traditional social life is built is the solidarity of kinsmen who trace descent from a common ancestor in the male line. Genealogies are thus of crucial significance in understanding Somali social structure, not merely as ambiguous records of the past, but as the primary idiom in which contemporary social and political relations are cast. Somalis readily compare their use of genealogies with the European practice of identification by name and address. In the Somali world, however, far more is involved than is conveyed by this parallel. By his genealogy, every individual is irrevocably placed in relation to all others, and identified in principle as friend or foe; and people regulate the character of their social and political relations with others in terms of their proximity or remoteness in genealogical terms. Indeed, the entire Somali nation is ultimately represented within a single national pedigree that traces its origin to Arabia, thus validating the shared attachment of all Somalis to Islam.

Within this national genealogy, the primary division is between those who descend from an ancestor Samale (whose name seems to have been extended to the whole people in the same fashion as the term English is extended to include all the inhabitants of the British Isles), and those who descend from an eponym called Sab. This division, which represents the deepest traditional cleavage in Somali society, corresponds partly to a distinction between cultivator and nomad. The Sab, who comprise two congeries of clans (or clan-families), the Digil and Rahanwin (also known as Digil Mirifle, and probably number about half a million, occupy the fertile regions between the Shebelle and Juba Rivers, where they are predominantly cultivators and agropastoralists. The Samale, by contrast, are mainly nomadic. In addition to other minor cultural distinctions, the Sab speak Af Maymay, a separate but closely related language to Somali, which differs from it by about as much as Spanish differs from Portuguese. Nevertheless, problems of communication are eased by the fact that many Sab are bilingual, northern Somali having the status of a *lingua franca*.

The Samale in turn divide genealogically into four main clan-families: the Dir, Isaq, Hawiye, and Darod. Being heavily engaged in the pastoral economy, these are much less firmly localized than the Sab clans. Some Dir (the Gadabursi and Ise clans) live in the extreme northwest of the Somaliland Republic, others are found in the south around the port of

Merca. The Isaq are their neighbors in the north. The Darod occupy the east of this area, most of the Ogaden region of Ethiopia, the northeastern part of Somalia, formerly known as Mijerteynia (named after one of their main clans), and now known as Puntland. They occur again in strength beyond the Digil and Rahanwin across the Juba River in the extreme south, and extend into northern Kenya. They are the largest single Somali group and may well number several million. Their wide dispersion across national boundaries is an important factor in contemporary Somali politics. Finally, the Hawiye, who boast probably about a million persons— live to the south of the Mijerteyn Darod in Mudugh, Hiran, and part of the Benadir in the centre and south of Somalia, including the important area in and around Mogadishu. The Rahanwin, and the less numerous Digil, are their neighbors around amd along the Shebelle River.

These vast genealogical units are too large and too widely dispersed to have acted as politically united groups in traditional Somali life, although, as will become apparent, in modern politics their segmentary solidarity is an important element in national politics. Internally, each clan-family is divided into a ramifying array of clans and clan segments, again all genealogically defined by descent in the male line. Although among both cultivators and pastoralists, and especially the former, clans have some weak degree of institutionalized political authority in the form of a clan-head, sometimes called by the Arabic term Sultan, the really effective units of political cooperation were (and are) generally smaller. Throughout the entire Somali region, the basic and most stable entity in traditional politics is the diya-paying group. This is made up of patrilineally related kin who collectively pay and receive damages (*diya)* for injury and death. The unity of the group depends not only upon common descent, but also upon an explicit treaty (*her)* in terms of which its members act collectively.

The vital importance of this grouping, in an environment in which the pressure of population on sparse resources is acute, and where fighting over access to water and pasture is common, can scarcely be overemphasized. It is upon his *diya*-paying group, and potentially on wider circles of clansmen within his clan-family, that the individual ultimately depends for the security of his person and property. This contractually defined circle of kinsmen, varying in size among the nomads between a few hundred and a few thousand men, extending to much larger groups among the southern cultivators,[2] does not, of course, exhaust the possibilities of political division and alliance. Lines of attachment, based on descent and following genealogical connections, ramify outside this relatively stable group, and in situations of conflict can be activated to mobilize much larger segments. Thus clans regularly unite against other clans, and eventually, in current politics particularly, clan-family divisions also play an important part in influencing the behavior of individuals and groups, and in proposing lines of alliance and antagonism. Despite the emergence of class and educational distinctions in contemporary society, it is no exaggeration to say that Somali life as a whole is still thoroughly permeated by these genealogical lines of cleavage in private as well as public lie. Hence, any attempt to understand contemporary politics that ignores their significance is doomed to failure.[3] They play an equally crucial role in traffic accidents in towns (when blood compensation is claimed), in the preferment of individuals in business or governments. They are not, of course, the only factors at work, but they are the most fundamental.

Another characteristic of this traditional system is the extreme democracy of policy-making at all levels of grouping. In conformity with the shifting and ephemeral character of their political allegiances, except in the military, there has been little development of institutional authority. In principle, every adult male has an equal voice in the councils of the groups with which he is aligned. The position of clan-leader, although it connotes status, carries little intrinsic authority. It is essentially a representative role. There is some difference here between the northern pastoral nomads and the southern agropastoralists. In their clan organization, the latter have a more formal hierarchy of political offices. But as a whole, and certainly in comparison with many other traditional African political systems, that of the Somali is characterized by the diffusion of authority, and by the practice of basing decisions on consensus. Thus politics, traditionally, is not a specialized art left to the care of a few individuals who hold particular positions, but a free-for-all in which every pastoral nomad has long experience. Not all men, of course, are equally eloquent in the debates that decide pastoral policy, nor equally acute in their choice and advocacy of policies where weight of kinship support and wealth may be persuasive. In these circumstances, it is individuals rather than the holders of hereditary office who rise to prominence by their superior sagacity, rhetoric, or support.

These features of the traditional Somali heritage are all strongly reflected in contemporary life, in urban contexts as well as the interior.[4] There has so far been no very extensive or far-reaching radical economic development; and with few exceptions urbanization, where it has taken place in centers such as Mogadishu and Hargeisa, has not utterly disrupted or changed beyond recognition the traditional fabric of society. In many respects, modernity has provided new scope for the adaptation, extension, and intensification of traditional social imperatives.[5]

From Colonial Rule to Independence

British Somaliland

Before the Second World War, the British Somaliland Protectorate, with its 60,000 square miles of largely semi-desert territory and its half million or so inhabitants mainly devoted to a nomadic existence, was governed on little more than a care and maintenance basis and not unfairly dubbed a "Cinderella of Empire". The twenty years (1900-20) struggle for independence from alien Christian rule led by Sayyid Mohammed 'Abdille Hassan had brought the Protectorate a few years' news value.[6] But this had been followed by a modest consolidation of colonial rule without any striking new economic or social developments. Attempts to establish a general system of Western education had met with a hostile reception of what was seen as further subversion of the ancient religious heritage of Islam. The principal exports at this time remained hides and skins and livestock on the hoof, valued in the late 1930s at only £279,940 in comparison with imports in the same period worth £535,210. The territory's minute budget was only £217,139 in 1937 and derived from imperial grants-in-aid and local revenue from import and export duties. There was no direct taxation.

The upheavals of the war, and particularly the local effects of the East African campaigns, in the course of which British Somaliland was briefly occupied by the Italians, greatly changed the general position. The channeling of traditional national Somali sentiments in a more progressive direction among the urban intelligentsia favored rather than opposed educational and other advancement, and in November 1945 the rehabilitation of civil rule in the Protectorate (under military government from 1941) inaugurated an entirely new phase. The break with the past was emphasized not only by a much more concerned and better-financed effort on the part of the government to promote development in all spheres, but also by the abandonment of the port of Berbera as the old capital in favor of Hargeisa in the center of the country.

The new destiny of the adjacent Somalia as a United Nations Trust Territory, administered by Italy with a ten years' mandate to independence, set a precise date for the autonomy of one segment of the Somali nation. But development in the Protectorate proceeded, initially, at a leisurely pace. Reports of the rapid pursuit of radical advances in distant Mogadishu merely served to reinforce the local Protectorate's administrative philosophy of the need for slow and thorough change and a gradualist approach to a distant and unspecified independence, probably within the British Commonwealth. In this spirit, the first secondary school for boys was opened in 1953, and the same year saw a notable innovation with the establishment of the first government school for girls at Burao. Changing attitudes toward the education of women were reflected in the many pressing requests for the marriage of their daughters, which the parents of the first batch of pupils received. In the following year the appointment of a Somali Education Officer marked the first promotion of a Somali official to the senior ranks of the civil service.

In other areas less was achieved.[7] The export of hides and skins increased to a value of £1,013,790 import cost £1,904,400 in 1953, but no new resource was discovered to augment the economy.[8] Agricultural and veterinary services were expanded, the most striking achievement being the excavation of a sorely needed chain of water basins along the southern boundary with Ethiopia. Hydrological and geological surveys were also intensified, and there was some experimentation with date cultivation. However, the total budget was still very small, providing in 1953 for an expenditure of £1,290,999 and revenue of £1,434,767, of which £445,729 derived from local customs dues and the bulk of the remainder from grants-in-aid (£580,000) and Colonial Development and Welfare grants (£161,180).

In the political field elected town councils were established at Berbera and Hargeisa, the two largest towns, while on a wider scale the only vehicle for the direct expression of public opinion remained the Protectorate's Advisory Council, a body with no statutory powers inaugurated during the period of military rule in 1946. The main political party was now the moderately progressive Somaliland National League (SNL), led mainly by prominent traders and with an intermittent history going back to 1935, although the Somali Youth League (SYL) with headquarters in Somalia also had some following. This organization, however, while having some attraction for those clans hostile to others supporting the SNL, did not have a very effective local leadership and was hampered by the disfavor in which it was held by the administration on account of its assumed communist leanings. These two parties were both committed to the principle of Somali unification, the SYL program being more detailed and specific in its aims on this issue.

A significant stimulus to this very modest range of activity was provided by Britain's final transfer of the Haud grazing lands to Ethiopia at the end of 1954. This region of some 67,000 square miles of rich pastureland had originally been included in the Protectorate, but in defiance of prior Anglo-Somali treaties, had been excised from it by the Anglo-Ethiopian Treaty of 1887, which in effect recognized Ethiopia as the local superpower. Since most of the area thus in effect relinquished to Ethiopia was not in fact actually administered by the Ethiopians before the Italian conquest in 1935 and the subsequent liquidation of Italian rule in 1941, it was only after this time and with the rise of modem Somali nationalism that its control became a vital issue. During the period of British Military Administration of the Protectorate and Somalia, the Haud (along with the Ogaden) was administered by British political officers on the basis of Anglo-Ethiopian Agreements of 1942 and 1945. The Ogaden was returned to Ethiopian control in 1948, but British administration in the Haud, though gradually reduced, was not finally ended until the end of 1954. It was only then that the full effects of the 1887 treaty became apparent to British-protected Somalis. Their natural indignation was little reduced by the knowledge that attempts would be made to protect their grazing rights by a British liaison office at Jigjiga.

News of the transfer was greeted with widespread public indignation, and led to the rapid mobilization of the National United Front (NUF) in an effort to concert all political activity toward the recovery of the Haud. A crucial side product of this quickening of wider political action, and one that gathered increasing momentum as the campaign to restore the territory was at every turn frustrated, was a growing and more articulate demand for independence. So, anxious to make amends where it could, the British government in 1957 authorized the formation of a legislative council with six unofficial members. Two years later this was modified to include twelve elected members, two nominated unofficial, and fifteen official members, with the governor as president.

By this time, partly due to the failure of the campaign to regain the Haud, the NUF ceased to be a national consortium and became a political party in its own right. The SNL, now representing the most forward nationalist position in the Protectorate and urging early union with Somalia (due to achieve independence in 1960), boycotted the attendant elections. Their requests for an immediate unofficial majority had not been accepted. This left the field clear for the NUF and SYL. In the event, however, no SYL candidate was returned and of the twelve successful contestants, one supported the NUF, four had no party allegiance, and one belonged to the SNL (despite the party's boycott).

This result and the victory of the moderately progressive and pro-Commonwealth NUF was bound to be short-lived. In response to the growing demand for wider representation, a new constitution providing ministerial responsibility was introduced early in 1960.[9] In the ensuing elections, still restricted to male suffrage, the SNL, representing most of the Isaq clans (except for Habar To1 Ja'lo voters who supported the NUF) gained twenty of the available thirty-three seats. The NUF in alliance with the SYL, gained one seat, and the new United Somali Party, associated with the SNL, won twelve. Two members of each of the winning parties were appointed ministers and the Isaq head of the SNL became leader of government business.[10]

This sudden constitutional step forward indicated that the British government at last recognized that the extent of public pressure in favor of independence had suddenly accelerated. In 1959 there were only two Somali full district commissioners, and a handful of district officers and police assistant superintendents. In the following year, all six districts in the Protectorate were administered by Somali officials and the assistant commissioner of police was also a Somali. Over 100 Somali students were studying overseas, a few at British universities, and Somaliland's second secondary school had been opened. The Protectorate had come a long way toward meeting outstanding aims. In 1957 Britain had already approved the eventual union with Somalia, which it reiterated two years later in 1959, so that all seemed set fair for the last years of British rule and rapid preparations for self-government.[11]

Somalia

In comparison with the Protectorate, Somalia experienced a more regular and predictable period of gestation toward independence and union, but one that despite the greater impact of colonization before the Second World War, still left the territory far from being economically viable. Unlike British Somaliland, which was a protectorate and had no foreign settlers, Somalia was a colony in the true sense with a significant Italian settler community. Much effort and expense had been expended in the hope of creating an attractive home for some of Italy's surplus population, and a worthwhile source of primary products for the mother country. The main enterprises developed by Italian settlers, with the help of government subsidies, were a chain of large banana plantations along the lower Juba and Shebelle Rivers, the Societa Agricola Italo-Somalia's fruit and sugar plantations and refinery at Jowhar (Villagio Duca degli Abruzzi),[12] the salt-extraction plant at Ras Hafun, and a number of cotton estates. The 1920s and early 1930s also saw a considerable expansion in road and building construction, and a general enlargement of government administration. This was especially the case under the fascists, who saw themselves as dedicated colonizers in the Roman tradition, bringing civilization to a benighted country.

From a figure of under 1 million lire in 1905 the budget rose continuously, reaching 21 million lire in 1908, and an average of 74 million in the early 1930s. Local revenue accounted for about half this figure and was derived, as in the British Protectorate, mainly indirectly from customs and excise tariffs. The remainder was furnished by grants from the Italian state in expectation of the benefits, at least in prestige and glory, which the colony was held to promise.

By this time, the export trade—chiefly of hides and skins, and cotton[13] and bananas—had at last begun to show some return. The adverse balance of trade had fallen from a peak of nearly 130 million lire in 1927 to just under 29 million in 1934.

The Italo-Ethiopian War of 1935-36, and Italy's subsequent involvement in the Second World War, changed the position considerably. The preparations for the Italian conquest of Ethiopia brought a brief period of unprecedented prosperity to the colony, but this was quickly followed by a sharp economic decline as Italian resources were stretched in the ensuing global conflict. Trade and commerce were now strictly controlled by a rigid system of governmental monopolies and parastatal organizations and by fascist legislation that excluded the participation of Somalis or other colonial subjects in any sector of the economy where they might compete with Italians. As in the British Protectorate in this period, local Somali personnel were recruited only into the lowest ranks of the administrative services. There was no room at all for such liberal ideas as those of Tommaso Carletti, governor of Somalia in 1907, who had proposed the formation of Somali municipal councils and eventually of an elected system of government. Education, though considerable, in comparison with the Protectorate, was in any case minimal: under 2,000 Somali and Arab pupils were enrolled in elementary schools in 1939.

Nevertheless, in thirty years of direct Italian rule significant developments had occurred. In the decade between 1930 and 1940 Mogadishu had doubled in size to a population of almost 60,000 inhabitants; more than 40,000 Somali recruits had seen service in the Ethiopian campaigns; and the Somali areas of eastern Ethiopia (including the Ogaden) were now incorporated as three separate provinces in the newly expanded colony of Somalia. The first stirrings of local Somali nationalism had also occurred, with a number of Somali junior officials and merchants forming patriotic betterment clubs and associations. And although these were naturally frustrated by the watchful fascist administration, the Italians must at least be given credit, whatever their motives, for having laid the foundations of a modern Somali state with a promising export trade and a stronger and more pervasive system of government than was ever attempted or achieved in British Somaliland.

The nine years of British military administration that followed the Italian collapse in Ethiopia and Somalia in 1941 were a time of great political turmoil. The new administration, which on the whole was welcomed by the population at large and made little secret of its admiration for Somalis and contempt for the defeated Italians, brought with it a new spirit of progress. District and provincial advisory councils were opened in 1946, and by 1947 there were nineteen government elementary schools in place of the thirteen mission schools that the British had found when they assumed control. There was now also a much-needed, but still inadequate, teachers' training center with an average enrolment of fifty students. And although Somali personnel were not promoted in the civil service to as high ranks, as was the practice in Eritrea under British military rule, something of this kind was achieved in the police force (the Somalia Gendarmerie), which received a great deal of attention. Thus, at the end of the British period, the police had a substantial cadre of well-trained Somali senior inspectors, many of whom were destined to achieve high positions later. (The two most outstanding in their subsequent careers were the police commander, General Mohamed Abshir, and army commander and head of state, General Mohamed Siyad Barre).

In politics the same trends were evident. The first constitution of the Somali Youth Club, destined to become the major Somali political party, was drafted with the assistance of the British political officer in Mogadishu in 1943 (later to become in the 1960s minister of African affairs in Zambia where I met him). The club's subsequent development in the form of the SYL after 1947 was regarded officially with sympathy and encouragement. Its progressive aims for development, educational advancement, and the extirpation of tribalism were all consistent with the administration's general policy, as was its wider aim of Somali unification and the creation of a Greater Somalia. The positive interest of local officials in this pan-Somali aspiration was increased further after it had become clear in 1947 that, despite the British foreign secretary's advocacy,[14] it was not going to win the support of the four powers (Britain, France, Russia, and the United States, which were initially charged with the disposal of the former Italian colonies[15]. Thus, by 1950, when the British Military Administration relinquished authority to the new Italian Trusteeship Administration, which had been given a ten-year UN mandate to prepare Somalia for independence, despite the existence of a number of rival organizations,[16] the SYL was the paramount Somali party. It was now an extremely well-organized movement with branches throughout the country and supporters in all branches of the civil service and particularly in the police.

Though it had raised Somali hopes of unification that had not been fulfilled, the British interlude had at least opened the door to progressive Somali advancement, and prepared the ground for a new era of social advancement. In economics the record was less encouraging. With its very scant resources in manpower and finances, the Military Administration had concentrated its energies on making good the ravages of war, and on setting the plantation export economy on its feet again as well as promoting the wider involvement of local merchants in trade and business. No dramatic advances had however been achieved.

It was to this mixed legacy that, despite widespread public opposition, the Italians returned in 1950. The new Trusteeship Administration, which included many former colonial civil servants, was mandated by the United Nations to "foster the development of free political institutions and to promote the development of the inhabitants of the territory towards independence". The agreement establishing the Trusteeship Administration's authority, approved by the United Nations General Assembly on 2 December, 1950, contained in an appendix full details of the administration's obligations. Additionally, provision was made for the establishment in

Mogadishu of a United Nations Advisory Council to act as a direct liaison with the Italian authorities.

These safeguards and the precise limitation of the period of the trusteeship to ten years, despite rumors to the contrary, helped to temper opposition to the Italian return. After an initial phase, lasting about two years, of mutual mistrust and recrimination, especially between the Italians and the SYL, a modus vivendi was reached. The development prospects were not unpromising. The Italians were returning to a colony with settler farming populations numbering several thousand, an established export industry in bananas, and a population who were to a considerable extent more accustomed to manual labor than their counterparts in Somaliland. There was another important difference: the Italians were in a hurry to get on with the task of development, but the British did not feel the same urgency. Quality, they considered, was more important than quantity. The Italian approach was in all fields based on securing large and dramatic results. In this spirit, in association with UNESCO, an elaborate program of general education was launched in 1952, free state schools replacing the mission education of the past, and by 1957 some 32,000 pupils were enrolled. In the same year, the School of Politics and Administration, opened by the Italians on their return in 1950, had produced its first crop of urgently needed Somali officials and was transformed into a Technical and Commercial Institute. Meanwhile, in 1954, a Higher Institute of Law and Economics had been established to provide a two-year Rome University diploma course, generally in preparation for further study in Italy. In 1960 at independence, this was upgraded to become a university college.[17]

By 1956, when there was only one Somali full district commissioner in the Protectorate, all Somalia's districts and provinces had become under the direct charge of Somali officials, often aided by Italian advisers and clerks. Elected representation on the expanding urban councils was introduced in 1954. Two years later, in step with the transfer of administrative authority in districts and provinces, elections took place for a newly established Legislative Assembly with seventy seats, ten of which were reserved for ethnic minorities (Arabs, Indians, Pakistanis, and Italians). Ministerial government was introduced, with authority in internal affairs, although the Trusteeship Administration held a right of absolute veto and retained control of defense. Of the sixty available Somali seats, the SYL won forty-three, the Hizbia Dastur Mustaqil Somali (HDMS),[18] representing the Digil and Rahanwin clans, thirteen, and the remaining four seats were filled by two smaller parties. The SYL's success was a testimony to its wider degree of representativeness as a consortium of the various clan groupings, with the exception of the Digil and Rahanwin (a few of whom, however, supported the SYL).[19] All this, as I found in the course of an extensive ethnographic tour of southern Somalia at this time, seemed impressive.

The first Somali government called to office after the elections was led by Abdillahi Ise (of the Hawiye clan-family), a former employee of the Italian colonial administration and prominent in the leadership of the party since 1947. Two other ministers were chosen from the same clan-family, and one from the Dir and two from the Darod. Beside the ten reserved seats, the Assembly itself was divided equally between Darod, Hawiye, and Digil Mirifle—each group having twenty members. On this basis, Adan Abdullah Osman, a leading member of the government party belonging to a small faction of the Hawiye, and a man with a high reputation for probity, was elected as president of the Assembly.[20] Notwithstanding its deep internal divisions, reflected in the range of cabinet appointments to represent the main groups, the SYL's dominant position in the country was further consolidated in the 1959 General Assembly elections.

The Assembly had been expanded to ninety seats (there being now no reserved minority seats)—of these the SYL won eighty-three. Of the remaining seats, two went to the small Liberal Party, and five to a breakaway offshoot of the HDMS. The latter, like the militant new Greater Somalia League (GSL), had officially boycotted the elections. This was partly in protest at government restrictions imposed upon GSL activity, after disturbances involving some members of that radical party and its electoral allies in the north, the Somali National Union. The Assembly seats were now distributed among the main clan contenders as follows: Darod thirty-three; Hawiye thirty; Digil Mirifle twenty seven. The SYL landslide, following intense campaigning among the Digil and Rahanwin, as well as the suppression of Darod-Hawiye rivalries within the League, placed a heavy burden upon 'Abdillahi' Ise, who had again been chosen to form a government. There were many disparate and competing interests and groups to reward, and it was impossible to please everybody. The prime minister, however, did his best, and the cabinet eventually formed consisted of four Hawiye, three Darod, one Dir, and one Digil Mirifle.

This distribution of ministries did not satisfy an important section of Darod within the party, which criticized the new government for, as they put it, sacrificing principles of ability and efficiency to clan expediency. From the formation of the government until independence and union with Somaliland in 1960, the main source of friction and disagreement was in the Darod camp. This was the final election to be held in Somalia before the merger with Somaliland and the first election to be held under universal suffrage.[21]

If the line of political and administrative progress was clear and unwavering, economic development followed a less definite course, although with generous (and not unself-interested) aid from Italy,[22] and the United Nations, more was attempted than in the British Protectorate. With little preparation, in 1954 a seven-year development plan was launched, envisaging a total expenditure of £4 million. Over half this was assigned to agricultural and livestock projects, including well-drilling, construction of public silos, and the creation of an agricultural credit bank designed to encourage mechanization and crop development. In the private sector, mainly in the fruit plantations, sugar refinery, and other small industries, Italian companies had by 1957 invested £3 million. By this time, sugar production at Jowhar had risen to the level where it supplied most of the country's own internal needs. Banana exports, exclusively through the Italian monopoly agency, ran at 50,000 tons annually—almost five times the volume reached in 1937. Revenue, based almost entirely on tariff dues, had doubled from £1 million, while expenditure ran at about £5 million.[23] In the British Protectorate income was £1.5 million, over half from grants-in-aid and from the Colonial Development and Welfare Scheme. Exports, still the staple hides and skins and livestock on the hoof, were valued at £1.25 million and imports at twice that.

However weak the economic position in both countries, with its plantation economy and vast interriverine arable area, and with its longer tradition of more radical political, social, and educational progress, Somalia seemed to possess greater advantages than the less-developed Protectorate. This was the generally accepted view of the relative positions of the two territories. While 'Abdillahi' Ise's government was committed to the pan-Somali principle and busy preparing a constitution that was designed to facilitate unification, it was from Somaliland that most of the pressure for union emanated. This was so despite the fact that some of the most enlightened northern political figures and officials believed that they had a long way to go before they could meet with Somalia on comparable conditions.

Following the decision of the United Nations General Assembly to advance the date of Somalia's independence to July 1, 1960, and a strong surge of public feeling in favor of immediate union, the Protectorate's SNL leaders were forced to throw aside their doubts and hesitations. They now campaigned strenuously for independence, with union as early as possible after Somalia attained sovereignty. Abandoning previous thoughts of some form of Commonwealth connection, accordingly, on April 6, 1960, the elected members of the Protectorate Legislative Council unanimously voted that "bold and definite action be taken, and that the date of independence and union with Somalia must be July 1, 1960, the date when Somalia will attain its full freedom". With no reason to delay further the independence of what, in relation to its size and utility had certainly been one of its least rewarding possessions, the British government readily accepted this request, leaving its local officials a few months of hectic scramble to make such preparations as were possible in the limited time available.

On the political level, the way had already been prepared by discussions between the party leaders of the two territories at the national Pan-Somali Movement Conference held at Mogadishu in July the previous year. At a further round of talks between delegates from the two territories at Mogadishu in April 1960, it had been agreed that the new state should have a unitary constitution with an elected president as head of state, and should be governed by a prime minister and council of ministers responsible to a single National assembly formed by the merger of the existing two legislatures. If the idea of a federal system was raised, it was quickly dropped in the nationalistic euphoria of the moment-which was almost palpable. Until they could be effectively integrated, the existing administrative, judicial, and fiscal regimes would remain in place with centralized control from the capital in Mogadishu. The constitution, which envisaged further unification as other Somali territories achieved independence, had been prepared with Italian assistance in Somalia.[24] The Italian bureaucratic model was strongly evident and no consideration had been given to the decentralized character of traditional Somali political units. Nevertheless, this typically Eurocentric framework, which no one at the time questioned, was accepted provisionally until it could be ratified by a national referendum after union had taken place.

Union and Unification

In the event, British rule in the Protectorate was terminated on June 26, and on July 1, 1960, the two territories formally joined together as the Northern and Southern Regions of the Somali Republic. The two parliaments assembled together in Mogadishu to form the new National Assembly of 123 members (33 from the north, 90 from the south). The southern Assembly President, Adan Abdullah Osman, was elected provisional president of the Republic, his place as leader of the Assembly being taken by a northerner, and the more difficult business of choosing a national government began. The southern premier, 'Abdillahi' Ise, failed to gain sufficient support, and leadership passed to the dissident Darod group headed by 'Abdirashid' Ali Shirmarke and 'Abdirazaq Haji Husseyn. The former, with an Italian degree in political science, became prime minister; and the latter minister of the interior, Abdillahi himself assumed the important office of foreign minister. The office of deputy premier was given to a northerner of the United Somali Party (USP), while another USP leader became minister of education; and the SNL leader of government business, Mohamed Haji Ibrahim Igal, assumed responsibility for defense (later education). The new minister of agriculture was also a northerner of the SNL. In the final cabinet of fourteen ministers clan-family representation was as follows; Darod six; Hawiye four; Digil Mirifle two; Isaq two. Two of the six Darod and both the Isaq were northerners.

The national jubilation that accompanied this rapid implementation of what had broadly been agreed to before union was increased by encouraging news on the economic front. Britain promised an annually negotiable subsidy that in the first year was to run at approximately £1.5 million;[25] Italy engaged to provide £3 million annually on a similar basis;[26] and there were offers of loans and aid from the United States, Egypt, and the communist bloc on a scale far beyond previous Somali hopes. Moreover, through its association with Italy, the Republic would become eligible for substantial European aid. Yet there was much to be achieved before this formal political union, however bright its economic prospects seemed, could be consummated. Before tracing how events developed subsequently in the direction of a more binding and organic union, it is necessary to review the implications of union at a more profound level.

However precipitate and incomplete it may have seemed at the time, the formal union of the two territories had at once profound implications for Somali politics. To appreciate what was entailed here it is essential to remember that, despite the patriotic fervor with which the Republic's formation was acclaimed, the most pervasive element in local politics remained the loyalty of the individual to his kin and clan. Before union, politics in the northern regions had been dominated by the numerically predominant Isaq clan-family supporting the SNL (with the exception of the Habar Tol Jalo clansmen), while the traditionally opposed Dir and Darod clans combined in opposition as the USP. Union with Somalia greatly reduced the political importance of the Isaq, but also made it possible for the USP Darod to acquire new significance through direct association with the Darod wing of the SYL. This possibility gave a novel prominence to the Darod Dulbahante clan who straddled the northeastern border with Somalia, who in their colonial experience were accustomed to playing off one colonial administration against the other. Because of their geographical position, the Dulbahante became the bridge joining the two former states and this gave them a special importance in the politics of independence. For the Dir (Gadabursi and Ise) on the western edge of Somaliland, facing French Somaliland and Ethiopia, traditional connections suggested alliance with the Hawiye wing of the SYL, as well as with the Isaq, and even the possibility of an Isaq-Hawiye-Dir "Irririst"[27] association in opposition to the Darod clans. For the Digil Mirifle HDMS the range of political maneuver on all fronts was greatly increased by the new opportunities for clan permutations. Despite traditional animosities toward them, their position was enhanced in the enlarged arena of national politics. Any group that could offer a compact bloc of voters could now exert significant leverage between the principal clan contenders in their search for political advantage and dominance. All this was indeed a new and unfamiliar world to explore for clan groups that previously, in some cases, hardly knew of each other's existence.

These, of course, were not the only potential lines of political engagement. As long as the SYL maintained a moderate and constitutional approach to the central national concern of further pan-Somali unification, other parties such as the GSL, SNL, and USP, which affected a more militant and often pro-Arab stance, or advocated a socialist regime, might be expected to be drawn together against the SYL. There was also the possibility of sharp regional cleavages between north and south, reflecting the different colonial legacies and other differences between these two regions. Despite their largely common cultural, linguistic, and religious heritage and the pervasive and overlapping character of clan ties, the two colonial traditions turned out to have left a more profound and enduring imprint than at first appeared. British exclusiveness and empiricism, the emphasis on quality rather than quantity in educational and social advancement, attachment to British ideas of justice and administrative procedures, the separation of politics from administration, all contrasted in northern eyes with the apparently less rigorous standards of political and public service morality in the south and with the convoluted Italian bureaucratic system.

With the lighter impress of colonial rule in the north, and no settler community to act as a leaven, the traditional attitudes of pastoral Somali society were more strongly ingrained in the north, while the south was, in many ways, more urban in outlook and in that regard more "modern". For northerners these contrasts provided a set of standards well-suited to express their traditions, pride, aloofness, and independence. This ex-colonial identity was also, of course, associated with English in opposition to the Italian spoken by those who had been educated in the south.[28] Southerners, however, also had a background in English through their experience of the British Military Administration before independence. A further common cultural bond, directly linked to the universal adherence to Islam, was of course knowledge of, if not always literacy in, Arabic taught in the local Quranic schools, that were omnipresent throughout the country and whose pupils were invariably males. These various influences provided a series of crosscutting ties that tended to reinforce pan-Somali cultural nationalism.

The Mechanics of Integration

Despite these common links, as soon as the two countries united politically, essentially on the basis of their common culture, their conflicting differences were highlighted and demanded attention. So, in administration, although the functions of Italian and British-trained personnel were similar, each operated under different conditions of service and rates of pay. This affected officials in all branches of government, including the police, and also the new national army formed by the amalgamation of the former British Somaliland Scouts and the Italian Somali military force. Northern district commissioners and assistant superintendents of police (now styled captains) received salaries equivalent to British expatriates and considerably higher than the wages of provincial commissioners (regional governors and military colonels in the south). Similar differences existed in the legal system. Law in the north was also based primarily upon English common statute law and the Indian Penal Code. In the south Italian colonial law was practiced. While prior to union, Somalia had its own appellate system, appeals from the High Court of the British Protectorate were heard by the East African Court of Appeal. Hence, until a unified judiciary could be established, separate sections of the Supreme Court had to be created to deal with litigation in the north and south. In fiscal and accounting, the position was even more complex because wide procedural differences distinguished the two colonial traditions. There were also significant differences in tariffs and customs dues and in the general organization of trade and trading regulations. Finally, in the northern educational program, Arabic and English were the principal foreign languages and media of advanced instruction: in the south Italian was the main vehicle.

These linguistically distinct traditions had wide practical implications. Since, at this time, there was no generally accepted script for Somali itself, English, Italian, and, to a lesser extent, Arabic were of necessity the only means of written communication in private as well as public and official business. From their experience and education during the British Military Administration, some southerners knew some English, but few if any in the north had knowledge of or much inclination to learn Italian. These circumstances and the value of its wider currency favored English in the long term but did little to alleviate the immediate practical problems created by this polyglot heritage.[29] In some government departments it proved necessary to duplicate English- and Italian-speaking personnel. These linguistic barriers tended to be aggravated rather than alleviated by the continued presence of a number of foreign advisers and technical assistants in most branches of government. Those several hundred Italian "experts", whose services formed part of the extensive Italian aid program, were naturally particularly sensitive to developments that tended to reduce the status of their native tongue or diminished the cultural attachment to Italy.

With this mixed legacy and the pattern of clan cleavages between north and south, it is hardly surprising that difficulties should have arisen between the two parts of the Republic shortly after independence. Nor it is to be wondered at that, in the main, dissatisfaction should have arisen first in the north. Although there were at this time four northern ministers in the cabinet, and senior northern officials were rapidly gaining senior positions in ministerial departments,[30] the north had obviously sacrificed far more than the south. Mogadishu had retained its position as the capital of the state and as a thriving commercial town, while Hargeisa had been reduced in status to little more than a provincial headquarters, and was declining in prosperity as business tended to gravitate south to the seat of government. These disparities were further aggravated by a rise in unemployment due to the exodus from the north of expatriates and their families shortly after independence.

All this quickly bred a strong sense of resentment that soon replaced the honeymoon period of euphoria of the first months of independence. Many northerners, particularly officials and nationalist politicians, began to feel that they had been in effect the victims of a confidence trick; and what was all the more galling, one to a significant extent of their own devising. It was they who had pressed for immediate union despite their misgivings over their lack of preparation. Since union, however, many of the northern elite who had been to the south, or were now rubbing shoulders with southern officials and politicians, were coming to consider that the southern reputation for progress and modernization, which they had hitherto accepted without question, was in many respects unjustified. Far from being better trained and equipped for independence, the ex-Italian Somalis turned out to be in many cases less prepared than they were. Northern popular songs, current at this time, expressed this disillusion in terms of a marriage where the husband found his new bride, on closer acquaintance, less satisfactory than had been anticipated.

This mood of disenchantment was clearly expressed in the national referendum held on June 20, 1961, to legitimize the provisional constitution that had been prepared in the south before independence. In the north, this occasion was interpreted as a test of confidence in the government, rather than in the provisions of the constitution itself, and more than half of those who troubled to register their view (100,000 men and women) voted against the constitution. Since this represented less than one tenth of the northern population, the result was hardly a ringing endorsement of the union.[31] In fact, northern ministers in the government were rapidly losing the support of their electors and, indeed, of the northern party organization. This trend was expressed more dramatically in the abortive military coup of December 1961. The revolt was led by a group of Sandhurst-trained lieutenants who, following the formation of the new national army, found themselves serving under Italian-trained superior officers from the south. As a whole, however, despite its grievances, the north was not prepared to take such a drastic step; and although some senior officials and ministers were assumed to be sympathetic to it, the rising was quickly quelled by the loyal action of a group of noncommissioned officers. So much for Sandhurst and northern Somali snobbery!

This incident at last convinced the government that the situation in the north had to be taken seriously, and that more effective measures to implement integration more fully were urgently required. Northern and southern personnel in all branches of the civil service, the forces, and the police were posted more widely on a national basis. Other measures took more time to accomplish. The new civil service law unifying salaries and conditions of service throughout the Republic, although already approved on March 15, 1962, was proving difficult to implement because it required the grading of all personnel from the two regions on some common basis. Moreover, although urgently required, its provisions were regarded by many of those concerned as a mixed blessing. Senior northern salaries were to be scaled down, and southern ones raised to a common point. A number of northern resignations of senior staff directly followed, while the salary scales of lower grades of employees in the north were to be raised to meet the rates current in the south. Later in 1962 new fiscal and accounting procedures, largely based on the British pattern, were adopted. The practice of purchasing government equipment and supplies by tender competition was also introduced, to the chagrin of many Italian companies in the south. More attention was also given to the development needs of the north, particularly in health, education, and economics.

Dissatisfaction, however, still continued and found new political expression when, following a disagreement over government policy in the north, two northern ministers resigned from the government later in the summer of 1962.[32] The political parties were now in a state of flux, and various new alignments were in the air. These moves culminated in May 1963 in the formation of the Somali National Congress (SNC), led jointly by the former northern chief minister,

Mohamed Haji Ibrahim Egal, and the former SYL minister and defeated presidential candidate, Sheikh Ali Jumale.[33] This represented the final rupture of the uneasy SYL-SNL-USP coalition government and left three main parties in the field: the SYL government with the SNC and Somali Democratic Union (SDU) in opposition. This last party had been formed in the summer of 1962 under the leadership of Haji Mohamed Hussen which, based on the old GSL, sought to amalgamate dissident elements of the SNL, USP, and HDMS.[34]

These developments brought the various currents of north-south antagonism more firmly into the party political arena. The SYL was now strongly represented in both regions, and so were its principal opponents, the SNC and SDU.[35] This was the position when the country went to the polls in the municipal elections of November 1963. Of the 904 seats at stake, the SYL won 665 (74 percent), the SNC 105, and the SDU the majority of the remainder. National Assembly elections followed in March 1964, at a time of unusually strong patriotism. Then the perennial border dispute with Ethiopia had flared up into open war, and the country was being exhorted to fight with one hand and vote with the other. The SYL gained 69 seats, the SNC 22, and the SDU 15. Still campaigning on the narrower front of their own region, the HDMS won 9 seats; and other smaller groups the remaining 8. Subsequent party changes by a number of deputies from the smaller groups—a recurrent phenomenon in Somali politics—served to increase the strength of the SYL bloc in the Assembly.

These results indicated how the cleavage between the two regions of the Republic had accommodated to other sectional interests and divisions. This trend was certainly reinforced by the country's increasing isolation in inter-African affairs,[36] associated with growing resistance from France, Kenya, and Ethiopia to the pan-Somali campaign for further unification. It was further encouraged by the choice of ministers in the new government formed following a lengthy period of nego-tiation. After intense turmoil within the SYL, 'Abdirazaq Haji

Hussen had eventually succeeded in gaining general support and had supplanted 'Abdirashid' Ali Shirmarke as premier. Like his predecessor, he was also from ex-Italian Somalia (actually from Mijertenia). But a third of those whom he invited to join his cabinet were northerners. These new ministers, most of whom were former civil servants who had only recently entered politics, were placed in charge of such important departments as foreign affairs, defense, finance, information, and agriculture. This was a novel achievement for the north and one warmly welcomed there.

These developments, both within the government and in the opposition parties, were less the result of a deliberate integration policy than part of a general trend toward a fuller accommodation between northerners and southerners. They appeared to mark a growing acceptance of union and a realization by northerners that the south offered many attractive opportunities for the exercise of their traditional political and business talents. In commerce, as well as in politics and administration, many northerners were moving south to compete in business and trade with southerners and Italians and opening up new lines of enterprise. Northerners had begun to penetrate the lucrative banana export trade, and some of the most successful businessmen were founding agencies for the import of foreign goods and machinery on a scale that brought them into immediate competition with Italian concerns. Already some remarkable successes had been achieved. Few, perhaps, could emulate that of a former northern store clerk in Hargeisa (where I first met him in 1955) who, some eight years later, had come to own a flourishing import and export business and was one of the richest men in the country and also an important political influence.[37] (His son, Ragge Omar, became a well-known TV news correspondent). Yet, although many others were not so spectacularly successful, on a smaller scale this story could be repeated for a considerable number of other enterprising northerners who had moved their businesses south. Figures of the numbers of northerners involved, or of the extent of their capital commitments, were unfortunately not available, but the trend was clear.

Many of those northern entrepreneurs who at the time of union were most hostile to the continuation of Italian influence in the south found it expedient to learn sufficient Italian to advance their business activities there. However, although the tussle between Italian- and English-speaking Somalis still continued, it seemed probable that, in the long run, English would supplant Italian as the dominant foreign language. While obviously secure as the language of Islam, the long-term general status of Arabic was difficult to predict. The cabinet formed by Abdirazaq Haji Hussen in 1964 was largely English-speaking, many ministers and senior officials sent their children to schools where English was the principal medium of instruction (and even to schools run by Christian mission societies); and adult classes in English were more enthusiastically attended than those in Italian. By 1964 English had begun to replace Italian in intermediate and secondary schools in the south, and the impressive new Russian-built secondary school at Mogadishu had English as its main medium of instruction. Thus in language as well as in administrative procedures, the country seemed to be moving increasingly toward the English speaking world, despite the lingering bitterness and hostility toward Britain engendered by London's support of Ethiopia and Kenya against Somali interests, and the rupture by Somalia of diplomatic relations in March 1963.

Other formal measures designed to integrate governmental and administrative practice in the two regions must be mentioned. In June 1963 customs and tariff regulations were established on a unitary basis with the effect, at least initially, of raising prices in the north. In May 1964 the International Monetary Fund (IMF) approved a stand-by agreement enabling Somalia to draw £1.6 million to facilitate the introduction of a unified exchange-control system. Already in the previous year the Assembly had passed legislation extending universal suffrage to the north, and in August had ratified a new Local Councils Bill regularizing the system of local government throughout the state. This allowed local authorities considerable powers, particularly in education, sanitation, and town planning, and enabled them to maintain their own budgets with a variety of local taxes on housing, and, licenses, and so on. Integration in the field of law had likewise not been neglected. In April 1964 legislation was approved introducing a unified code of criminal procedure on which work had been proceeding since shortly after independence. All these measures establishing uniformity between the two regions were prepared with the advice of a Standing Advisory Committee on Integration appointed in October 1960 under the chairmanship of a United Nations legal expert.

Finally, the Establishment Commission, appointed at the end of 1962 to give effect to the provisions of the Civil Service Law coordinating salaries and conditions of service had, after three years of work, prepared new unified salary scales that were introduced in January 1966.[38] The Commission's activities over this period had shown that the original version of the law left much to be desired, and there was certainly much still to be done before conditions of service could be placed on a satisfactory footing. Although the drafting of a national system of legislation regulating pensions and gratuities had commenced in 1963, the civil service still lacked these benefits three years later.

These developments, both formal and informal, should now be viewed in the wider context of the total economic situation. As far as external trade was concerned, the position remained much as it was before union. The export trade of the two regions continued on complementary rather than competitive lines. The livestock and livestock products trade of the north, mainly with the sterling area, ran much as before, augmented by some export of the same commodities from the south. The main trade of the south, however, remained the banana crop marketed almost entirely in Italy, and shipped by Italian vessels. Efforts were being made, of course, to expand production and to improve transport and shipping facilities.[39]

Although the grain resources of the north were expected to be augmented by the development of a large state farm at

Tug Wajale producing wheat and sorghum, it seemed probable that the region would still need to import grain from abroad. This demand might be partly met by the intensification of agriculture planned and already in progress in the great arable belt between the Shebelle and Juba Rivers.[40] At the same time, work begun in 1964 on the expansion of sugar production and modernization of equipment at the Jowhar estates[41] aimed to meet the whole country's needs and provide some sugar for export. These projects seemed likely to consolidate national economic interdependence.

This trend toward economic complementarily between north and south was encouraged also by the provisions of a general Five Year Development Plan, launched in 1963. With a budget set at £70 million, this aimed at promoting the general diversification of development projects throughout the country, and included much-needed north-south road works to facilitate interregional mobility and trade. Expenditure on development, which rose from under £1 million in 1962 to £2.7 million in 1964, was charged to a separate special budget. Funds here derived almost entirely from foreign aid and loans, of which £26 million had been received by the end of 1963.

Meanwhile, with an ever-increasing range of general commitments and the added financial burden imposed by a series of famine years and armed conflict with Ethiopia, ordinary budgetary expenditure rose steadily from £8.2 million in 1961 to £12.7 million in 1966.[42] Improved fiscal and accounting procedures and a slight increase in revenue from direct taxation narrowed the budgetary gap from £2 million in 1961 to less than half that in 1965.[43] Nevertheless, this improvement was not sufficient to enable funds to be diverted from the ordinary to the special budget to finance development projects under the ambitious Five-Year Plan. In view of this obstacle and the difficulties confronting attempts to raise development revenue through commodity aid from friendly countries, the government decided in March 1966 to abandon the Five-Year Plan, and to concentrate its energies on a narrower and more realistic range of objectives. The main aims of the resulting "emergency plan" were:

1. the attainment of self-sufficiency in food-production,
2. the improvement of the livestock industry and the expansion of its export value,
3. the improvement of the banana industry to enable it to compete successfully on the world market,
4. other measures to abolish the recurrent deficit in the ordinary budget.

Responsibility for the detailed preparation of the necessary measures was assigned to a new Ministry of Planning established in the spring of 1966. By the summer of that year, two new organizations were being formed to deal with the most outstanding development needs. An Agricultural Development Agency was being opened to provide technical assistance to cooperatives and other progressive farmers in the riverine area between the Shebelle and Juba Rivers. A parallel Livestock Development Agency would concentrate on raising productivity, and improving watering facilities for the livestock sector. These new arrangements were assumed to require UN specialist technical support in financial administration, budget and government accounting, and taxation. Meanwhile, the government continued to follow the existing policy of maintaining 100 percent reserves in convertible foreign exchange to support local currency.

Conclusions

In the first half decade of its life, the Somali Republic appeared to have consummated the marriage of its two original territories quite successfully. The elections of 1964 seemed to mark a turning point, indicating the fusion of government and opposition politics on a national basis. This matched the developing economic links, formal and informal, between the two regions and the increasing uniformity of law and practice throughout the state.

That it had proved possible to hold and increasingly bind together Somaliland and Somalia, without so far the introduction of authoritarian rule or abandonment of parliamentary democracy, is some indication of the strength of traditional cultural nationalism. National cohesion was undoubtedly also reinforced by the new state's external difficulties with its neighbors over the question of further Somali unification.

Their traditional ethnic identity had thus given the population of the new Somali state a political framework that in its initial phase, encouraged the parliamentary democracy, inherited from the trusteeship period, to survive. This derived added vitality from its strong roots in the traditional pastoral social system. But if this traditional system is essentially democratic in character, its democracy is of an extreme form, in which the shifting character of political alignments and divisions militates against the ready formation of stable units. It also inhibits the smooth and efficient working of modern government on a national level.

This was no doubt partly alleviated by the omnipresent character and strength of following of the SYL government party throughout the state.[44] Yet it would be misleading to regard this organization as a monolithic machine dominating all aspects of life in the state, and seamlessly directed from above by an exclusive clique. The party was too loosely structured, and encompassed too many divergent lineage interests, to have this character; nor was the state's civil service simply an offshoot of the party. Although the majority of civil servants were probably SYL supporters, by no means all, at any level in the official hierarchy, were affiliates of the government party. Thus, as was evident at the 1964 elections, district and provincial commissioners did not by any means all support the government in a political sense; and the same holds true of the police. Many senior civil servants, indeed, tended to regard politicians skeptically with the distrust they displayed toward all those who held power. Moreover, as the constitution actually worked in practice, and with the funds they could discreetly disburse to influence votes, Somali governments were highly sensitive to the pressure of public opinion, not only from their own dissident ranks inside and outside the National Assembly, but also from their opponents. Parliament was, of course, an ideal theatre for Somalis with their love of argument and debate. Securing consensus was another matter, and traditional methods of reaching agreement required a large expenditure of time to enable everyone present to express his opinion.

With the difficulties regularly experienced in securing a parliamentary majority, there were naturally advocates of a more highly centralized and authoritarian system to facilitate decision making, and as necessary to respond to the country's internal and external needs. As events proved, those who took this view were ahead of their time. For the moment, opinion seemed to be satisfied by the promise shown of the new government led by Prime Minister Abdirazaq Haji Hussen, an SYL stalwart, widely respected for his dynamism and determination.[45] His ministers were young men, largely chosen for their technical expertise, and, as he insisted, would thus enable his administration to establish and maintain higher standards of probity and efficiency than his predecessors. Their first actions sought to improve the civil service by introducing in-service training and weeding out corrupt and inefficient staff.

Those who had been adversely affected by these changes, and those of the old government who were excluded in the new administration, naturally trended to be hostile to the premier. Where changes within the ranks of the civil service led to the replacement of officials belonging to other clans by men of the premier's own clan-family (Darod), his critics charged him with tribal favoritism —despite his own vehement denunciations of this practice.[46] When this resulted in the displacement of northerners of the Isaq and Dir groups, it tended to drive them into the arms of the Hawiye; or at least such of the Hawiye as opposed the government. This helped to ease relationships between these northern and southern groups, where they were strained by conflict over the language issue; we see how rivalries based largely on clan cleavages lead to new temporary associations of perceived advantage within a common system, founded, upon the union of the two territories.

When this chapter was originally written (June 1966), the opposition parties were again in disarray, a situation from which they seemed to emerge as distinct groupings only at election, and attempts were being made to transform the SNC into a new party with a more specifically socialist policy, advocating firmer ties with Russia and Eastern Europe or China. These moves seemed to be led by part of the former SNC leadership (while other leading members of the party appeared to be on the verge of throwing in their lot with the government), and by those elements within the SYL who were hostile to 'Abdirazaq's leadership. Whether or not this would result in a radical split within the SYL as a whole remained to be seen. It seemed a little unlikely, however, since some of those who opposed the premier shared his clan connections and the SYL had weathered many similar storms in the past.

How these trends might develop in the future would depend to a considerable extent on the resoluteness with which the government pursued the popular issue of further Somali unification. This would surely remain a major test of any Somali government's popularity until public opinion learned to understand the difficulties of the situation and accepted national dismemberment with greater fatalism. As far as the relations between northerners and southerners were concerned, with their many complicated facets, these promised to remain a source of continuing rivalry with explosive potential.

Notes

1. Camels are not ridden. But some are trained as burden animals and used to transport the nomad's ten (and its contents) from place to place as families move with their livestock.

2. In some cases here whole clans, with populations as high as 100,000, act as single diya-paying groups. This extension of solidarity seems to be associated with cultivation and landholding on a clan basis.

3. For fuller analysis of traditional Somali social structure see my *Pastoral Democracy*, Oxford: Oxford University Press, 1999.

4. Compare A. Castagno's excellent study of Somali party politics in J.S. Coleman and CG. Rosberg, *Political Parties and National integration in Tropical Africa* (Berkeley: University of California Press, 1964, pp.512-59.

5. It should be understood here that in the modern setting as well as the traditional, poetry provides an important vehicle for affecting political attitudes and sentiments, the effectiveness of which is increased rather than decreased with modern means of mass communication by radio broadcasting. See Colin Legum, "Somali Liberation Song's", Journal of Modern African Studies, 1, 1963, pp.503-519; and B.W. Andrzejewski and I.M. Lewis, *Somali Poetry*, Oxford: Oxford University Press, 1964.

6. See I.M. Lewis, *A Modern History of the Somali*, Oxford: James Currey, 2002, pp.63-91 on this period. This religious rebellion with its analogies to that in the Sudan arose in circumstances of increasing Christian and particularly Ethiopia encroachment in Somaliland, and was as much directed against the Ethiopians as against the British and their allies, the Italians.

7. The only development of significance was the increasing adoption of agriculture in the northwest and this was unconnected with any government action.

8. A modest and by no means exhaustive survey of the resources of the Protectorate conducted by a former administrative officer and geologist had proved disappointing. See J.A. Hunt, *A General Survey of the Somaliland Protectorate, 1944-1950*, (London: 1951).

9. For an original and perceptive view of conditions in the Protectorate at this time, see the Canadian novelist M. Laurence's *The Prophet's Camel Bell* (London: 1963).

10. These were selected by the Governor from a list of twenty-four candidates proposed after a series of public meetings. Those proposed were nominated on a clan and not a party basis, which reflected current political realities at the time.

11. For a fuller discussion of this and the issues involved, see Lewis, pp. 59-62; J. Drysdale, *The Somali Dipute*, (London: 1964), pp.74-87.

12. For further details, see Lewis *A Modern History*, pp.153-155; Castagno, in Coleman and Rosberg. *Political Parties*, pp.542-546.

13. Although the cotton trade was at first promising the world slump in cotton prices caused the emphasis to shift increasingly toward banana cultivation after 1932.

14. Frnest Bevin proposed a union of the former British, Italian, and Ethiopian Somali territories under a trusteeship administration by Britain or some other friendly power.

15. The issues involved in the final decision to consign Somalia to Italian administration for a ten-year period under UN mandate are discussed in Lewis, pp.124-28: see also Drysdale *The Somali Dispute*, pp.65-73.

16. The most important of these was the Hizbia Digil-Mirifle, founded in 1947 and drawing most of its support from the Digil and Rahanwn clans of Southern Somalia (the Sab) between the rivers.

17. For further details of educational developments here and in British Somaliland, see A. Castagno, in Helen Kitchen, ed., *The Educated African* (New York: 1962).

18. Somali independent constitutional Party, the new sanitized name for the old HDMS. Clan names for parties having been banned by the national assembly.

19. Whereas the previous municipal elections had seen sixteen parties in the field, in these first national elections, wider interests and alliances had reduced the number of competitors to six. For a detailed account of the procedural aspects of the elections, see AFIS, *Le prime elezioni politiche in Somalia* (Mogadishu: 1957).

20. For fuller details on the political circumstances at the time see, Lewis, *A Modern History*, pp.157-160; and Castagno in Coleman and Rosberg, *Political Parties*, pp.536-540.

21. In the previous municipal elections of October 1958, women had voted for the first time in Somalia and, despite all predictions to the contrary, shown by the extent of their participation, expressed extreme interest.

22. The annual Italian subsidy in the period 1950-55 was approximately £3 million spent mainly on reconstruction and public works, communications, education, and health, and in the initial period on public security.

23. For an excellent study of Somalia's economics during the trusteeship period, see Mark Karp, *The Economics of Trusteship in Somalia* (Boston: Boston University Press, 1960).

24. The constitution was prepared by a series of committees after consultation with other African governments, see G.A. Costanzo, *Prob-*

lemi constituzionali della Somalia nella preparazione all'Independenza, (Milan: Giuffire, 1962).

25. Britain's interests in the new Republic were restricted to the granting of over-flying rights and to the retention of its powerful BBC Middle Eastern Service relay transmitter at Berbera.

26. Italian interests, as well as those of the well-being of its few thousand plantation settlers, were concerned with the maintenance of the Italian Monopoly in the banana trade.

27. In the traditional national pedigree, ultimately these three groups share a connection with an ancestor called Irir and the term "Irirism" had crept into political discourse at this time.

28. On the vexed question (as it then was) of written Somali and the rival claims of the Arabic and Roman scripts, as well as of indigenous orthographies, see Lewis, "The Gadabursi Somali Script", *Bulletin of the School of Oriental and African Studies,* 1958, pp.134-156.

29. The foreign advocates of English were the few British officials retained for a short period after independence in the north, the UN staff, and the American aid mission.

30. By 1963, half the heads of departments in ministries were northerners.

31. In the south, the only area where the vote went against the constitution (and the government) was Hiran province occupied mainly by the Hawiye. As Castagno points out (in Coleman and Rosberg, pp.548), this may be interpreted as a swing of Hawiye opinion, led by a former Hawiye premier, against the Darod dominated government.

32. For further details see Lewis, *A Modern History,* pp.175-77.

33. Sheikh' Ali Jumaleh was Adan Abdullah Osman's main rival in the election in the assembly held in July 1961 for the presidency of the Republic.

34. The HDMS remained in scope principally concerned with its own peoples in the region between the rivers and had no national organization.

35. For further information on the GSL, see Castagno, (in Coleman and Rosberg), pp.549-550.

36. Cf. Lewis, *A Modern History,* pp.178ff, and "Recent developments in the Somali Dispute", *African Affairs,* 66, 1967, pp.104-112.

37. The primary function of well-endowed business interests here is frequently in supporting the electoral campaigns of selected candi-

dates for election to the national assembly. Businessmen are often said to have built up particular deputies and ministers.

38. See Presidency of the Council of Ministers, *Revision of the Somali Civil Service*, Mogadishu, October 1965.

39. New arrangements for the export of the banana crop introduced in 1965 resulted in a widening of the international market, Italy being no longer the sole but still the main importer. See "The Banana Crisis" in *Dalka: The Homeland*, July 1965, pp.8-9.

40. This fertile area of some 210,000 sq. km. was subjected to an intensive agricultural and water survey under the joint auspices of the UN Special Fund and the FAO. Indications both for the expansion of irrigation cultivation along the rivers and for the improvement of dry-land farming between them were promising. Small improvements in farming methods and improved fertilization could easily treble current yields and enable the Republic to be self-sufficient in grain. See Agriculture and Water Survey, Somalia: Interim Report of Agriculture and Economics: Afgoi-Bur Hacaba-Hoddur Regions (Mogadishu: State Printing House: 1964). With Russian aid a state farm covering 20,000 hectares of land was under construction between Jelib and Jamama along the lower Juba. Crops to be planted included sesame, sunflower, groundnuts, and cotton. A cotton gin and an oil extraction plant were to be included.

41. These were run by a partly nationalized company in which the government held half the shares.

42. The main heads of expenditure were: transport and communications, agriculture, industrial development, housing and water supplies, and irrigation and drainage. In the period up to 1965, road improvement was mainly concentrated in the south. Different sections of the long tarmac road linking the U.S.-aided port developments at Kismayu with the lower Juba banana plantations, and these in turn with those on the Shebelle and on to Mogadishu, were under construction by the Germans, Chinese, and the European Economic Commission.

43. The budget deficit was made good by directs grants from Italy and Britain in 1962, by Italy and China in the following year.

44. As was well-known, the independent-mindedness of many SYL members of the Assembly proved financially rewarding during Dr. Abdirashid's Premiership. The power of deputies was further enshrined in the constitution, which required votes to be recorded in secret, so creating formidable problems for party discipline.

45. The president's opponents claimed that this action was influenced by his desire to secure a prime minister favorable to his reelection as head of state: his relations with the previous premier had deterio-

rated. Later to consolidate his personal position and also coordinate policy within the SYL in and outside the Assembly caucus, the premier was elected secretary of the party in December 1964.

46. Following the resignation of the minister of finance, a cabinet reshuffle took place in the spring of 1966. This slightly increased the proportion of Darod Ministers, but left the representation of other clans much as before. More significantly perhaps, the northern region president of the Assembly was replaced in March 1966 by a southerner of the Digil Rahanwin group.

Two

THE BLOODLESS COUP (1969)

✦

In the lives of nations, as of men, reputations all too often achieve their widest currency when they are already out of date. The Somali Republic is no exception to this general rule. Although the real circumstances had already significantly altered before the military brusquely seized power in October 1969, Somalia was still generally known for democracy at home and trouble abroad. The first of these characterizations referred to the striking persistence of a vigorous and effective multiparty parliamentary system. The second related to the seemingly uniquely intractable nature of the "Somali dispute", which committed the Republic to supporting the secessionist claims of the contiguous Somali populations of Kenya, Ethiopia, and French Somaliland, at the price of severely strained relations with these neighboring states. These and other attributes unusual amongst the new states of sub-Saharan Africa appeared to be closely connected with the Republic's exuberant sense of national identity, a quality all the more remarkable in being firmly grounded in a long-standing and entirely traditional cultural nationalism.

This chapter seeks to analyze the political precipitants of the 1969 *coup d'etat*, to assess its significance, and to reconsider the relationship that has previously been assumed to exist in Somalia between internal democracy, external irredentism, and traditional nationalism. In pursuing these themes here it is necessary first to elucidate the relationship between the Somali nation on the one hand, and the Somali state on the other, and to outline the main linkages that had grown up between traditional and modern political interest groups and institutions.

State and Nation

As is now glaringly obvious, most of the new African countries are states rather than nations, in the sense that they generally lack any uniform national culture to serve as an effective basis for a fully fledged patriotism transcending their numerous internal tribal divisions. At a popular level, African politics have become virtually synonymous with tribalism and the same circumstance explains the vogue that the euphemistic if more comprehensive term "pluralism" currently enjoys in erudite circles. It is easy to exaggerate and oversimplify, but there is little doubt that most African states have witnessed an intensification of their internal tribal and other divisions since independence. Against their background the Somali Republic appears at first sight as a striking anomaly. In contrast to its neighbors, the state owes its very existence to the sense of common identity and destiny that the Somalis displayed as a people and that while sharpened by colonization, was certainly not created by it.

This sense of community is anchored in the possession of a broadly homogenous and largely pastoral culture, a common language (with one major cleavage), and a fervent and deep-rooted devotion to Islam, which reached their shores over a thousand years ago. These attributes in Somali eyes distinguish them clearly from other neighboring ethnic groups in northeast Africa. Self-determination has always meant Somali-determination; hence, as I have argued previously, the only form of pan-Africanism that has ever enjoyed much support follows the principle that charity begins at home, and is limited in scope to the surrounding Somali areas.

On the basis of this traditional cultural unity, in 1960, as we have seen, the former British Somaliland Protectorate and UN Trust Territory of Somalia (administered by Italy) joined together as the northern and southern regions of the Somali Republic. The formation of this new state left many Somalis outside the fold and still under foreign rule—as part of eastern Ethiopia, northern Kenya, and French Somaliland (known since 1967 as the French Territory of the Afars and Isas, and subsequently as the Republic of Djibouti). The Somali Republic was thus in its terms from the outset incomplete, and this encouraged its leaders to embark on a process of external expansion, which is the opposite of that pursued in other African states.[1] The abiding preoccupation of most African states has been with internal nation-building, with the foundation and development of an integrated national culture capable of transforming politically independent states into culturally distinctive nations or, where that fails, federal structures.

For the Somali Republic, however, the problem was very different. In its truncated circumstances, the aim was from the first to expand the state so that it fully comprehended the nation: nationhood had already been achieved, and political fulfillment was awaited as a single all-embracing Somali state. This desire to continue and bring to fruition a process that received international sanction with the formation of the Republic seemed perfectly natural in Somali eyes; but it was, of course, the basis of the Somali dispute with Ethiopia, Kenya, and France. This aim was pursued with varying degrees of militancy, if with little success, by successive Somali governments in the period from independence until 1967, for these countries were as reluctant to cede territory and subjects as the Republic was anxious to acquire them. In this context the fact that the Somali people—estimated to number some

4 million—did not form a single, united political group in the precolonial era was scarcely relevant (except, perhaps, to those who confounded the concepts of state and nation). They considered that the significant thing was their possession of a vigorous sense of cultural nationalism of a kind familiar to students of nineteenth-century European nationalism and that in the colonial period, gained new political meaning. Here we see an example of the politicalization of an existing cultural identity. This is the reverse of the elaboration of cultural distinction to give substance and moral weight to political interests—a process that although already well known to historians, has received a great deal of attention and emphasis in discussion of politics in the Third World.[2]

It is also, I consider, equally pointless to debate whether the Somali people are a tribe or a nation. While in political rhetoric the first is currently a term of abuse and the second of approbation, this simply serves to highlight the essential relativity of the two concepts, which is indeed self-evident when one considers the meaning attached to the term "nation" in an international context. Clearly both words connote the same thing—a group—and the only significant distinction that might be conceded is that of scale; in that case, tribes are little nations and nations are big tribes. When, however, we are dealing with populations several million strong, we are surely entitled to use the larger more inclusive term.[3]

The Nation and Its Traditional Subdivisions

If then, as I argue here, the Somali people are to be considered a nation, part of which achieved independent statehood in the Republic, is the implication that their national, cultural homogeneity has saved them from the vicious tribal factionalism that plagues the political life of other African states? Somali nationalist politicians certainly do not think so. Indeed, since the birth of modern political parties in the 1940s, these leaders have consistently, if in the nature of things vainly, inveighed against the sectarian evils that have so often jeopardized their efforts to unite. These divisive and constricting forces are identified as tribalism and equated with similar particularistic attachments in other African states. If, however, the effects are much the same, the institutions that produce them differ. The linguistically and culturally distinct ethnic divisions that threaten the fragile cohesion of most African states are here replaced by kinship-based ties that if they lack the trappings of cultural uniqueness, are arguably even more deeply entrenched and paralyzing in their effects.

It is thus clanship in the technical sense, rather than tribalism that commands allegiance and frustrates the achievement of much that is in the national interest. Strictly, all the units referred to here are conceived of by the Somali as lineages, based on common descent traced in the male line from an eponymous ancestor. I use the terms "clan-family", "clan", and "lineage" for convenience to indicate groups of descending size and to emphasize, however, that these analytical distinctions refer to essentially relative levels of lineage allegiance. These ties, moreover, are the more crippling in that they are embedded within the existing structure of nationhood. They represent the price that Somalis pay for their preformed national identity founded upon these very divisions. The position is further complicated by the fact that each individual is bound not merely to one specific clan group, but to an almost infinite and homogeneous series of such subgroups. One's loyalties ebb and flow between different levels of lineage allegiance according to the context in which one is acting.

The patrilineal genealogies that record these kinship ties are thus not conserved simply for antiquarian or historical reasons. Their significance is primarily political, and their function to place the individual socially and politically in a world of transient and shifting loyalties. Clan and lineage genealogies thus essentially define friend and foe, and the character of the relations between people is in principle a direct reflection of their closeness or distance in genealogical space—of the "number of ancestors counted apart" as Somalis express it.

At the highest level, the genealogies that each person learns in childhood converge in a single national pedigree. Hence the entire Somali nation can ultimately be represented on a single all-embracing family tree. This is one aspect of traditional Somali nationalism.

Beneath this level, the most significant groups in the national genealogy are six large clan-families. Of these the *Dir* live in the northwest, extending into French Somaliland and with one small pocket in southern Somalia; and the Isaq occupy the center of Somaliland. The Darod, who alone number well over a million, form a bridge between the former British Protectorate and northeastern Somalia, and also extend in force into eastern Ethiopia and northern Kenya. They are at once the largest and most widely distributed Somali group with the most direct stake in the pan-Somali campaign for union with the missing territories, a fact that has not passed unobserved by hostile governments seeking to refute Somali nationalist claims in Ethiopia and Kenya. The Hawiye, who live in a wide area in and round the capital city Mogadishu, also occur again in the south of the Republic and extend into Kenya. The people of these four groups are traditionally and still overwhelmingly today pastoralists, herding sheep, goats, camels, and in some areas cattle, over vast expanses of territory. Produce from this pastoral economy provides the largest single component in Somali exports.

The remaining two groups in the national genealogy are the Digil and Rahanwin, who occupy the comparatively fertile area between the Juba and Shebelle Rivers—the only permanent watercourses in this otherwise largely arid land. They practice a mixed economy with an emphasis on cultivation. Their region provides Somalia's other main export: the plantation banana crop. These two clan-families speak a distinctive dialect (or even separate language, '*Af May-may*), and retain special cultural features that set them apart from the rest of the nation. They constitute in fact the only division with sufficiently developed cultural differences to warrant the term "tribalism". But the significance of their regional distinctiveness is offset since, unlike their nomadic countrymen, they are of very mixed origin. They represent in fact an amalgam of ancient cultivating stock and more recent and once nomadic immigrants from the other Somali clans. Almost every other Somali lineage has some offshoot living among them. This mixed constitution gives the Digil and Rahanwin potential ties with the other four clan-families. And such unity as their heterogeneous structure possesses has been further eroded by legislation (adopted in 1960) to maintain the right of every Somali to live and farm where he chooses, irrespective of his relationship with other local people. This official abolition of the status of client-tenant has thus encouraged many partially assimilated lineage fractions to assert their original identity, and to participate on this basis in national politics.

These are the main units within the nation. In their traditional setting, however, these entities were generally too large and too widely dispersed to act as effective political units. They represented a largely unrealized political potential. Within them, individuals identified with and acted as members of smaller units that we can usefully distinguish as clans, these having a maximum population of some 100,000 and being often considerably smaller. Clans in turn did not exist on a permanent footing; rather, in Chinese-box fashion they comprised a series of smaller lineage subdivisions that might be mobilized at any level of grouping. This fluid pattern of shifting loyalties, well adapted to the exigencies of the nomadic life that discouraged the formation of permanently established units, was accompanied by an equally loose and highly democratic process of government. Whenever, at any point in the series of segments, a lineage was mobilized, its policy was determined in ad hoc assemblies attended by all the adult men concerned, or their representatives. Men of energy, valor, and wealth, as well as sagacity and wit, were highly respected; and these and other factors enabled certain individuals to build up temporary followings and spheres of influence, thus becoming "big men". Some clans, admittedly, had leaders (sometimes dignified with the Arab title

Sultan), but these were essentially mediatory and ritual figureheads; and with the general exception of the southern Somali cultivators (the Digil and Rahanwin), there was no clearly defined hierarchy of established chiefly offices. This, of course, did not prevent the colonial administrations from appointing salaried headmen and chiefs at various levels of lineage division.

Nevertheless, as in other highly egalitarian cultures, traditional Somali attitudes toward power and authority were distinctly ambivalent. For all their hardy republicanism and individualism, and perhaps indeed because of the very difficulties involved in wielding effective power in such unpropitious conditions, the figure of the tyrant and despot seems always to have held a curious fascination for the pastoral nomads. To some extent this is also a facet of the martial character of traditional Somali society, where the display of force, however brutal and merciless, is associated with manly virility and contrasted with weakness, a quality, which though despised, is in principle held to possess a certain compensating mystical virtue.

In this generally turbulent society with its mercurial political formations, a certain stability was provided in the basic traditional political unit, the so-called diya-paying group. Rarely boasting more than a few thousand warriors, these groups consisted of closely related patrilineal kinsmen who had combined together for mutual support and were parties to a specific treaty (her), which contained many features comparable to those of the social contract of the political philosophers. The crucial bond here was the common obligation to pay and receive damages for injury and death (Arabic, diya) in concert. If one member of a group was killed or wounded, his comrades rallied together until revenge or satisfactory damages had been exacted. Fighting, when it occurred, tended to spread rapidly, however, soon involving the members not only of the dia-paying groups directly responsible, but also those of more distant kin and allies. With such rapidly escalating hostilities, where group identities were constantly being enlarged as the more inclusive levels of lineage patriotism became involved, whole clans would eventually be mobilized to defend their component lineages against their foes.

In this context of internal conflict, constituent dia-paying group loyalties would be set aside for the duration of the wider confrontation. As soon as fighting between clans ceased and tension at this level abated, these units would again fall apart into their component lineages. In such a conflict-ridden culture, peacemakers had clearly an important role to play, and here appropriately religion came to the aid of a divided society. Local Muslim leaders were expected to intercede between men, as much as between men and God. These Sheikhs symbolized the transcendental brotherly love of the Islamic community, and although ultimately forced to rely on traditional lineage ties, they were ideally committed to the furtherance of peace between warring clans and lineages. The complementary character of the two roles was reflected in the traditional Somali view that mankind comprised two fundamental categories: men of the spear, and men of God. (Thus, the ethnocentric development studies concept "civil society", invoked with such hackneyed regularity by development workers, is of highly questionable validity in this Somali case. Strictly, it applies theoretically only to men of God. Women are not fully included, either, since their allegiance is primarily to their father's kin, or after marriage to their husband's).

This segmentary political system continues to provide the basic framework within which modern Somali political organizations operate. To a significant extent, this is a tribute to the traditional structure's capacity to absorb innovating influences and modernizing trends with a minimum of dislocation. For although the region attracts substantial development funds, except in a few urban settings, radical socioeconomic change on any appreciable scale has scarcely taken place. Certainly little has so far occurred to diminish the strength of these traditional imperatives, which, as with tribalism elsewhere, thrive on increasing competition for scant resources, whether these are of traditional or modern origin. Where, after independence, the government was still the main employer, but no general pension scheme existed and material conditions were generally precarious, clansmen naturally continued to regard their traditional kinship ties as their ultimate safeguard and protection. Consequently, despite the existence of an unusually well-trained and effective police force, fights and feuds in the rural areas remained a characteristic if commonplace feature of life, and towns were not immune from their politically polarizing consequences. Only the rich could sometimes afford to disregard these lineage bonds, and more typically sought to employ them selectively to advance their own personal interests. Here, however, they had to be prepared to come to terms with the claims that would inevitably be made on their resources by their less successful clansmen.

The principle that, irrespective of education or ability, kinship ties should be recognized and honored permeated all aspects of life. It affected the composition and working of political parties and intruded forcibly into every government department and private enterprise. It also cut completely across the largely nominal division between urban and rural society. Hence, before the 1969 coup, cabinet ministers and wealthy urban merchants were still strongly bound to their rural cousins, who looked to them for employment and preferment. The former in turn benefited from this rural support in situations—such as elections—when they needed it. Equally, although it had become fashionable to invest in banana plantations, rich and powerful men often continued to maintain profitable livestock interests (and therefore viable social and political connections) in the rural economy.

The wealthy townsman was frequently not only a nomad at heart but also in pocket, and in urban life itself kinship continued to play an important role. So, for instance, in the absence of any general system of comprehensive motor insurance, the traditional (diya-paying group) procedure of life insurance was extended in the towns to cover traffic accidents. In this, and many other respects, despite rural-urban cultural distinctions, the continuities between town and country were more binding and significant than the discontinuities.

The enduring appeal of these traditional imperatives posed serious problems for those who sought to overcome their divisive implications and to replace them by a steady attachment to the transcendent nation. A revealing issue here concerned the necessity to find a formula to elicit and express clan identity that was both compatible with modern nationalist aspirations and, at the same time, in tune with the realities of clanship. Where members of the elite maintained that clanship was as dead as the dodo, it was clearly impossible to employ the old brusque expression "What is your clan?" in order to establish a person's most basic political affiliation. This difficulty was tackled with typical Somali ingenuity. Clanship was kept at arm's length by consigning it to the past, and so, in the heady days prior to independence, it became fashionable to speak of a man's ex-clan, the English word "ex" being even adopted into the Somali language expressly for this purpose! Nationalist solidarity had become *a façon de parler* if nothing else.

Party Politics Before The Coup

These were the general political conditions with which party politics and bureaucratic government had to come to terms if they were to relate meaningfully to social and political realities. Immediately prior to independence and the union of the two ex-colonies to form the Republic, as we have seen, there were four main political parties. In the south (the Italian sphere) the Somali Youth League, originally founded in 1943 during the British Military Administration of Somalia (1941-50) held a secure monopoly of power and represented a loose consortium of all the main clan groups. Its chief rival was the Digil Mirifle party (HDMS) catering for the separatist interests of the *Digil* and *Rahanwn* clans and with no following outside that area. While the SYL also had at this time adherents in the north (British

Somaliland), the principal parties there were the Somaliland National League (with a tradition going back to 1935) and the more recently formed United Somali Party. The former represented the Isaq clan, which had dominated the life of the British Protectorate since its inception. The latter catered for the interests of the Dir clans of the west and the Darod of the east. Although far apart geographically and scarcely interacting at all, these two clans had at least one thing in common: joint distinction from, and potential antagonism toward the Isaq. They thus acted on the well-tried Somali political maxim that one's enemy's enemy is one's friend.

When, amalgamating the ex-British and ex-Italian territories, the Republic was proclaimed on July 1, 1960, as we have seen in the previous chapter, the two existing legislatures combined to form a single National Assembly at Mogadishu. The southern assembly president, Adan Abdulle Osman, a Hawiye politician of great esteem and experience, was elected provisional head of state and confirmed in office by a referendum a year later. Dr. Abdirashid Ali Shirmake, a prominent member of the Darod leadership of the SYL, who had recently returned from a course in political science in Rome, was appointed prime minister and formed a coalition cabinet containing SYL, and U.S.P. members. The new government included four northern (ex-Protectorate) ministers, two of whom were Darod and two Isaq.

At this time, it will be evident that the identity of the northern region as a whole was reflected in the existence of the two northern parties, neither of which had any direct support in the south. At the same time, the separate interests of the main northern clans, the Isaq on the one hand, and the Dir and Darod on the other, were faithfully mirrored in their two distinct parties. In the south, apart from the HDMS, comparable particularistic clan interests were catered for within the omnibus SYL (see Chapter One for details).

The creation of the Republic radically altered the position of the northern regions, and also affected the balance of power between opposing clan groups in the state as a whole. The capital both of politics and of business was now in the south, and northerners were forced to adjust to this situation, and to adapt their British colonial experience to fit the Italian pattern in the south. The resolution of the inevitable problems that this process involved, and particularly those posed by the northerners' attachment to English and that of the southerners to Italian, was to some extent eased by the ten-year period of British administration, which the south had experienced after the Italian defeat in East Africa, before independence. Nevertheless, there was initially considerable friction between the exponents of these two rival colonial traditions. The northern political, administrative, and commercial elite did not immediately accept that to further their interests effectively they had now to work through Mogadishu.

As we have seen, the first two years of the Republic's life were consequently marred by many signs of northern discontent and disaffection. The most dramatic was the short-lived and unsuccessful coup staged by a group of young Sandhurst-trained officers. By 1963, however, the north appeared to have come to accept the Republic as an established framework within which to pursue its interests. The political parties, which had become more and more out of touch with current political realities, now adjusted to this situation. The uneasy SYL-SNL-USP alliance fell apart with the formation of a new party called the Somali National Congress (SNC). This was led jointly by a former Isaq minister, and a prominent ex-SYL politician of the Hawiye clan (see Table 1). The USP was disbanded, its members joining either the SNC or the SYL, some also joined forces with a more radical new party called the Somali Democratic Party.

TABLE 1: Groups, Parties, and Personalities

Parties
SNC (Isaq, Dir)
SDU (Dir, Darod)
HDMS (Digil, Rahanwin)
SYL (Darod; all clans)
Personalities
Dr Abdirashid Ali Shirmarke,
Darod: Premier, 1960-67; President, 1967-69, assassinated 1969
Adan Abdulle Osman, Hawiye: President, 1960-67; arrested 1969
Abdirazaq Haji Hussen, Darod: Premier, 1964-67; arrested 1969
Mohamed Haji Ibrahim Egal, Isaq: Premier, 1967-69, arrested 1969
General Mohamed Abshir, Darod: first commander of the Somali police; forced to resign and placed under house arrest at the time of the coup
General Jama Ali Korshell, Darod: commander of police from 1969; involved in coup and made Vice-President of Supreme Revolutionary Council, denounced as a traitor and arrested 1970
General Mohamed Siyad Barre, Darod: Army Commander 1969; led coup and became President 1969, overthrown 1990

The alteration in party alignments was highly significant. The formation of the SNC on a basis of Isaq Hawiye, and Dir elements represented a new attempt to capitalize on the close genealogical relationships of these three groups in opposition to the Darod-led SYL. It signified the collapse of the northern-southern regional political axis, and indicated the common commitment of all the political leaders to the Republic as a unitary state. It demonstrated that the Isaq and

Dir of the north apparently now recognized that they shared common interests not only with the southern Dir but also with the Hawiye. This was all the more striking in that, prior to the formation of the independent state there had been no effective contact at all between the Isaq and northern Dir on the one hand, and the Hawiye of the south on the other. The viability of this new pattern of party allegiances was put to the test in the general elections of 1969. These coincided with a period of maximum nationalist fervor, when the Republic's perennial dispute with Ethiopia flared into open warfare. Twenty-one parties and 973 candidates contested the elections, which the SYL won by gaining 69 of the available 123 seats. The SNC won 22, the SDU 15, while the HDMS secured only 9 seats.

The new SYL government formed after these elections had far-reaching implications. The previous premier was replaced by another leading Darod politician, but from a different lineage. Again, the new government contained northern as well as southern ministers, and representatives of all the main Somali clans. But the split in the ranks of the Darod leadership of the SYL had profound consequences, which were all the more embarrassing to stable administration since they existed within the government party itself. Here it is necessary to appreciate that, except on special issues, voting in the Assembly was usually conducted by secret ballot. This allowed individual deputies great freedom of maneuver and immense power, severely hampering the maintenance of party discipline. Members of the Assembly who had promised their support for the government might, in fact, not give it if they found sufficient encouragement to do otherwise. The government of 1964 was severely harassed in this fashion and, despite a number of cabinet changes, actually resigned in 1966 following its defeat over an unimportant issue. With the encouragement of the president, however, it was reappointed, and a determined effort was made to patch over the party's persistent internal cleavages. But the respite this brought was short-lived. The fact that it now counted 105 members in the Assembly (following defections from other parties) paradoxically only compounded its many difficulties.

Matters came to a head with the election by the Assembly of a new president of the Republic in 1967. The existing Hawiye incumbent was supported by the Darod premier and opposed by the latter's Darod predecessor, Shirmarke, who was now campaigning in alliance with the Isaq ex-leader of the SNC. This experienced politician, Mohamed Haji Ibrahim Egal, had in fact recently joined the SYL and was one of those siding with Shirmarke in opposition to the premier, Abdirazaq Haji Hussen. In the event, Shirmarke turned the tables on his opponent and was elected president by the National Assembly. So the 1969 government resigned, and Egal was summoned to replace it with a new team of ministers.

These developments greatly reduced the significance of the SNC. For the first time a northerner was premier and his government, like all its predecessors, was built on the tacit principle of clan balance. The Dir-Isaq-Hawiye alliance represented by the SNC was now decisively shattered with the continued division of the Darod bloc within the SYL. Indeed, these large groups had temporarily lost their significance in party politics, and effective allegiance had fallen back to the smaller constituent lineages, which were now combining across their parent divisions. Apparently the hostilities and animosities between the smaller lineage groups, which had necessarily been suppressed to some extent in the situation of wider national solidarity against Ethiopia and Kenya, had now come again to the fore.

This reemergence of small-group particularism coincided with growing disillusion among the urban elite about the effectiveness of the methods that hitherto had been applied in the campaign to secure the missing Somali territories. So, arguing that if he could first secure the friendship of Ethiopia and Kenya, his government would be more likely to meet with success in furthering Somali nationalist claims, Egal at once embarked on a policy of détente with his powerful neighbors. Although this new policy initially aroused hostility at home, with the financial resources at his disposal the new premier was soon able to secure a favorable balance of cautious support. While he was obviously vulnerable on this ground, his personal position vis-à-vis his main Darod opponent (the ousted premier, Hussen) was entirely secure. Because the president was now Darod, the premier must of necessity belong to a different clan.

The elections of March 1969 confirmed all these trends. Despite new electoral regulations designed to discourage one-man lineage parties, sixty-two parties—mainly of this type—fielded 1,002 candidates.[4] This was a record even for Somalia. The SYL won three seats, and the emasculated SNC only one. The Digil and Rahanwin, whose cohesion had been progressively eroded through their members' increasing participation in other parties (especially the SYL), gained only three seats for their local party, the HDMS. With such intense competition involving an unprecedentedly large number of senior civil servants who had resigned from their posts to enter the lists, electoral expenses had been unusually heavy, and those who had succeeded in gaining a seat in the National Assembly were naturally anxious to recover their costs at the earliest possible opportunity. In a nation where the annual budget ran at approximately £15 million, some candidates were estimated to have spent as much as £15,000!

So when the Darod president, Dr. Abdirashid Ali Shirmarke, again summoned his Isaq ally, Mohamed Haji Ibrahim Egal, to form a government, and the latter selected a group of ministers representing the main clan blocs on the standard pattern, no one imagined that this new administration would founder for lack of support in the national assembly. Few, however, can have anticipated the enthusiasm with which the new government would be received. At the very first meeting of the assembly, with the sole exception of Abdirazaq Haji Hussen, all the opposition members crossed the floor to join the SYL government. If this haste to demonstrate their unqualified support for Egal and his colleagues appeared unseemly to some critics, those deputies concerned could protest, not without truth, that they knew where the interest of their constituents (as well as their own) lay. Thus with surprisingly little fuss or clamor, the Somali Republic had at last joined the ranks of African one-party states.

The Military Revolution of October 1969

In this situation where the Republic was now completely dominated by the longest-lived and most comprehensive party organization in Somali political history, it is clear that the big clan blocs had, for the moment at least, lost much of their political identity. Two factors seem of major importance here. First, the Republic's markedly improved relations with Kenya and Ethiopia very much reduced the external pressures bearing on the state as a whole, and thus tended to encourage the mobilization of loyalties at the lowest levels of lineage organization. Secondly, within the state, the continuing schism in the ranks of the Darod elite and the fact that the head of state was drawn from this group, reinforced the same trend. For as long as the leading Darod politicians were incapable of working together there was little incentive for those of other equivalent lineage blocs to unite against them. But although this might be taken to imply that tribalism in its special Somali form had also disappeared, this was far from being the case.

As the 1969 elections so forcibly showed, effective political solidarity had simply reverted to much lower levels in the segmentary system. Polical commitment was indeed mainly—although not solely—engaged at levels that were so parochial that they could be directly served only by one-man parties that in the national political context were simply not viable entities. Nor, of course, were there sufficient seats in the National Assembly to accommodate a representative from each primary lineage in the country. Yet the very large proportion of disappointed candidates (almost 90 percent) cannot be taken as any direct measure of the disequilibrium between the total number of grass-roots constituency units seeking representation and those who actually managed to return a member to the Assembly. Most of the competing local units fielded several candidates under different party banners, some of which were frankly parochial electoral formations, whereas others were truly national organizations.

The situation was further confused and complicated by the provisions of the new electoral laws modifying the existing system of proportional representation. In a vain effort to discourage the proliferation of small lineage parties, each constituency had been assigned an electoral quotient, which was determined by dividing the number of votes cast by the number of seats available. On this principle, only parties that polled more votes than this figure were allocated seats. The precise effect of this procedure is hard to establish: certainly it did not achieve the aims for which it was claimed to be designed. With its 122 deputies, the SYL government was almost literally bursting at the seams, and could not be other than an extremely heterogeneous assemblage of competing personal, family, and lineage interests. The maintenance of any semblance of unity with such an ill-assorted crew would clearly prove a most costly business.[5] Stability has never been a conspicuous feature of Somali governments, but on no previous occasion since independence had the internal forces favoring instability been so many or so menacing. In the backlash of discontent and frustration following the elections, therefore, the president had been steadily consolidating his position by every means at his command, and the premier was acting in the same fashion with little regard for the steadily mounting public criticism that his actions encouraged.

It had now become plain that if the government had not completely rigged the elections, it had certainly done its best to do so, and that numerous irregularities had occurred. Disturbances that were hushed up during the electoral campaign were subsequently reported to have accounted for as many as forty deaths—although this figure may be exaggerated. The chief of police, the widely respected General Mohamed Abshir, had himself resigned before the elections in protest at increasing political interference in his work. And under its newly appointed president the Supreme Court now conveniently reversed a previous decision and denied that it had the authority to judge the mass of electoral petitions alleging irregularities that complainants brought before it.

There was still also the delicate issue of the government's increasingly cordial relations with Kenya and Ethiopia, which did not seem to bring Somali unification any nearer and certainly offered a convenient stick with which to assail Egal's policies. Finally, official corruption and nepotism seemed to be flourishing on a scale hitherto unknown in the Republic. Some previous governments (and particularly that led by Hussen) had attempted to curtail these activities, but there was little sign that either the premier or the president were unduly disturbed by their persistence.

This complacent abuse of power, as it seemed to many critics, enraged some of the country's leading intellectuals, and particularly those who were not closely associated with the government, or who had failed to secure a seat in the last elections. The democratic parliamentary system that had seemed to combine so well with traditional Somali political institutions, and had begun with such verve and promise, had turned distinctly sour. The National Assembly was no longer the symbol of free speech and fair play for all citizens. On the contrary, it had been turned into a sordid marketplace where deputies traded their votes for personal rewards with scant regard for the interests of their constituents. Its members were ferried about in sumptuous limousines bearing the magic letters AN (Assemblea Nazionale), which the inveterate poor of the capital translated with bitter humor as annanolahay: "I'm all right". Where even such enlightened and inspired politicians as Abdirazaq Haji Hussen had tried to improve the system and had failed, more drastic remedies seemed the only possible recourse. In the view of the most disillusioned critics, democracy had lapsed into commercialized anarchy, and strong rule of a new type was desperately needed if the state was to be rescued from its present morass of poverty, insecurity, and inefficiency, and set on the road to progress. Rumors of military intervention were thus inevitably in the air.

The immediate precipitants of the impending coup were, however, entirely unexpected. While the premier was out of the country travelling abroad, Shirmarke, the president, was assassinated by a policeman on October 15, 1969. The murderer belonged to a lineage that had been persistently ill-treated by the president and sought revenge rather than revolution—or so at least it seems.[6] Nor was the death of Shirmarke followed immediately by a coup. The next event in the rapidly unfolding drama was the hasty return to Mogadishu of the premier to mastermind the National Assembly's election of a new president who would safeguard his own position. Naturally a Darod candidate was put forward—in the event, an old campaigner whom the government's critics saw as sharing most of the vices of his predecessor. When at their late-nights sitting on October 20 the party caucus had reached agreement to support this man as their official candidate, and it was thus virtually certain that he would be elected by the Assembly the following day, those army officers who had been closely watching the situation decided to act.

In the early hours of the morning of October 21, 1969, the army occupied key points throughout the capital, and—with the aid of the police, who seem, however, to have been initially at least somewhat reluctant accomplices—the members of the previous government and other leading politicians and personalities were rounded up.[7] The National Assembly was closed, political parties were declared illegal, and it was announced that the state would be governed by a Supreme Revolutionary Council. Corruption and tribalism would be eliminated, and true justice and democracy restored. While honoring existing treaties, the military regime would support national liberation movements and the struggle for Somali unification. As an earnest symbol of its intentions, and of its hopes, the country would henceforth be known as the Somali Democratic Republic.

The membership of the Supreme Revolutionary Council was announced on November 1; predictably its president turned out to be General Mohaned Siyad Barre, commander of the army, who was supported by twenty-four other officers, listed in descending order of rank from major-general to captain. Of the two initial vice-presidents, one was significantly General Korshell, General Abshir's successor as police commandant. These members of the SRC were to be assisted by a fourteen-man civilian secretariat of secretaries, fulfilling much the same function as previous civilian ministers, but without their power. The appointments initially announced were certainly promising, and included a high proportion of the ablest civil servants.

Insofar as it is possible to discern any general public response to these dramatic events that had taken place very quickly, and apparently without a single shot being fired, the sudden and triumphal entrance of the army onto the political stage appears to have been greeted with cautious optimism and with a mixture of respect and fear. Prior to this, the army had played no direct part in the internal affairs of the Republic; although its leaders had their links with politicians, the army had not been directly employed to support any of the previous civilian governments. Its significance lay primarily in external affairs as a shield against the Ethiopians and Kenyans, and as a symbol for the vigorous pursuit of the Somali unification struggle. It had in fact been in action against Ethiopia in 1964, and had also participated more or less clandestinely in the Somali guerrilla campaign in northern Kenya. It is only fair to point out, however, that much of the day-to-day border patrolling was carried out by special units of the armed, carabinieri-style police force.

This raises the important issue of the relationship between these two bodies. Historically the army was largely an offshoot of the police, formed initially in 1958 and strengthened by the incorporation of the former British Somaliland Scouts unit after independence. As with the police, its officers had been trained in Italy, Britain Egypt, and Russia, and sometimes in several of these countries. Both forces probably contain an equally representative cross-section of the general Somali population with, however, in each case very few recruits from the southern Somali cultivators.[8] Their distinctiveness as separate organizations with different roles was accentuated by the fact that the first commander of the army was Hawiye (General Abdulla Daud, who died in 1965), while the police commandant (General Abshir) was drawn from the Darod. These differences bred a tradition of comradely rivalry between the two forces, and made it seem perfectly logical that while until 1969 the United States should be the main source of arms and support for the police, Russia should fulfill the same role for the army. This, of course, did not prevent both forces jointly drawing on further aid from other friendly countries, including Italy, Egypt, Britain, and Germany.

By 1969 there was no doubt which of the two competitors had become the senior partner, both in size and military equipment. But, as their mutual support in the coup demonstrates, their rivalry had by no means exhausted their capacity to cooperate. The at least tacit help of the police was also, I think, very important for the military as an additional source of legitimacy for their intervention in the affairs of the nation. What might have happened had fighting actually broken out, either as the civilian politicians were rounded up or with the intervention of the police, is impossible to predict. Any open conflict would, however, have severely tested the esprit de corps of the army. It is also, I am sure, highly significant that at no point since assuming power did the Supreme Revolutionary Council seek to suggest any link between the revolution and he assassination of the late President Shirmarke—Indeed quite the contrary. Far from becoming a hero, the assassin was swiftly brought to trial, sentenced, and executed; and the many allegations of corruption and nepotism that have been so freely applied to their civilian predecessors have most noticeably not been directed at all at the ex-president. He remained an official hero; after all he was dead.

The military thus assumed power with the declared aims of cleaning out the Augean stables and restoring Somali virtues. They brought a new energy and dynamism, and also a much-wanted sincerity, to public affairs. In the ministries headed by civilian secretaries, military officers were posted as watchdogs, and close inspection of ministry accounts revealed an impressive if unedifying list of malpractices; this led to the arrest of many former civil servants who were tried and sentenced for embezzlement, tribal nepotism, and other allied offenses.

The large floating urban population of tribal dropouts, accustomed to living by their wits and at the expense of their more fortunately placed kin in the civil service and the National Assembly, were rudely shaken to find themselves faced with the alternative of engaging in useful but strenuous public works, or returning to the interior. A strong endeavor was thus made to clean up the towns, both literally and figuratively, and to make the social services operate more effectively and fairly. In the interior itself, district and provincial administrative officials were recalled to the capital for retraining in development and discipline and were replaced by military personnel. Abroad, diplomats were similarly recalled and posted to new stations immediately after the SRC had assumed power. Further measures were taken in 1971 when senior members of the diplomatic corps were summoned home for a period of military training and familiarization with the socialist ideas and aspirations of the leader of the revolution, General Siyad.

Despite the very explicit emphasis on efficiency, self-help schemes, and the value of work, and despite repeated appeals and threats to all and sundry on the part of the new president, the military soon found the task of social reclamation arduous and unrewarding. Although it could dispense with the scruples of previous parliamentary governments, and had the power to command obedience for its directives, the SRC, like its predecessors, soon came to recognize the intractable character of the problems it faced: poverty, climatic uncertainties, limited natural resources, and a turbulent, predominantly nomadic population whose divisive clan and lineage attachments were as stubbornly unyielding as the stark physical environment.

In attempting to deal with these impediments to progress, General Siyad developed his own rough-and-ready brand of socialism, which he saw as the necessary alternative to these parochial conservative forces. Thus, on the first anniversary of the revolution on October 21, 1970, the head of state publicly declared that henceforth Somalia would be dedicated to socialist goals and to the complete eradication of tribalism: the positions of government-stipended tribal chiefs and headmen would be abolished, the practice of paying blood money (*diya*) would be forbidden, and those who indulged in tribalism would incur serious penalties.[9] These exhortations were later followed in December 1970 and early in 1971 by demonstrations in the Republic's main centers when tribalism, corruption, nepotism, and misrule were symbolically buried and thus eliminated, and in some cases effigies representing these evils were also burned. More pragmatically, the regime promised to provide financial expenses for those who died in the towns without relatives at hand who could perform these services. This innovation was realistically aimed at providing an official substitute for one of the functions served by lineage ties in the urban centers.

The regime's unremitting struggle against traditional conservative forces in Somali society (including many of its religious leaders) was accompanied at a more intimate level (and one much less directly accessible to observativation) by General Siyad's personal battle with the hidden tribal enemy within the Supreme Revolutionary Council itself.[10] For, of course, as the new president had himself scornfully declared, the general public (both rural and urban) tended to regard the SRC, as it had done previous civilian governments, and expected it to be equally representative in lineage composition. Thus the Council was largely assessed in terms of the lineage identities and assumed loyalties of its members, and changes in its ranks were interpreted in light of this all-pervasive lineage logic. If, for example, as was said to be the case initially, the SRC dealt less strictly than might otherwise have been expected with former politicians of the Digil and Rahanwin groups, then that was reportedly because they were underrepresented on the Council.

Similarly, when the former police commander and first Vice-President General Korshell was abruptly arrested and charged with organizing an imperialist counterrevolution, some commentators interpreted this as a shrewd move devised to correct the SRC's supposed overrepresentation of senior Darod members. And those critics who at the time of the coup smugly asserted that General Siyad was a mere Negib who would be swept from power into obscurity once the real militants of the revolution (the young majors and colonels) came to the top, soon found it necessary to revise their opinions. The astute maneuvers within the SRC that led to the appointment as army commander of one of his closest dependents, and to the expulsion or neutralization of many of his potential rivals, greatly enhanced the head of state's reputation as a master of political strategy, and contributed to his personal image as an outstanding example of the Somali conception of the "Big man". Further evidence of General Siyad's political adroitness could be seen in his creation in November 1971 of a personal advisory board, or cabinet, of three leading members of the SRC to debate policies before their submission to the Council as a whole.

Those who adopted this traditionalist approach in analyzing the fortunes of members of the SRC in terms of an internal power struggle along lineage lines, saw confirmation rather than contradiction in the actual charges that were employed to discredit Council members who had fallen from grace. Most Somalis are far too sophisticated to take seriously the accusations of "failing in revolutionary zeal," which accompanied some unexpectedly abrupt demotions. The rapid turnover of vice-presidents on similar counterrevolutionary charges also tended to reinforce the public's impression of a cutthroat struggle for power, which if conducted in a tougher style, recalled the endless factionalism of previous governments. Speculations of this sort, however, were best kept secret, since the airing of any opinion that could be construed as hostile to the regime was a serious offense.

The inveterate tea-shop gossip, with its scandalous accounts of the latest escapades of politicians, which had been such an engaging feature of the urban scene in the "bad prerevolutionary days," abruptly disappeared. Idle chatter was certainly silenced, and with it the freely voiced public criticism of previous years. The voice of the dead could not be so easily silenced, however. One expression of public criticism about this time took the form of a series of letters addressed to the head of state by his old colleague, the assassinated former President, Dr. Abdirashid Ali Shirmarke! These sinister messages from the grave ended by expressing the hope that Mohamed Siyad would soon be joining the sender. Copies of these interesting documents were found lying about Mogadishu's main market where they quickly attracted attention.

If efforts to galvanize the citizens of the Republic into approved revolutionary activity were not as successful as originally anticipated, at least the new regime could claim to have made some impact in foreign relations. Following its Russian military connections, it leaned to the East where previous governments had leaned to the West. Thus at the price of alienating the US and jeopardizing a large component of U.S. aid, the new Somali leaders entered into relations with North Vietnam, North Korea, and to the embarrassment of Bonn, with East Germany. These moves did little, however, to affect existing links with Italy and the European Community, nor, for what it was worth, with Britain. Nor did the Republic's increasing economic dependence on Russia seem to have much impact on its relations with China, which remained cordial and inscrutable. In the more immediate Middle East context, Siyad's vigorous espousal of "Socialism"[11] which he found compatible with Islam, seemed likely to place Somalia among the radical Muslim states. In inter-African affairs and in the Organization of African Unity (OAU), Somalia appeared to play a more effective role than previously, and initially sought to build upon improving relations with Kenya and Ethiopia.

Nationalism, Tribalism, and the Revolution

The Supreme Revolutionary Council's obsessive preoccupation with treachery and betrayal and its growing reliance on harsh repressive sanctions, inevitably suggest that its leaders no longer enjoyed the public confidence that they claimed when they seized power in October 1969. The strident, almost hysterical tone of the leader's repeated denunciation of tribalism, which he sought to link with colonialism and sinister neo-colonial plots, is also a measure of the frustration and desperation that those who sought to achieve dramatic changes in the socioeconomic conditions of the country must have felt when they considered the glaring discrepancy between their aims and what had actually been achieved.

Previous civilian governments also sought to replace poverty by prosperity and to eradicate tribalism and other sources of nepotism and injustice. These ambitions and slogans were not new; and dissatisfaction with the previous civilian leaders centered not so much on their stated aims but on their failure to implement them. Strong authoritarian rule and charismatic leadership, which General Siyad sought to apply, raised the hopes of many by promising a new and more effective method of tackling old problems. But the most difficult and fundamental of these remained unresolved. Whatever the intended consequences actually were, however, the full evaluation of Siyad's rule must be left to future Somali historians.[12] We must simply note that when Siyad was swept away by an extremely bloody and chaotic coup in 1990, most people seemed to have reached a powerfully negative evaluation. But, in the anarchic and violent years following his disappearance in this second Somali coup, it is a measure of many peoples' desperation that they should have looked back with such nostalgic longing to the oppressive Siyad era. More objectively, although it ultimately destroyed Somalia, jumping forward three decades after the date at which these lines were originally penned, it can be said that Siyad's ill-

fated regime left one universally acclaimed positive achievement in introducing written Somali across the nation. But
what a price to pay for this!

Notes

1. See I.M. Lewis, "Pan-Africanism and Pan-Somalism," *Journal of
   Modern African Studies* (Cambridge), I, 2, August 1, 1969.

2. In the work of Africanist anthropologists, this emphasis was especially marked in the writings of Abner Cohen, as notably in *Custom
   and Politics in Urban Africa* (London: Reutledge and Kegan Paul
   1969).

3. As is evident, I disagree with those who hold that nations are quite
   distinct from tribes. Compare, for example, P.H. Gulliver (ed.),
   Tradition and Transition in East Africa (London: Reutledge and
   Kegan Paul 1960), pp.28-91.

4. The number of candidates was roughly the same as my estimate
   of the total number of **diya**-paying groups in the whole country.
   This my be a fortuitous coincidence, since most candidates were
   presented by coalitions of such groups. In any event, this reflected
   the overall political situation of Somalia at that time and did not,
   of course, signal any permanent change in the general pattern of
   segmentary allegiance. Clans and higher level agnatic groups
   retained their situational relevance to be evoked when segmentally
   appropriate.

5. According to a detailed statement made after the coup by a spokes-
   man of the Supreme Revolutionary Council, and based "on a close
   study of the accounts of the Premier's Office," Egal expended
   £500,000 of public funds in payments to members of the assembly
   between January and October 1969.

6. See Anglo-Somali Society Newsletter 1970, for a report of the trial
   of the culprit who was found guilty and sentenced to death.

7. These included Mohamed Haji Ibrahim Egal, as well as his opponent Abdirazaq Haji Hussen, and the former head of state, Adan
   Abdulla Osman. This oddly assorted house-party of politicians and
   dignitaries was confined in the presidential guesthouse at Afgoi
   outside the capital, and remained there in reputedly reasonable
   conditions until the 1970. The former police chief, General Abshir,
   was placed under house arrest and was later transferred to prison.

8. From the earliest days of colonization, the bulk of recruits to the
   police, and indeed to other government employment, had come

73

from he nomadic population of Somalia. This is a direct reflection of the pressure of population on resources in the most nomadic regions (e.g. Mijerteynia now Puntland).

9. In January 1971, for instance, a number of people were sentenced to 18 months of hard-labor for fostering tribalism' by a district court in a remote northern part of the republic.

10. Some of General Siyad's early speeches are conveniently collected together in two official publications entitled *My Country and My People* (Mogadishu: State printing Agency, 1970).

11. Following General Korshell's disgrace, in May 1971, General Mohamed Ainanshe (another vice-president) and General Salad Gavaire were arrested and charged with engineering a plot to kill the revolution. They were brought to trial, and publicly executed on July 3, 1972. Official reports emphasized that the firing squad was multitribal in composition, and that the government would see to the funeral arrangements—traditionally a lineage responsibility.

12. It is interesting to record the skeptical assessment of a Polish Marxist: A. Wolczyk, "I1 'socialismo' Somala: un industria per il potere," *Concretezza*, Rome, January 1972, pp. 23-26; for less sophisticated treatments see L. Pestalozza, *Somalia: Cronaca della Rivoluzione*, (Bari: Dedalo Libri, 1973); and B. Davidson, "Somalia: Towards Socialism," *Race and Class*, Vol. 17, no. 1 (Summer 1975), pp. 19-38. For a well-informed, detailed account of Siyad's dictatorship, by a former CID officer and subsequent minister of the interior, see Jama Mohamed Ghalib, *The Cost of Dictatorship: The Somali Experience* (New York Lillian Barber Press, 1995). See also Chapter Three of this volume, where the full-blown version of Siyad's system of oppression is examined.

Three

SCIENTIFIC SOCIALISM— SOMALI STYLE

✦

Western Marxist social anthropology has seemed more concerned with its own parochial pursuits than with analyzing the transformation of traditional institutions in self-defined Marxist states.[1] It is thus largely left to others, of questionable ideological credentials (like the present writer), to undertake this task. This chapter attempts to explore and assess the main currents of structural change in the Somali Democratic Republic, which, before it collapsed in 1990, had been under military rule since 1969 and officially Marxist since 1970.[2]

Here, as in so many other parts of the world today, the immediate problem confronting the student of contemporary politics was that of successfully penetrating the official rhetoric to discover the underlying political realities. The difficulty was not simply the usual one of finding out what really happens in high places. There was the further and wider issue of ascertaining how, and according to what principles, ordinary people ordered their lives, because their thoughts and actions were carefully monitored and apt to be self-censored. This inevitably raised delicate interpretative problems as well as concerns about the safety of informants. Even in such conditions, fortunately however, informants tended to be delightfully indiscreet, so that it was usually possible to test interpretations by direct questions—with trusted friends and sometimes also by direct observations.

The Somali Revolution and its Ideology: Scientific Socialism

After nine years of clan party politics following independence in 1960, there was undoubtedly public support for the "bloodless" coup d'état with which the army seized power on the propitious date of October 21, 1969.[3] The new military leaders naturally sought to distinguish themselves as sharply as possible from their venal civilian predecessors (many of whom were summarily imprisoned). Hence while generally maintaining the neutralist stance of previous Somali governments, where the latter had tilted toward the West, they tilted the balance in the opposite direction toward Russia (already the main source of military aid), China, and Korea. As the initial wave of public enthusiasm subsided, the new rulers' implicit mandate to govern lost much of its force. They were, consequently, under increasing pressure to produce a coherent and explicit political ideology[4] at once legitimizing and consolidating the "Revolution" (ka'an, as the coup was retrospectively styled) that had brought them to power. In any case, as the president declared in response to criticism from conservative Muslims, in a speech delivered in the middle of 1972: "The founders of scientific socialism were not against religion in particular but they exposed and disproved the reactionary elements of religion that dominate [the] sound reasoning of mankind and hence hinder [the] progress of society".[5]

If socialism did not exclude religion and was actually part of Islam, the founders of scientific socialism were not against religion in particular, but they exposed and disproved "the reactionary elements of religion that dominate (the) sound reasoning of mankind and hence hinder (the) progress of society".[6] If socialism does not exclude religion and is actually part of Islam, there is, however, no question about the unique transcendental status of the latter. As the president explained on another occasion (January 1972):

> As far as socialism is concerned, it is not a heavenly message like Islam but a mere system for regulating the relations between man and his utilization of the means of production in this world. If we decide to regulate out national wealth, it is not against the essence of Islam. God has created man and has given him the faculty of mind to choose between good and bad, between virtue and vice. We have chosen social justice instead of exploitation of man by man and this is how we can practically help the individual Muslim and direct him to [a] virtuous life. However, the reactionaries want to create a rift between socialism and Islam because socialism is not to their interest.[7]

There is no question of the death of God here, or of the vulgar secularization of Islam. With this emphatic religious grounding, scientific socialism Somali-style, known literally as "wealth-sharing based on wisdom" (*hanti-wadagga 'ilmi ku disan*)[8] was closely linked with such key concepts as "unity" or "togetherness" (*waddajir*), "self-reliance" (*is ku kalsonan*), and of "self-help" (*iska wahu qabso*).[9] As these associated principles suggest, scientific socialism was first and foremost an ideology for development designed to annihilate the three major enemies that General Siyad repeatedly insisted confront his people: poverty, disease, and ignorance. These scourges could be overcome only by a sustained effort of the national will in which all sections of the population set aside their selfish interests, shrugged off contaminating neocolonial influences and joined the common struggle for national prosperity. Women had as much to contribute as men: and the young, "tomorrow's leaders" had a particularly important part to play.

Here tribalism and multipartyism were singled out as anachronistic barriers to progress to be discarded in favor of a new and mature sense of national integrity. As General Siyad incisively stated the issue in a minatory address to regional judges: "Tribalism and nationalism cannot go hand in hand. It is unfortunate that our nation is rather too clannish: if all Somalis are to go to Hell, tribalism will be their vehicle to reach there.[10] Tribal nepotism and corruption hence became equally heinous offenses, incurring severe penalties, and the nonkinship term jalle (comrade, or friend) was pressed into circulation to replace the traditional polite term of address "cousin" (*ina' ader*), which was strongly discouraged because of its kinship associations. Earlier nationalists, religious and secular, had appealed to the transcendent brotherhood of Somalis, regardless of clan or lineage. The new stress on friendship appealed for cooperation and unity in which ties of blood counted for nothing. The productive energy that would thus be released was to be harnessed in a carefully planned sequence of national campaigns designed to achieve success on all the fields of battle destined for victory by the glorious revolution.

These major national campaigns (s. *olol*, battle-formation) were reinforced by more specific local crash programs (*s. parnamaj*) throughout the country. Salvation lay in honest toil: each worker benefiting in direct proportion to his efforts (*hawl iyo hantiwwadag*), spurred on by the terse slogan: "Less talk and more work" (*haddalyar iyo hawlweyn*). This tight-lipped new dynamism was epitomized in the word chosen to express the revolution itself: *ka'an* which meant literally "rising" or "standing" and refers originally to nomadic movement.[11]

The dynamism that the sublimation of archaic lineage loyalties should yield received direction and was brought to a final climax of enthusiasm in the personality cult that had been assiduously developed round the head of state. "The Victorious Leader" (*Gulwadde*) General Siyad was presented in the official hagiography and iconography as dauntlessly leading his people in the unremitting war against all their foes. Countless posters, poems, songs of praise, and speeches proclaimed his sublime role as the "father" of a nation whose "mother" was the revolution. Inspired by scientific socialism, this mystical union, dissolving mundane kinship loyalties, was the source of all prosperity and the infallible guarantee that the nation's struggle would be successful.

Among its most precious progeny were the "flowers of the revolution," those destitute children, often without parents, who had been gathered into Youth Revolutionary Centers all over Somalia where they were fed, clad, and trained to serve their country. Their gratitude to the nation and its beneficent head (*il buono condottorre*)[12] was unquestioned and, unsullied by divisive lineage constraints, set a shining example. It was this transcendent dedication to the motherland and her virile consort that was to replace the old genealogies that divided the nation into so many hostile camps.

The government newspaper, the *October Star*, printed since 1973 in the new Somali (i.e., Roman) script, supplied its readers with an edifying thought for the day, often in the form of a pithy exhortation culled from the long dramatic perorations of a man who, before his elevation in 1969, was better known for his blunt military epithets than for polished oratory.[13] A selection of these thoughts and sayings, in the form of a little blue-and-white (the national colors) pocket manual, published in 1973,[14] enjoyed wide circulation. Wherever he went, the president was greeted by mass applause and adulation, feted and saluted by his loyal subjects who literally danced before him with Korean choreography. Every public occasion, no matter how small or trivial, ended with its participants reaffirming their pledge of loyalty to the revolution and to its beneficent architect.

This lofty image of invincible power contrasted sharply with the disarming humility and directness that the head of state reserved for his face-to-face encounters with his comrades, his much publicized eagerness to listen to and share their problems, and his humble life-style and edifying compassion for the poor and underprivileged whose plight was a recurrent theme in so many of his speeches. The refreshing absence of ostentatious luxury or pomp and ceremony, when the president received visitors for homely man-to-man exchanges, emphasized the sincerity and directness of a leader who succeeded in conveying the impression that he was genuinely a little bewildered by the populist cult surrounding his public person. And like the splendid conductor he was, in his speeches praising the proud achievements of the revolution he regularly, self-depreciatingly reminded his audience that their success reflected their efforts as much as his and called upon them to congratulate themselves on their exemplary dedication to the cause.

The Maoist Facet

Many of these features, particularly this elaborate personality cult so foreign to the traditional egalitarian values of the Somali nomads,[15] with the associated emphasis on public pageantry, mass rallies, sports, and gymnastics, conveyed an intriguingly oriental flavor. Local parallels could of course be found in such relatively accessible sources of influence as Nasser's Egypt and, less significantly, Tanzania. More remote parallels seemed even more striking. In addition to the obvious Russian influence, there was certainly more than a trace of Maoism in the cult that had been created a round "Chairman" Siyad, and the North Korean model was equally relevant. Although Kim II Sung had not yet set foot in Somalia, general Mohamed Siyad had twice visited North Korea, where he was cordially received, and numerous senior officials had been to Korea on training courses, as others had been to Russia and China.

On ministerial bookshelves in Mogadishu the works of Kim II Sung far outnumbered those from any other communist source. There was, in addition, the shared military emphasis of the two regimes. Other significant parallels included the Korean unification issue, recalling Somalia's own struggle to extend its frontiers to embrace those nationals living under foreign rule over the border in Ethiopia,

Kenya, and the French Territory of the Afars and Isas,[16] and, crucially, North Korea's remarkable success in maintaining its independence while enjoying both Russian and Chinese patronage.

Kim II Sung's much-publicized *juche* principle of "being true to one's inherent character," which so closely resembled the paired Somali concepts of self-reliance and self-help, gave a more specific ideological edge to these correspondences and further enhanced the appropriateness of the North Korean model. We shall be in a better position to judge how illuminating this diffusionist perspective is when we have looked more closely at the implementation of socialist policies in Somalia.

The Control: The Official Structure

After the coup, Somalia was ruled by an all-military (including some police officers) Supreme Revolutionary Council (SRC), aided by a largely civilian Council of Secretaries, the latter exercising quasiministerial functions but not possessing ministerial power. Key departments, such as Defense, Information and National Guidance, and Internal Affairs,[17] however, remained in the hands of members of the SRC. Unlike its more recently formed Ethiopian counterpart (the Derg) which was said to include ordinary soldiers, the SRC consisted, from its inception, entirely of officers of the rank (then) of captain and above. Since the arrest of one of the initial vice-presidents, General Korshell (then police commander) in April 1970,[18] and the public execution of another (General Ainanshe) with other counterrevolutionary plotters in July 1972,[19] the composition of the SRC remained remarkably stable. As might be anticipated, there were more frequent changes and reshuffles in the personnel of the subordinate Council of Secretaries. This unequivocal pattern of military dominance at the center was replicated at all levels of administration throughout the state. Shortly after the army had seized power, all civilian district and regional governors were replaced by military officers. From the beginning of 1974, however, civilian officials began to resume these functions.

The command structure of the Somali army thus formed the backbone of the state, which was literally a military rather than a police state;[20] and much symbolic play was made of the fact that the term for the armed forces, *hogga*, means literally "force, might and power." This martial structure was fleshed out, both at the center and in the provinces, with a formidable array of ancillary agencies, each with its own power structure leading back ultimately to the president, in some cases directly and in others via other members of the SRC. Crucially significant here were: the President's Political Office (formerly his public relations service and the provisional nucleus for a contemplated party organization); the National Security Service (NSS); and the National Security Court with virtually limitless power to try a wide spectrum of political offenses ranging from tribalism to treason.

The heads of all these organizations were members of the SRC, that of the NSS having, as we shall see later, a particularly significant position. The Political Office shared with the Ministry of Information and National Guidance (headed until December 1974 by an energetic vice-president), the important task of national thought control. These agencies were, as it were, primarily concerned with the preventive medicine for the revolutionary health of the nation. Where they were unsuccessful, the NSS and National Security Courts stepped in. The young apparatchiks of the Presidency Office, partly trained in Moscow, were specifically charged with the delicate task of expounding Marxist Leninism in its local, Somali version. Additional intellectual support was provided here by the Somali Institute of Development Administration, the political studies nucleus of the national university.

The most prestigious center for instruction in the aims and implementation of the revolution was the former military academy in the capital, Mogadishu, renamed Halane after a young Somali lieutenant who reportedly gave his life trying to save his country's colors in the Somali Ethiopian conflict of 1964. Here regular in-service training for all categories of officials was organized, including courses for the highest ranks in the civil service. Thus, for instance, the many ambassadors retained from the previous civilian regime were recalled shortly after the coup and sent for intensive training to Halane.[21] There, in addition to Spartan paramilitary discipline (which some found a tonic), they were taught the meaning of the revolution and how its aims were to be implemented in their service abroad. Halane had great symbolic and functional importance; it was, to quote the zealous secretary of state for Information, Vice President Colonel Jalle Ismail Ali Abokor, "almost synonymous with the October Revolution". All secondary school leavers now spent six months in compulsory military training and "socialist orientation" at Halane before proceeding to do their national service as teachers in remote parts of the country. (Vocational training generally, it should be added parenthetically, reflected the self-reliance ideal and was realistically geared to the nation's needs. So, for instance, medical and veterinary training specialized in the locally relevant areas rather than trying to comply with international standards).

Practical orientation for the public at large was provided by the people's militia, the so-called Victory pioneers or revolutionary youth (*gulwadayal*), with their bright green unisex uniforms and sinister Orwellian-eye, symbol of vigilance.[22] Formed in 1972 and recruited largely from the urban unemployed, this organization provided revolutionary training facilities and the prospect of employment. The latter was an important consideration where, in urban centers particularly, the government sought to control the labor market, and unemployment and inflation posed serious problems. These official volunteers were expected to play a leading role in local development projects and crash programs, as well as helping to organize routine civic affairs and social welfare. Their women's branches were prominent in community work. Since some members were popularly supposed to have had close links with the security services, it was generally felt to be dangerous to ignore their appeals for voluntary cooperation in kind or cash to help with the latest campaign.

These organs of thought control were augmented by the carefully calculated propaganda that poured forth on the national radio and press—the daily *October Star* and monthly *New Era*. Although the impact of the latter had become more important since the introduction of written Somali,[23] the radio was still the principal instrument for disseminating propaganda among the population at large, especially among the nomads. Radio controllers had successfully adapted the now-established pattern of broadcasting to include the new revolutionary message in such a way that it seemed a natural and inevitable extension of traditional Somali values and Islam. Indeed in the typical structure of the daily program, readings from the Quran were followed by a Somali commentary, then by exhortatory proverbs, and finally by passages from speeches of the head of state and his colleagues, presented in such a way that all this material coalesced in a seamless continuum. In this fashion, ends and beginnings were constantly juxtaposed, and scientific socialism was made to appear the cornerstone of Somali traditional culture, a transformation not as implausible as it may appear.

So much for the central organization of government. Outside the capital, in 1974 Somalia's former eight provinces were reconstituted (and where necessary renamed to exclude clan names) as fifteen new regions (from 1975, sixteen), comprising sixty-four districts, excluding the fourteen districts of Mogadishu). Each province had its regional revolutionary council, presided over by the military governor acting as chairman (*gudonshiye*) and assisted by the local military and police commanders, the regional NSS chief, and the representative of the President's Political Office whose main task was to see that the local orientation center was properly organized and well-attended. As I observed myself in the summer of 1974 and on later field trips, in some major urban centers the routine evening meetings at local orientation centers were often poorly attended. In the provinces, however, I have seem impressively large turnouts at the weekly Friday meetings in the provincial orientation center. With the help of locally recruited vigilantes, workers' committees, local dignitaries, and women's representatives, the official apparatus of the central government was brought into the life of the community. Some regions had well-trained and efficient local government officials. But there appeared to be considerable variation in the effectiveness of local government institutions. A key issue here was naturally the role of the traditional clan heads, formerly known in southern Somalia by the mongrel Arab-Italian term *capo qabila*. These tribal leaders were officially abolished, or at any rate rechristened "peace-seekers" (*nabad don*), and had become theoretically bureaucrats capable of being posted to any part of the country. This regional pattern was replicated on a smaller and more modest scale at the district level with again the same combination of military and other security officials and local dignitaries.

As will be evident, great stress was placed on propaganda and thought control. Even the smallest permanent settlement in thee countryside was expected to have its orientation center with, ideally, a suitable complement of Marxist-Leninist literature and portraits of the reigning trinity: Jalle Siyad, Jalle Markis (Marx), and Jalle Lenin. Orientation centers with their public-spirited attendants, were intended to provide an approved alternative basis for social and political activities, indeed to replace the old lineage structure that the government sought to destroy. They represented the new nationalism based on friendship and patriotism, not kinship, and were designed to form the nerve centers of the vibrant new revolutionary life. In some urban areas, they did appear to have become a focus of neighborhood social life in competition with that based on mosque or lineage association (officially banned).

People were encouraged to arrange their weddings at these centers, thus (theoretically at any rate) marrying in revolutionary rather than clan style and without exchanging marriage payments, traditionally collected and disbursed on a kinship basis. Other associated measures designed to undermine lineage loyalties and to increase the individual's dependence on the state included: government provision of burial expenses, the banning of collective blood-compensation payments, the penalty of execution by firing squad for murder, and other tough sanctions to control crime. All these, clearly, were more likely to be effective in towns than among the elusive nomads who make up the major part of the population.

This formidable apparatus extending from the president's office to the grass roots throughout the country seemed more designed to ensure that national policies were faithfully followed than to establish a creative dialogue with ordinary citizens. The latter was, however, something on which the president claimed to set great store and regularly emphasized in his perorations to administrative officials. The following extract from an address to a national seminar of district and regional officials (chairmen, representatives of the President's Office, and NSS officers) delivered by General Siyad on April 3, 1973, conveys the message in the general's own inimitable style:

It is incumbent upon me to explain to you the aim behind the Local Government Reform Law and how serious its implementation is considered. The law is based on the just policy of socialism, which stipulates that the people shall take part in running their own affairs. The way this could be done is not to let all power be concentrated in Mogadishu, or on one man, but for the people to have their say. Secondly, we used to be a one-city state. We want to fight against this tendency and establish a country of many regions and towns that are living and thriving. This is intended to create self-sufficient districts that can erect self-sufficient councils that can erect their own factories, to create local employment and finance their own education. How can this and other revolutionary decisions be implemented? The people can attain this, and run their own affairs and not be dictated to by colonial style administrators. The provincial people should participate in the task fully till self-sufficiency is attained ... the management of the people's affairs should be put in their own hands. The Chairman is just to oversee and not to interfere.[24]

The periodic arrests and exemplary sentences that followed murmurs of local dissent or questioning suggested a rather one-sided exchange. And when striking local developments were achieved, as in some districts they had been, these could often be attributed in large measure to the energy and ambition of a particular governor or other key official.

Development and the Management of the Economy

If the population was so extensively and minutely controlled so, in theory, was the economy. Briefly, the position here was that imports and exports were generally controlled by government agencies, a notable exception being the export of livestock on the hoof (the main trade item). Bananas, the principal cash crop, were marketed and exported solely through government agencies. Hides and skins from the pastoral sector were dealt with similarly. All grain grown privately was bought by a government agency, the Agricultural Development Corporation, and sold at controlled prices through retailers or distributed directly through orientation centers. Each farmer was allowed to keep a proportion of his crop for his own domestic consumption. This system, which also provided regional storage facilities, sought to destroy the parasitic activities of mercenary middlemen. But it was not clear whether the amount of grain the producer was allowed to keep was sufficient, under existing market conditions, to provide a sufficient incentive for maximum production.[25]

Private enterprise was not restricted to small-scale farming: there were many privately owned large-scale banana estates; and despite halfhearted occasional attempts to portray the nomads as herding their livestock in pristine communes, virtually the entire nomadic economy retained its traditional status with private ownership of livestock. The economy was thus, in practice, mixed. Nationalized industries such as the Jowhar sugar complex[26] (the seat of many scandals), and the Kismayu meat-canning factory, existed cheek-by-jowl with private companies and interests, the official emphasis on cooperatives being most ostentatiously displayed in such small urban businesses as pharmacies, many of which boasted appropriate revolutionary-style names.[27] The largest and most successful spontaneously formed agricultural commune was, ironically, El Birdale, a traditionally based religious settlement in the north. According to a sympathetic and to the best of my knowledge accurate Russian report,[28] this involved some 600 families with a population of about 4,500 people who grew their own food as well as rearing their own livestock, and produced cash crops that included grains, citrus fruits, coffee, and the narcotic plant, *Catha edulis*, chewed as a stimulant in Somalia and Ethiopia. The cooperative had its own tractors, bulldozers, trucks, and other equipment, and at least one qualified agricultural officer; it received substantial support from the Somali Development Bank.

The stress placed on agricultural development, particularly in the relatively rich riverine Juba-Shebelle basin in the south of Somalia, with the minimum aim of achieving self-sufficiency in grain production, was strongly reflected in the Five-Year Plan (1974-78) in which, prior to the disastrous 1974-75 drought, almost 30 percent of the budget (£200 million) was earmarked for agricultural development (in comparison with 5 percent for education).[29] Special attention was given both to the reactivation of the previously unsuccessful state farms, and to the formation of further cooperative and crash-program farm settlements designed to absorb surplus unemployed population from the towns and nomadic areas (a matter of critical urgency after the 1974-75 drought).

If the showpiece of the nation's effective self-help schemes was the impressive sand-dune stabilization project near Merca to the south of Mogadishu,[30] the largest, most ambitious crash program was unquestionably the Rural Development Campaign launched in February 1975 (which

I had the good fortune to witness). This was a logical extension of the "Cultural Revolution" achieved in 1973 in the urban areas through the quite successful mass literacy campaign using the new Latin script (adopted in 1972). After long and careful preparation, this ambitious rural campaign was launched with appropriate pomp and ceremony in July 1974, when virtually all the urban intermediate and secondary schools were closed to provide a task force of over 30,000 students and teachers that at an estimated cost of £10 million poured into the interior in triumphant truckloads.

Grouped in parties of eight, with a teacher as leader and assisted by visiting veterinary and medical personnel, these young pioneers sallied forth to teach the nomads how to write their own language in the new script, basic hygiene (not practiced in government hotels!), modern techniques of animal husbandry, basic civics, and the aims of socialism. Equipped with blankets, a folding blackboard (which did not open properly), water bottle, and other basic kit and drawing a daily allowance of two Somali shillings, these privileged urban students were to share the fruits of the revolution with their neglected nomadic comrades, staying as guests with nomadic families and repaying hospitality by teaching their hosts to read and write.

Here as in the previous urban mass literacy campaign, the president provided the guiding motto: "If you know, teach. If you don't learn". As he explained in a speech marking Women's International Day on March 8, 1974:

The key is to give everybody the opportunity to learn reading and writing. It is imperative that we give our people modern revolutionary education.... to restructure their social existence. It will be the weapon to eradicate social balkanization and fragmentation into tribes and sects. It will bring about an absolute unity and there will be no more room for any negative foreign cultural influences.[31] The interrelated goals of modernization, nationalism, and independence were here all combined, a modern integrated nation comprising not merely those who speak the same language,[32] but who also read and write it. Nor was this simply urban utopianism, since there was some evidence that the urban literacy campaign had quickened sentiments of national identity and self-awareness.

As might have been anticipated, this unprecedented assault on the refractory nomads turned out to involve an exchange of knowledge between the young urbanized students and those they set out to teach. It was certainly a character-building experience, and while there is no doubt that the nomads demonstrated they could learn to write as quickly as their urban countrymen, it remained to be seen how many of the 1,750,000 new recruits to literacy would retain their command of writing.[33]

An enterprise of this scale was bound to encounter technical difficulties, which in practice varied from region to region. In some cases the nomads turned out not to be where they were expected. It was also often difficult to persuade them to combine their normal herding tasks with regular instruction, even when charges were waived for watering at government wells to attract the nomads to join settlements where they would be more accessible for indoctrination. What was totally unforeseen, although it might have been, but in the end turned out to enhance the impact of the program, was the intervention of the worst drought in recent Somali history.[34] In contrast to the earlier Ethiopian drought, once the extent of the devastation became apparent, the government made no attempt to hide the disaster and mobilized its resources to save the lives of drought-stricken nomads. A state of emergency was declared, a "holy war" proclaimed against the drought, and energetic appeals mounted for international famine relief.

In these circumstances, the first priority of the development campaign became simply that of securing and distributing famine relief supplies. The majority of the young nation-builders found themselves helping to set up and staff the famine relief camps needed to house almost a quarter of a million of almost destitute nomads. Once the camps had been established and stocked with supplies, their inmates became a conveniently captive audience that could be taught the aims of the revolution and also educated in local self-help schemes.

Thus, if the drought transformed the Rural Development Campaign[35] into a massive famine relief operation, the original aims of the enterprise were partly recovered by converting famine relief camps into orientation centers. This, naturally, was a temporary expedient. The long-term future of these totally impoverished nomads posed a new challenge. As the government was quick to see, here was a golden opportunity to pursue the long-cherished aim of sedentarization, and settlements were opened as crash-farming schemes in the fertile interriverine area of southern Somalia and fishing settlements along the coast. Both involved the movement of people to new locations, hundreds of miles from their traditional grazing areas, and their settlement among clans and lineages with which they were unlikely to have any immediate connection. This unprecedently vast movement of people was actually effected by a Russian airlift (and not with Arab aid as the Somalis had earlier hoped). As President Siyad's speeches at the time indicated, the government realistically feared that its nationalistic objectives might be jeopardized by a backlash of clan and lineage feeling on the part of those so abruptly uprooted and juxtaposed.

The long-term impact on traditional kinship ties of this dramatic movement of population was likely to be considerable. To set it in perspective, however, it must be appreciated that the existing population of the southern interriverine area was of extremely heterogeneous composition and included a very substantial proportion of people of nomadic origin who, over the centuries, had made their home in this region and had become more and more involved in cultivation. Their very mixed composition, reflected in the name of their largest tribal unit, the Rahanwin, literally "large crowd," made these partly sedentary southern Somali the epitome of the new transcendent nationalism that the revolution sought to realize. It was difficult, however, for the government to hold them up as a shining example of the ideal nationalistic community without referring to their own synthetic clan identity. There was also the additional consideration that they were traditionally disparaged by the arrogant nomads, precisely because they were both sedentary and of mixed-lineage composition. Of course this had not prevented northern nomads settling among them as clients, probably under acute environmental pressures such as the 1974 drought.

Similarly, although the proud nomads do not traditionally eat fish and use "fish-eater" as a term of abuse, fishing communities (as the somewhat despised Rer Manyo) have for centuries existed on the edges of the nomadic world in the coastal ports. The boundaries between nomadism, cultivation, and fishing are thus far from being as hard and fast as they are traditionally drawn by the nomads. Historically, there have certainly been movements back and forth between these economic categories: in their capriciously arid environment the Somalis would scarcely have survived at all without such flexibility in adaptation.[36]

The Infrastructure: Traditional Constraints

If the drought made the Rural Development Campaign much more than the mere ritual exercise it would largely otherwise have been, it did not have the revolutionary force of its Ethiopian counterpart. A few heads rolled: but not that of leader. However, it does seem to have contributed to the major change in the structure of government instituted in December 1974. This involved the replacement of a large proportion of the secretaries of state and the formation of five new Coordinating Committees (for politics, social affairs, economics, justice and law, and security), with a membership drawn from the SRC and the Council of secretaries augmented by additional advisers (some ex-secretaries of state). The widely publicized intention here was to bring into the center of government and policy-formation a fresh infusion of new blood in the shape of the young, ideologically oriented intellectuals, and to clear the decks for the concerted achievement of the objectives of the revolution.[37] It was also announced that a political party of a kind unique in Africa was about to be launched. This evidently took longer to realize than was originally expected, for it was not until July 1, 1976, that the party, under the title Somali Socialist Revolutionary Party, was formally inaugurated.

Sufficient has now been said of the formal framework that had been created in Somalia in the name of scientific socialism. We must now shift out emphasis to try to establish what lay behind this imposing edifice, directing our attention toward those bastions of the traditional order: Islam, and tribalism in its particular Somali lineage form. Both of these have an external as well as an internal component, so we cannot exclude foreign policy from our examination. Here the unifying perennial issue remained that of the future status of the Somali-inhabited areas adjoining Somalia, the French Territory of the Afars and Isas,[38] the Ethiopian Ogaden, and the northern districts of Kenya. Like all its predecessors, the military government protested its dedication to the goal of Somali self-determination in these regions but, in contrast to the incisive vigor of its internal policies, pursued the issue with marked restraint. The constraints imposed by General Siyad's chairmanship of the Organization of African Unity during the critical period of Ethiopia's extreme vulnerability in 1974-75 may, as some commentators argue, have exerted some influence here. If so, this was reinforced by a number of other considerations. One was the fact that the new Ethiopian military regime had developed a strong socialist orientation, adopting policies remarkably similar to those in Somalia and hailed (predictably) by some Somalis as imitations of their own revolutionary efforts (as, e.g., in sending all the students into the countryside to preach the revolution).

There was also the equally complicated issue of Russia's priorities. The Russians had a considerable strategic investment in Somalia, which was reported to include nuclear-weapon-servicing facilities near the port of Berbera and, after their massive drought aid, more reason than ever to expect (though not necessarily to receive) a grateful Somali response.[39] At the same time, like the Chinese, they were also keenly interested in current events in Ethiopia where their chances of ousting the Americans were greater than they ever were under the imperial regime in 1976. Russia controlled Somalia's oil supplies as well, of course, as replacements and ammunition for the sophisticated equipment used by the Somali army and air force.[40] In seeking as advantageous a position as possible here, the Somali regime was acutely aware that the closer and more explicit its dependence upon Russia the more complicated and less rewarding its links with the right-wing, oil-rich Arab states became. Then there was the question of Chinese aid and interests, which, again, were not limited to Somalia but also embraced Ethiopia. In these circumstances, it was not surprising that Somalis of varying political conviction looked with envy at Kim Il Sung's remarkable success in performing such a delicate balancing act on the Sino-Russian tightrope.

Somalia's opportune chairmanship of the Organization of African Unity in 1974 brought, at considerable local expense,[41] a significant increment of diplomatic glory and increased bargaining power and freedom to maneuver. Here Somalia attempted with some success to usurp the role previously played to good effect by the Sudan as mediator between Black Africa and Islamic North Africa. On a longer term basis Islamic identity itself suggested another option, but one entailing reconciling the recalcitrant problem of Mohamed and Marx. If this posed delicate internal issues, it also raised equally acute and less easily controlled external difficulties, and these compounded each other as had become increasingly obvious since Somalia had joined the Arab League in 1974.

The obstacles encountered in assuaging Arab doubts about scientific socialism were thrown into sharp relief by the extraordinarily ill-timed execution of local religious leaders at the height of the famine when the Somali foreign secretary was pleading for emergency aid in Arabia and the Gulf States. Their crime, which in the Arab point of view made the Somali treatment of it even more heinous, was that they had allegedly preached in the mosques against the president's plan, announced on Somali Women's Day (December 1974)[42] to grant women equal inheritance rights, this being contrary to traditionalist interpretations of Islamic law. The execution of these Somali sheikhs astonished the Somali public and outraged many of the more conservative Arab governments. When on the same day, two Somali air force MIGs crashed in Mogadishu after colliding in the air, many saw this as divine intervention. Others suggested that one plane had set out to kill the president, while the other had been sent up to intercept it.

No wonder that the Somalis' urgent wooing of the Arabs had little success and led to the indefinite postponement of the Mogadishu Arab League meeting planned for the summer of 1975, when the Somalis had hoped to secure sufficient Arab assistance to enable them to settle the destitute nomads without calling on other sources. If this enabled the Russians to seize the further opportunity of demonstrating Siyad's dependence on their help, it also encouraged him to show that he was master in his own house by locking up a number of leading procommunist figures, including for good measure one of his own kinsmen.

If the outcome of the tempestuous union between Islam and scientific socialism was still in doubt, what of the fate of that other major traditional constraint—kinship? Banned shortly after the coup, officially buried in April 1971, and resurrected from time to time in President Siyad's numerous ominous warnings to backsliding neocolonialists, Somali tribalism, as we have seen, was clearly a perversely persistent force. If it did not continue to exist, it would scarcely have been necessary to wage such a relentless battle against it. The Marxist theory of power would suggest that we should start looking for the roots of this sinister antirevolutionary force at the very heart of the state. When we do this we discover at once that, in common with its predecessor civilian governments, the SRC contained representatives of all the major lineage blocs in the country. The only striking difference was a marked increase in the proportion of members of the president's own clan family, the Darod.

Although it was an indictable offense to say so publicly, it was in terms of this wide-ranging representativeness that the SRC continued to be regarded and assessed by the majority of the Somali population. Even more revealing was the fact that in 1974 (and up to the late 1980s), the clandestine code name for this military regime was MOD. M stood for the patrilineage (Marrehan) of the president; O for that of his mother's clan (the Ogaden who extend into the critically explosive neighboring territory of Ethiopia); and D for the Dulbahante clan who straddled the old Somalialand/Somalia border and to whom the head of the dreaded NSS, the president's son-in-law, belonged. All these groups are members of the Darod clan-family, which irrevocably branded Siyad's regime as an extension of his clan. The implications were succinctly expressed in an ironic popular formula that I heard on many occasions: "The Marrehan are drunk on power; the Dulbahante are drunk on pride; the Ogaden (whose clansman was in charge of the famine relief program) are drunk on powdered milk."

Earlier generations of Somali nationalists found it convenient to clandestinely acknowledge the persisting significance of lineage ties by ostensibly consigning them to the past through the expedient of qualifying them with the English prefix "ex." Now however, as I found by direct exploration, there was no room in Siyad's tightly controlled regime for this playful piece of doublethink. Resort had to be made to other subterfuges, that as soon as their use was reported to the NSS, rendered those who uttered them open to criminal charges. Thus, one woman I heard about, the chief witness against a man arraigned on a charge of tribalism before a National Security Court, was asked by the court chairman to declare the basis on which she could testify against the accused. With reluctance but considerable ingenuity the witness conceded that before the revolution she and the accused had belonged to the same "ex"! In such a minatory climate, ingenious Somali sophists developed a new idiom for expressing the regime's code-name MOD. They spoke of October 21 (=M for Marrehan), of October 22 (=O for Ogaden), and of October 23(=D for Dulbahante). These interesting fruits of the literacy and numeracy campaigns offered a more comprehensive exotic formula that could be extended to express a wider range of key groups in power and register changes in their precedence and relative position at different times.

Leavened as it was by the wider representativeness of the SRC, MOD was a powerful recipe for rule in Somalia. If it is part of the Somali political tradition that a man should depend for his ultimate security upon the loyalty of his agnates, his mother's brothers are also very important allies. His maternal ties with the Ogaden thus gave the president a lever with which to modulate the level of clan pressure for the liberation of those Ogaden who languished under Ethiopian rule. Despite the acute vulnerability of Ethiopia during the internal turmoil and chaos of 1974-75, General Siyad's apparent reluctance to take this desperate course suggested that he set more store by staying at home to lead the revolution than by engaging in uncertain adventures on Somalia's borders. Evidence of the pressure to which this tie also made him subject was indicated by reports current in late 1975 of a threatened purge of high-placed Ogaden clansmen in the Siyad administration.

The Dulbahante symbol in the national monogram was perhaps even more immediately important, for the Dulbahante formed the bridge linking the two ex-colonial territories that as we have seen, in 1960 united to form the Somali Republic.[43] They thus combined the British and Italian colonial heritages that still produced competition between Anglophone and Italophone factions and played a far from negligible role in the political structure of modern Somalia. Despite all the anticolonial rhetoric, the Italian connection retained its significance and, as well as harking back to the earlier totalitarian tradition of Mussolini, was conveniently adaptable to both communist and anticommunist Italian political trends.

97

Hence, when we look closely at the composition of the SRC and the connections of key figures and interest groups in Siyad's government, we find an inner core bound together by traditional loyalties and surrounded by an outer circle drawn from opposing groups carefully balanced so that none should gain an influence that could not be counteracted by others. If, for the moment, ascendency appeared to lie with the MOD trinity, those who were outside this charmed circle philosophically observed that others had had their chance in the past and found comfort in the reflection that every dog has its day.

Socialism and Siyadism

It would be easy to exaggerate the importance of this infrastructure that was so different from the external appearance. But the fact that it was entirely suppressed—forbidden knowledge that was a kind of public secret—and that the general public believed these ties to be crucially significant is not something we can ignore. President Siyad did not disregard them and we should take our cue from him, noting the suspiciously strident tone of many of his public condemnations: of course, the total political reality we are attempting to disclose was more complicated than this. It is not simply a question of Marxist rhetoric at the surface level and lineage ties underneath. The significant factions that jostled for power in the Somali hierarchy and sometimes acted independently, and in defiance of others, were not solely based on lineage. Doctrinal and ideological issues, Marxist and Islamic, entered the picture, as well as competition between the Italophone and Anglophone parties.

The very fact that there were, in his ideological harangues, stern official warnings of the "theoretical confusion and hesitation [which occur] when demagogy takes over some of the Marxistically educated youth" indicate that ideology was, for some, a real issue, which, if pursued too enthusiastically, could have dangerous consequences. It is this audience that

General Siyad addressed when he sternly announced that there was only one universal form of scientific socialism that was pragmatically adaptable to all conditions including those of Islam. The general understandably had little patience with those who presumed to question his interpretation of the doctrine. As he contemptuously observed, such slavish textbook ideologues miss the point when they say that Comrade V.I. Lenin confiscated such and such property after the Great October Revolution; or in [the] 1940s Comrade Mao Tse-tung did this and that in his country against the reactionary forces. These people are totally ignoring the historical context of the teachings of the great socialist thinkers. They recite quotations from the founders of scientific socialism out of their proper context.[44] And woe betide them in Somalia, he might have added.

All this of course requires some reformulation of the conventional Marxist dialectic of class struggle that in its simplistic, literal form, as General Siyad forthrightly declared, had little relevance to the traditional Somali social structure. In the struggle to liberate the nation from the oppressive evils of ignorance, disease, and poverty, the most intractable and pernicious enemy was not capitalism but tribalism. As the president exclaimed in his 1974 May Day address, Capitalism has no power in our midst, none of its basic pillars are evident among us. The explosive arsenal is TRIBALISM, which benefits the reactionaries that care the least about the progress of their nation. I urge all Somalis to wage a war against tribalism and [to] spearhead the struggle against this social evil that is contrary to out unity and socialist belief, in order to enhance our future chances of social, economic and technical achievements.

What so far seemed to be generally accepted by the various factions—ideological and tribal—that are obliquely attacked in these and other public utterances was, paradoxically, the ultimate supremacy of General Siyad himself as the primary source of legitimate authority. In this sense his writ seemed unquestioned, although to judge from his often violent public denunciations it did not prevent nepotism and corruption among his senior colleagues.[45] Such charges, one might have though, would have naturally been followed by exemplary punishments, but this does not always appear to have been the case. This, of course, would again be consistent with a fragmented power structure in which, within certain ill-defined and apparently shifting limits, factions with some degree of freedom of action pursued their own particularistic interests. Cynical interpreters might also say that the head of state found it convenient publicly to censure malpractices that he could not control or that enjoyed clandestine protection.

Particularly in such conditions of *Sturm und Drang*, there were traditional precedents for the kind of leadership General Siyad provided. Personal authority of this kind and on this scale had, however, in the past usually only been accorded to national religious heroes waging the holy war jihad against the infidel. There are two outstanding examples of this tradition who are relevant here. The first is the great sixteenth-century Muslim leader, Ahmed Gran (1506-43) who nearly succeeded in permanently subjugating Ethiopia and whom some Somalis regarded as a direct lineal ancestor of the head of the head of state[46] (a view Siyad did not discourage). The second is Siyad's maternal (Ogaden) relative (who was also connected by marriage to the Dulbahante), Sayyid Mohamad Abdille Hassan, the famous "mad mullah" who led the remarkably successful guerrilla war against the British, Ethiopian, and Italian usurpers between 1900 and 1920.[47]

The charisma of these two great heroes, which General Siyad sought subtly to subsume and appropriate, drove him constantly to present himself as a perennial crusader in the endless struggle against all of Somalia's foes. In this fashion, the lay and the religious (which Somalis, traditionally, strictly distinguish in their opposition between "man of God", and "warrior", merged in the reverse direction as General Siyad proclaimed himself the divinely guided leader of his people. No wonder some Somalis said, under their breaths (necessarily), that Somali socialism was a religion. No wonder either that religion should have been such a sensitive issue and one directly touching the legitimacy of a leader who sought to transform his secular uniform into the glorious raiment of those who fight in the army of the Prophet.

Life in Somalia was indeed a battle in which victory could be achieved only through the heroic efforts of the rightly guided savior of the nation. Not only did natural calamities such as the 1974-75 drought and the government's response to it confirm this, but so did internal acts of treachery within the state. As the head of state's speeches incessantly reiterated and as the arbitrary arrests and unpredictable rehabilitations of his subjects confirmed, the state was filled with potential adversaries, dedicated to the destruction of socialism. As the general himself proclaimed: socialism could not exist without opposition, which must be overcome by a ceaseless struggle for victory. In this war it was General Siyad who defined the enemy and kept the battle score. Thus though Lenin, Mao Tse-tung and Kim Il Sung all had their place in the home-spun philosophy of development and power that General Siyad and his coterie had constructed,[48] the local political realities suggested that "scientific Siyadism" might be an apt description for what was done in Somalia in the name of scientific socialism.[49] Certainly whether one looks at it from an economic or political point of view, socialism was a means rather than an end.

The Death of Tribalism?

Since they were elected, however fraudulently, and because they relied on public support, the previous civilian politicians were ultimately dependent upon the loyalty of their clan and lineage kinsmen whose interests and demands they could not totally ignore. Lineage ties no longer had this official franchise.

As long as he could safely control the means of destruction with loyal servants in key positions to do his bidding, General Siyad could theoretically disregard traditional lineage loyalties. However the evidence we have reviewed indicates that, despite the official campaign against tribalism (which may have had its roots in a serious endeavor to promote national solidarity), clan and lineage ties still carried a high political charge, not least within the SRC and in the innermost sanctum of the president's coterie.

More generally, while the public had good reason to know that it could be extremely dangerous to be seen to press lineage claims for position or profit, it was still in these terms that the government's representativeness was ultimately assessed. How could it be otherwise when the majority of the population were pastoral nomads whose whole social structure was based on the segmentary lineage system I have described elsewhere? It would be unrealistic in the extreme to suppose that, even with the help of the drought, this traditional order could have been drastically transformed by the 1975 rural development campaign. Moreover, while many of the measures we have mentioned (the official abolition of blood money and bridewealth, the attempted substitution of orientation centers for segmentary sociability, etc.) discouraged these traditional forces, other factors worked in the opposite direction. So, for instance, before the 1974 drought, state rent control in the towns encouraged businessmen and civil servants to invest in livestock cared for by their kin in the interior.

Tribalism in its special Somali lineage version maintained much more than a mere residual presence. Indeed, thriving, as President Siyad rightly acknowledged,[50] on insecurity in these uncertain political conditions, it waited in the wings, ready for emergencies and sudden changes of political fortune that could come at any moment.

As I discovered in 1962,[51] people of northern extraction settled among the southern cultivating Somali for generations and, absorbed in local tribes there, had not forgotten their original lineage genealogies. This bespeaks remarkable powers of endurance.

Thus, while in comparison with feudal Ethiopia, Somalia scarcely offered propitious conditions for a genuine socialist revolution, its traditional institutions appeared to present more refractory and challenging obstacles to radical change than those across the border. It is not too far-fetched to suggest that the direction of transformation from anarchic democracy to a monolithic militarism was actually in the reverse direction, and brought the military power structure of Somalia in some respects closer to that of the *ancient regime* in Ethiopia. There were also, perhaps, significant analogies with the prerevolutionary Chinese form of oriental despotism, where, as Maurice Freedman elegantly puts it, "Government existed, but its political and legal abstentions promoted self-help. Lineages depended on one another, ... and they might make common cause in the face of a common danger.[52] And if we invert K. Wittfogel's famous "hydraulic hypothesis" connecting centralized despotism with irrigation,[53] further confirmation of this oriental association might be found in the understandable enthusiasm of the Siyad regime for vast irrigation schemes—however difficult it proved to implement them successfully.

Notes

1. Serious discussion of this issue is conspicuously absent in such symposia as T. Asad (ed.), *Anthropology and the Colonial Encounter* (London: Ithaca press, 1973); D. Hymes (ed.), *Reinventing Anthropology* (New York: Vintage Books, 1974); and M. Block (ed.), *Marxist Analyses and Social Anthropology* (London: Malaby, 1975).

2. This chapter, which draws on the results of my earlier research in Somalia (principally in 1955-57, 1962, and 1964), relies particularly on data collected at the height of the regime's dedication to scientific socialism in the 1970s and 1980s.

3. This timing seems largely fortuitous since the coup was precipitated by the apparently unconnected (and unexpected) murder of the previous civilian president on October 15, 1969. It should also be noted that the five points on the Somali national star represent the five Somali territories (see note 16) and have no relation other than coincidence to counterparts elsewhere. For a fuller account of the precipitants of the coup, see I.M. Lewis, "The Politics of the 1969 Somali Coup", *Journal of Modern African Studies*, Vol. 10, no. 3 (1972), pp 383-408.

4. Somalia, Ministry of Information and National Guidance, *My Country and My people: Selected Speeches of Jaalle Major General*

Mohamed Siyad Barre (Mogadishu: State Printing Agency, 1974), p. 284.

5. Ibid, p. 83.

6. Ibid, p. 75.

7. Although he had numerous advisers, who helped to prepare major policy speeches, the president frequently spoke without notes.

8. The term *hanti-wadagga* was invented by announcers on the British Broadcasting Corporation Somali program in the late 1950s to refer to communism.

9. This term was in circulation in the mid-1950s in the British Somaliland Protectorate where the expatriate administration strongly encouraged self-help schemes for school construction, farming, and other development projects. The booklet prepared on the subject by the Somali Ministry of Information for the Organization of African unity conference in Mogadishu of June 1974 points out that self-help policies were also applied in the Soviet Republic, China, and North Korea.

10. Here the guiding slogan was: "Tribalism divides, Socialism unites".

11. This term replaced the Arabic loan-word *tawri*, which was used initially but subsequently discarded, partly because it can mean revolution in the sense of circular movement, it also suggests an upsurge that could later collapse. *Ka'an* has none of these negative connotations. It suggests a relentless force whose progress can neither be arrested nor deflected.

12. Literally, "the good leader". In describing the aims and objectives of the Somali revolutionary regime, I have deliberately used officially current words and phrases to give as vivid an impression as possible of the political rhetoric. This is how the leaders of the regime saw and described their aims.

13. Unlike the ex-Red Army Major, Kim Ii Sung, General Siyad had no official communist background. He served as a police inspector during the British Military Administration of Somalia (1940-50) and received most of his subsequent military training (including courses in politics and administration) under the Italians. See Jamal Umar Ise, *Thawra 21 Uktuubir: Asbaabuhaa, Adlwafuhaa, munjazaatuhaa (The Revolution of 21 October: Its Causes, Its Objectives, Its Achievements)* (Mogadishu: State Printing Agency, 1972), pp. 57-8.

14. *Khawalbaahii Madaxweynaha – G SK-Ee Soomaaliya, Jaalle Siyaad,* 1969-1973 (Mogadishu: State Printing Agency, 1973).

15. The nomads made up approximately three-quarters of Somalia's population of about five million. For a detailed account of their

uncentralized traditional political system in Somalia, see I.M. Lewis, A *Pastoral Democracy* (London: Oxford University Press for the International African Institute, 1961).

16. These three missing communities were symbolized in the Somali Star, the national emblem, whose two remaining points represented the former British and Italian Somalilands united in the Somalia state.

17. In the reorganization of December 1974, however, this post was allocated to the police commandant who was not a member of the SRC. Many would interpret this as a move sideways.

18. Reportedly he was released in the general amnesty of October 1975 on the occasion of the celebration of the Sixth Anniversary of the revolution.

19. An interesting account of the ideological disputes within the SRC, and the conflict between pro-and anti-Western factions that were contributory factors in these events, is offered by the Italian communist journalist Luigi Pestalozza, *Somalia: Cronaca della Rivoluzione* (Bari: Dedalo Libri, 1973), p. 141.

20. The head of state was, naturally, ultimately commander in chief of the armed forces whose immediate responsibility, however, lay with the secretary of state, General Mohamed Ali Samanter, who was reputed to be an undisguised atheist. It is noteworthy that there were a few older generals of higher rank who were not members of the SRC.

21. Somalia, Ministry of Information and National Guidance, *Our Revolutionary Education* (Mogadishu: State Printing Agency, 1974), p. 40.

22. This symbol is identical to that which appeared mysteriously in 1974 in the map symbolizing national unity adopted by the Armed Forces movement in Ethiopia.

23. See section titled "Development and Management of the Economy."

24. *My Country and My People*, p. 270.

25. For information on these topics in the agricultural areas of the northwest, see A. I. Samatar, *Socialist Somalia*. London, Zed Books 1988.

26. Before the coup, the state held the controlling share in this enterprise.

27. Further nationalization measures were announced in October 1975, affecting the importation and distribution of vehicles, machinery, textiles, and household utensils.

28. See P. Kuprijanov, "Somalian village: Social and Economic Transformation," *Proceedings, Third International Congress of Africanists* (Addis Ababa, 1973).

29. For comparative purposes it is interesting to note that in the ordinary budget of 1975 for approximately £30 million, defense expenditure was costed at £7.5 million.

30. Somalia, Ministry of Information and Guidance, *Somalia's self-help for Self-freliance* (Mogadishu: State Printing Agency, 1974).

31. Published in *New Era* (Mogadishu), no. 13, March 1974, pp. 9-18.

32. This is the most succinct definition of nationalism usually proposed by political scientists. See K. Minogue, *Nationalism* (London: Batsford, 1967), p. 154. See also Gellner, *Nations and Nationalism* Oxford: Basil Blackwell, 1983.

33. This item was included along with other notable achievements of the revolution in General Siyad's opening address to a seminar at the People's Hall, Mogadishu, on October 20, 1975.

34. See I.M. Lewis, *Abaar: The Somali Drought* (London: International African Institute, 1975); and Somalia, Directorate of Planning and Coordination, *Revised Programme of Assistance Required to the drought stricken Areas of Somalia* (Mogadishu: State Printing Agency, 1975).

35. The original title of "Rural Prosperity Drive" was quickly changed in view of the drought to the more neutral Rural Development Campaign.

36. Cf. I.M. Lewis, "The Dynamics of Nomadism: Prospects for Sedentarization and Social Change", in T. Monod (ed.), *Pastoralism in Tropical Africa* (London: Oxford University Press for the International African Institute, 1975), pp 426-42.

37. For a detailed description of the form and responsibilities of the new committees, see *New Era* (Mogadishu), January 1975, pp. 11-12.

38. Formerly known as French Somaliland, this tiny overseas territory had a local population of some 120,000, divided between the Isa and other Somali and the politically dominant Afar. See V. Thompson and R. Adloff, *Djibouti and the Horn of Africa* (Stanford, Stanford University Press, 1968).

39. For an apparently well-informed but obviously anticommunist assessment of these, see B. Crozier, "The Soviet Presence in Somalia", *Conflict Studies*, no. 54, February 1975.

40. Somalia was reputed to possess the finest military force in sub-Saharan Africa, fifth in manpower after Nigeria, Ethiopia, Zaire,

and Uganda, but with much superior equipment, including over 200 tanks, 300 armored cars and personnel carriers, 200 heavy guns and SAM missiles. The air force was reported to have 60 MIG fighters and a squadron of Ilyushin light bombers.

41. This included the purchase of a fleet of Mercedes Benz limousines to ferry the visiting heads of state about in the comfort to which they were accustomed. A Somali intellectual commenting on this and other extravagances pointed out to me that there is such a thing as "gross national pride" as well as gross national product.

42. The speech is published in *New Era* (Mogadishu), January 1975.

43. This refers to the British Somaliland Protectorate, and the Italian-administered (and former Italian colony) of Somalia, under United Nations trusteeship from 1950 to 1960. For the history of these territories and the legacy they bring to the political life of Somalia, see Lewis, *A Modern History of the Somali*, Oxford, James Currey 2002.

44. This is from a speech to the 6th Orientation Course at Halane on June 9, 1972. See *My Country and My People*, p. 83.

45. Some of these colleagues, like their counterparts in other uncertain political conditions elsewhere, are alleged to have had numbered Swiss bank accounts. I have reason to believe that some of the allegations of this kind are well-founded.

46. Here Somalis usually confuse two historically separate individuals, the great Muslim champion, the Imam Ahmad "the left-handed" as the chroniclers of the period and present-day Ethiopians and Somalis alike call him, and his Somali namesake and lieutenant, a valiant battle leader of the Muslim forces. The latter is not referred to in the chronicles as *Imam*.

47. Sayyid Mohamed is also immortalized as the greatest poet in recent Somali history. For a brief account of his life and nationalist struggle, see Lewis, *A Modern History of the Somali* 2002, pp. 63-91.

48. Basil Davidson's wistful proposal that we should also see the influence here of the MPLA freedom fighters in Angola seems rather implausible; see, B. Davidson, "Somalia: Towards Socialism", *Race and Class*, Vol. 17, no. I (Summer 1975), pp. 19-38. His utopian assessment of modern trends in Somalia was also, in my opinion, optimistic, to say the least. For a better-informed assessment see Samatar, *Socialist Somalia*, 1988.

49. Compare for an interesting Marxist critique reaching similar conclusions, A. Wolczyk, "Il 'socialismo' Somalio: un industria per il potere," *Concretezza* (Rome, January 1972), pp. 23-26.

50. Speech of April 19, 1971, in *My Country and My People*, p. 177. For the same interpretation of the role of lineage, compare Lewis,

A Pastoral Democracy 1961, p. 302. The widespread insecurity and lack of food resources associated with the collapse of Siyad's rule in 1991 prompted what is probably the most vicious upsurge of clan loyalties in the history of the Somali people. See Chapter Eight of this book.

51. Lewis, 'From Nomadism to Cultivation: the expansion of political solidarity in southern Somalia', in Kaberry and Douglas (eds.), *Man in Africa,* London, Taristock Press, 1969, p. 68.

52. M. Freedman, *Chinese Lineage and Society: Fukein and Kwangtang* (London: Athlone Press, 1966), pp. 114-15.

53. K. Wittfogel, *Oriental Despotism: A Comparative Study of Total Power*, New Haven, Yale University Press, 1957.

Four

NOISES OFF: ETHIOPIA AND SOMALIA CONFRONT EACH OTHER IN A CONTROVERSIAL CONFERENCE

✦

We live in an era in which, under the baneful influence of political correctness and postmodernism, especially in Anglophone social anthropology, it is customary to emphasize the powerlessness of Third World peoples in the colonial and postcolonial periods. This often results in an emasculation of individual and collective initiative, since the agency of such peoples is denied—rather ironically given the fashionable rhetoric of agency in anthropological discourse on religion and ritual favored by the same anthropologists. From my perspective, denial of Third World agency in this manner amounts to a kind of implicit racism and promotes cultural ethnocide!

Although Joseph Tubiana and I were affected by such denial of agency what I thus take some comfort from is the skill with which representatives of one Third World state dealt with those of powerful Western nations to safeguard their perceived national interests. My account concerns my efforts in cooperation with Professor Joseph Tubiana to organize a conference on Nationalism and Self-Determination in the Horn of Africa in 1980. The initiative for this and modest financial support came from a Ford Foundation project at the Anti-Slavery Society, which sought to illuminate issues of self-determination in regions of the world where national identities were in conflict.

In accepting this task from the Anti-slavery Society in the spring of 1979, I was naturally very conscious of my situation as a Somali specialist, and so particularly anxious to secure active participation by scholars attached to the Ethiopia centralist position (or positions), as well as by those who were experts on Eritrean and other separatist nationalisms. Also, of course, I had to try to recruit specialists spanning a range of disciplines: language studies, social anthropology/sociology, history, politics, law, and international relations. With these considerations in mind, I asked Joseph Tubiana if our proposed workshop might be held at the Laboratory Peiresc, the National Scientific Research center near Nice which he directed. This seemed to me a particularly appropriate venue because it would enable us to hold our conference under the roof of the most distinguished Ethiopianist and Amharic scholar in France. This would establish an important international dimension at the outset and more than balance my association with Somalia.

I had already secured the support, as I understood, of Richard Pankhurst, the British Ethiopianist and antiquarian with whom I had been discussing how best to obtain a balance between the opposing sides in the selection of participants. I had now arrived at a preliminary list of participants that included five Ethiopianists (one from Ethiopia and one from Eastern Europe the others from Europe, an Eritrean legal specialist, an Italian historian of southern Ethiopia, a geographer working on Oromo language, an Africanist specialiszing in Pan-Africanism, and myself (a social anthropologist specializing in Somali studies). Once Joseph Tubiana had formally agreed that we could hold the workshop at his institute, preliminary invitations were sent out in late November and early December. Particularly in view of the obvious political sensitivity of these issues, my invitations took care to emphasize the academic and unofficial nature of our proposed meeting.

Our project engendered an immediate and impressively dramatic reaction. The Ethiopian ambassador in London (who had been sent a courtesy copy of the letter inviting political scientists from the University of Addis Ababa) peremptorily summoned me to his embassy for discussions and, at the same time, urgently requested a meeting with the chairman of the Anti-Slavery Society. The ambassador was extremely indignant; the fates of Eritrea, the Oromos, and Somalis in Ethiopia were internal matters, and not matters for external scrutiny or discussion. Besides, the time was not ripe: the parties were at war, killing each other. How would we like it, the ambassador asked, if Ethiopians were to take up and debate the issues of Northern Ireland? I thought that this was an interesting idea and said so, but the ambassador did not welcome this reaction.

In the course of the ensuing discussions, we did our best to explain that the workshop was a serious academic exercise, of little importance to anyone except other academics, and we emphasized, that we were especially concerned to provide adequate scope for the presentation of the Ethiopian government's official policies on these matters. Indeed I had already invited a professor of political science at the University of Addis Ababa (an old colleague and friend) to present the official Ethiopian position and he had accepted. Despite the risk of tipping the delicate balance between opposing views in favor of the centralist position, with some reluctance we invited the ambassador, following consultation with his government, to propose the names of up to four centralist scholars acceptable to the Ethiopian authorities.

These concessions that we hoped would calm the Ethiopian ambassador's fears did not suffice. A few days later a strongly worded follow-up letter arrived from the ambassador addressed to the chairman of the Anti-Slavery Society.

With no acknowledgment of our proposal of increased centralist participation, and apparently without understanding the purpose of the Ford foundation grant to the Anti-Slavery Society, which was to pay for the conference, the ambassador's letter denounced our workshop as a reactionary American and Somali expansionist exercise, designed not to promote scholarly understanding but to discredit the Ethiopian revolution. This somber document concluded with the rather threatening pronouncement that his "government cannot remain indifferent in the face of imperialist machinations and gross abuse and contempt for scholastic practices."

Because the chairman of the Anti-Slavery Society was absent in West Africa, the Society's secretary, who had been present with me at the meeting with the ambassador, replied, rebutting these colorful allegations, and emphasizing the lengths to which we had gone in trying to ensure effective participation by Ethiopian academics associated with the Ethiopian regime of Mengistu Haile Mariam. When I casually mentioned all this feverish diplomatic activity to a friend of mine who was the Somali ambassador in London at this time, he was intrigued and offered to protest to the British government. But I managed to persuade him not to do this because it would surely have complicated matters further.

At about this time, Dr. Richard Pankhurst, with whom I had been liaising closely and who had earlier indicated his willingness to participate in the seminar, but who was now under heavy official Ethiopian pressure, withdrew from any further involvement in these proceedings. It also became apparent that the Council of the Anti-Slavery Society was itself harboring a staunchly pro-centralist Ethiopianist "mole" in the shape of the late David Hamilton, whose aim was apparently to sabotage the conference.

While these lively exchanges were taking place in London, Ethiopian ambassadors in other parts of Europe, egged on by various pro-Amhara "friends of Ethiopia," were busy trying to discourage scholars and students, in the countries to which they were accredited, from attending the workshop. Particularly strong and sustained representations were made at various levels to the French government in France and through the French embassy in Addis Ababa, as well as direct protests to Joseph Tubiana and the Laboratory Peiresc, the planned site fot the conference. The Laboratory was, of course, financed by the French government through the CNRS and the latter organization's director-general came under heavy pressure to discourage Tubiana from hosting the conference. Eventually, the CNRS received an impressive instruction from the French government, forbidding the "holding of the conference on French soil"! This was transmitted to Tubiana with an offer to pay his reasonable travel costs to the eventual site of the (relocated) conference. Joseph Tubiana (Tubiana's elder son was a sea captain) and I discussed what to do in these circumstances. We considered chartering a boat to station it just outside French territorial waters off the shore of Nice. Unfortunately our financial resources were insufficient to meet the costs of this solution to our problem!

Since the British government (fortunately) had maintained a position of sublime indifference to all these maneuvers by Mengistu's emissaries, and no one from our Foreign Office had been in touch to express disquiet or reservation about out doings (or even curiosity), we decided to relocate our meeting to Oxford University. Here we successfully held our workship in St. Edmund's Hall in April 1980 with the participation of a wider range of colleagues than had originally been anticipated, as well as a lively group of students from the Horn of Africa (centralist and anti-centralist). These included someone who became a minister in Mellas Zenawi's government after Mengistu's overthrow.

The results of our meeting were published in 1983. And seem to have been generally judged by reviewers as a balanced analysis of the competing nationalities in the Horn at this time.

This record of the political initiatives, aggressively pursued by a Third World government to suppress an academic conference in Europe, whose modest objectives and relative insignificance were grossly misunderstood by the men of affairs, illustrates the influence that may be exercised by those who are all too readily ethnocentrically written off as subaltern victims by neo-Marxist political economists. (Of course, the response might have been different if important European interests had been involved.) It also reveals interesting differences in the response to Third world pressure of two European countries with very different political and educational systems. British academics regularly complain of their lack of influence on U.K. policymaking, and of the tendency of politicians to regard them as eggheads with little to contribute to practical affairs. At the same time, this is coupled with the relative (but increasingly diminishing) independence of institutions of higher education from government control in Britain in contrast to France. In this case-history of a potentially controversial academic conference with foreign policy implications, we see that there are also positive benefits here in the British system—the benefits we might say of official indifference.

Note

1.   I.M. Lewis, ed. *Nationalism and self-determination in the Horn of Africa*, London, Ithaca Press, 1983.

Five

RESTORING HOPE?: THE FAILURE OF TOP-DOWN INTERVENTION

"War and famine: peace and milk."

–Somali Saying

Introduction

The UN Secretary-General Boutros Ghali's operation in Somalia was by 1993 the largest (28,000 personnel) and the most costly in the world ($1.5 billion annually, more than twice Yugoslavia). This chapter explores how the crisis arose, how the international community became so deeply involved, and the remarkable series of new departures in international behavior that arose in the process. It will also consider weaknesses in the international response that should be addressed in future action.

It will be as well to begin by briefly highlighting these new departures in international activity. In responding, very belatedly, to the challenge of mass starvation and famine in a country torn apart by wars, whose statehood had lapsed, and whose economy and public services had collapsed, the

United Nations found itself in the unexpected position of administering what was virtually an undeclared trusteeship known as the United Nations Operation in Somalia, or UNOSOM II). This astonishing development, bizarrely retracing Somalia's history as a UN trusteeship from 1950 to 1960, was largely triggered by the equally surprising initiative of the United States in mounting, with hasty UN legitimation, the heavily armed 30,000-strong operation, Restore Hope, to force food supplies along roads regularly menaced by trigger-happy Somali militias. Security Council resolution 794, of December 3, 1992, authorized the U.S.-led Unified Task Force (UNITAF), whose operations were directed by Robert Oakley, a retired U.S. ambassador to Somalia, to employ "all necessary means to establish as soon as possible a secure environment for humanitarian relief operations in Somalia."

If this was the first instance of unilateral UN military intervention in a (theoretically) sovereign state, this development was pushed even further by the successor UN, and more directly, military administration that took over in May 1993 as UNOSOM II, with even wider powers to act against any faction violating the [warlords] cease-fire and disarmament agreements. Very much in contrast to the situation in Yugoslavia (the Somalis had no operational military aircraft, and were much poorer in equipment and organization), in its efforts to secure the implementation of the disarmament agreements, the UN was drawn into extended military action against the most formidable of the Somali warlords, General Mohamed Farah Aideed. A further significant development, however poorly handled, was to accuse Aideed of war crimes, to proclaim him an outlaw, and to offer a reward for his arrest, to which the Somali warlord responded by issuing similar threats to the commander of UNOSOM II. It was, of course, somewhat ironic that all this should have led the UN to being criticized for intervening militarily in Somalia and for not doing so in Yugoslavia.

In the course of these unforeseen and unintended consequences of seeking to deliver humanitarian aid effectively (I discount theories of hidden agendas here), the United States had for the first time conceded that its national forces could serve in a multinational UN force under UN (and not U.S.) command. Admittedly, the second in command of the UN troops was an American, and UNOSOM II as a whole was directed by an American admiral, the former U.S. security advisor who became the UN secretary-general's special representative in Somalia. In responding to the appeal for international cooperation, Germany similarly made a unique, and controversial, concession in committing a military unit to provide technical services in the UN force—a landmark decision to post military personnel outside Germany for the first time, the legality of which was inevitably contested in the courts.

Somalis and the World

Traditionally, the Muslim Somalis (some 6-8 million) are, for the most part, nomadic herdsmen, moving with their camels, sheep, and goats (and sometimes cattle) over the inhospitable semideserts and arid plains of the Horn of Africa. In this region of scarce resources, where exploration for oil has proceeded apparently unsuccessfully since the 1940s, Somalis are accustomed to fight for access to pasture and water. Prior to European colonization, they did not constitute a state, and their uncentralized political organization was based on what anthropologists call a "segmentary lineage system" in which political identity and loyalty were determined by genealogical proximity or remoteness.[1] The ideological principle here was the same as that embodied in the famous Arab Bedouin political axiom: "Myself against my brother; my brother and I against my cousins; my cousins and I against the world." With their lack of chiefs and absence of centralized government, the nineteenth-century English explorer and Arabist, Richard Burton, who understood them well, characterized the Somalis as a "fierce and turbulent race of republicans." Had he been a modern travel writer, he might have added that, with their constantly shifting political loyalties, the Somalis lived in a state of chronic political schizophrenia, verging on anarchy. Instead, Burton rightly noted as a redeeming positive feature, the extraordinary prominence of poetry in Somali culture,[2] although he neglected to emphasize the crucial role of poetic polemic in politics and war.[3]

So constituted, as a proudly independent people with a strong sense of ethnic exclusiveness in terms of language[4] and culture—despite their myriad internal divisions—the Somalis have for centuries lived outside, or on the margins, of world history. They have, rather characteristically, usually impinged on the outside world in contexts of conflict. The first extensive reference to the Somalis in written history is a sixteenth-century document recording their role on the Islamic side in the religious wars of the period between Christian Ethiopia and the surrounding Muslim principalities.[5] This describes the Somali warriors as being especially expert in road ambushes, a tradition they have maintained up to the present! Just after the French, British, Italians, and Ethiopians had carved up the Somali nation at the end of the nineteenth century,[6] a fiery Somali fundamentalist sheikh who was also generally judged the most brilliant poet of his age mounted a *jihad* against the Christian colonizers that lasted for twenty years.[7] This rebellion attracted four major British military expeditions and the first use of air bombardment in Africa before it collapsed when Sayyid Mohamed—dubbed by the British the "mad mullah" (a term unused by Somalis)—died of influenza. During this period, the Somalis frequently figured in English newspaper headlines. So, for example, the terrible battle of August 1913, in which the British camel constabulary was routed by the Dervishes with heavy losses on both sides, was announced on the London news stands as "Horrible Disaster to Our Troops in Somaliland."

This long-drawn-out conflict was concentrated in the north of the Somali region, mainly in the British Somaliland Protectorate and eastern Ethiopia, inhabited by the ethnically Somali Ogaden, the clan to which the dervish leader himself belonged. Further south, the Italian colony of Somalia was largely unaffected. Somali conscripts, however, were drafted into Mussolini's armies for the conquest of Ethiopia and the Italo-Ethiopian War of 1935-36, which was part of the run-up to the Second World War. The Italo-Ethiopian War developed from a minor confrontation between Ethiopian and Italian forces at the oasis of Walwal in Ogaden territory, claimed by Ethiopia. The defeat of the Italians in 1941 brought their Somali colony together with those of Ethiopia and Britain under a single British military administration, which encouraged Somali nationalism, directly and indirectly, especially through the famous "Bevin plan," which proposed that all the Somalis should be administered as a single state and prepared for independence. This proved incompatible with the wider interests of the big four (Britain, France, Russia, and the United States), so the Somali territories resumed their former status with the exception that the Italian colony of Somalia became a UN trusteeship, administered by Italy, with a ten-year mandate (1950-60) to independence.

The next Somali intrusion on the world scene was in 1977-78 and again involved the Ogaden clansmen. With the overthrow of Haile Selassie in Ethiopia in 1974, General Mohamed Siyad Barre, who had come to power in a successful coup in Somalia in 1969, came under increasing pressure to support his kinsmen in the Ogaden in their struggle against Ethiopian rule.[8] He waited until 1977 when Ethiopia seemed to be falling apart and then pitted his forces behind the Western Somali Liberation Front (Ogaden) guerrillas in their uprising against the weakened Ethiopians. The ensuing Ogaden war precipitated a remarkable superpower somersault. The Americans, Ethiopia's traditional allies, had already distanced themselves from the revolutionary regime in Ethiopia, creating an interesting opportunity for the Soviet Union, which had been supporting and arming Somalia but balked at Siyad's dangerous adventure in the Ogaden. So the Soviets moved out of Somalia into Ethiopia, reputedly taking with them details of the structure and ordinance of the Somali armed forces.

Forced to concede defeat and pull out of the Ogaden, Siyad desperately sought American help, claiming now (rather suddenly) that he was bravely confronting the menace of communism in the Horn of Africa, and dangling the bait of the former Soviet port facilities at Berbera in the north. So grudgingly, the United States contrbuted Western equipment to Siyad's Soviet arsenals. Additional arms supplies from the European Economic Community (EEC), sometimes paid for by Somalia's local super-power patron, Saudi Arabia, added to the stockpile of weapons that kept Siyad in power through the 1980s, as he strove to suppress insurrection by clan guerrilla movements in the north (former British Somaliland, which had joined Somalia at independence in 1960) and the northeast. Widespread disaffection against his increasingly tyrannical rule had developed in the wake of the Ogaden debacle, and his survivalist, divide-and-rule tactics relied heavily on the unreliable expedient of bribing and arming friendly clans to attack his opponents. The ferocious fighting in the north powerfully eroded the strength of Siyad's forces, which became dominated by his own clansmen and other kinsmen.[9] Like the rest of the state, these forces depended heavily on supplies of food aid, officially for the huge refugee population (estimated at over 500,000), which had followed the retreating Somali army from the Ogaden in 1977. The official economy, heavily dependent on the export off livestock from the war-torn north, was collapsing and had been eclipsed in importance by the informal sector based on livestock trading and migrant labor (what Somalis called the muscle-drain) in the Gulf States. The Civil Service, still paid at essentially the same rates as in the 1960s, before the years of hyperinflation, had virtually disintegrated by the end of the decade.

Somalia had virtually fallen apart before the actual overthrow of the dictator Siyad in January 1991. Human rights pressure on Western governments, appalled at the ferocious internecine conflict in the north,[10] had led to the virtual stopping of aid by 1990, when Siyad's authority was increasingly isolated to the area adjoining the capital, Mogadishu. Thus, when he was finally dislodged from an already severely battle-scarred Mogadishu by United Somali Congress (USC) forces (of the Hawiye group of clans) led by General Aideed, Somalia had already disintegrated into its traditional component units.

A vivid illustration is provided by the experience of an acquaintance of mine, a former Interior minister who belongs to a northern clan. As he recounted, he and a group of relatives and friends decided to leave Mogadishu and return to the north. They formed a convoy of over seventy vehicles and took two months to complete a journey that, in time of peace, required little more than twenty-four hours. The convoy had its own paid armed escorts and was also forced to hire local guides and protectors while traversing the different clan territories. Four vehicles were looted en route—one by the convoy's own armed escort when it had completed its mission. Other vehicles had to be abandoned along the way, and only fifty-one reached their destination. Eighteen people died on the journey and thirty were injured; however, nine babies were also born en route.

This situation, of loosely articulated clan political units, was very similar to that described by Burton and other nineteenth century foreign explorers in the course of their travels in the Somali hinterland. The only significant differences were the superabundance of modern automatic weapons, which had long replaced the traditional spear, and the associated increase in the number of gangster big men. Visiting parts of the Somali interior in March 1992, every man and youth that I encountered was very visibly armed with a Kalashnikov, or American equivalent, and there appeared to be plenty of heavy weapons in the background. Additional supplies, including tanks, in which there was a lively trade, had flowed across the border from the arsenals of the former Ethiopian dictator, Mengistu Haile Mariam, whose American-supported overthrow in 1992 did not include any properly managed arrangements for the disbanding of his huge army, much of which disappeared with its weapons into the countryside. Other more recent supplies of arms had come into Somalia from Kenya, despite an official international arms embargo.

The Deepening Crisis

Having overthrown Siyad, the USC leaders, Aideed and Ali Mahdi (a prominent businessman) started fighting over their respective positions, Ali Mahdi having already set up an elaborate phantom government. This conflict, which literally split Mogadishu into two armed fortresses polarized along clan lines, soon engulfed what was left of the city in a protracted bloodbath in which (between November 1991 and February 1992) 14,000 people are estimated to have been killed and 27,000 wounded,[11] often by indiscriminate artillery fire and antitank missile fusillades.

Fighting was not limited to Mogadishu and spread devastation and starvation throughout southern Somalia. The USC Hawiye had engaged in clan-cleansing Mogadishu, butchering or driving out the remnants of people belonging to Siyad's own clan or associated clans (the Darod). The latter regrouped in their home region south of Mogadishu under the leadership of another of Siyad's former generals, "Morgan" (Mohamed Siyad Hersi). Each side laid waste the agricultural region between the rivers, which is Somalia's breadbasket, killing and terrorizing the local cultivators who are less bellicose than the pastoralist Somali. As the conflict widened, Aideed struck up an alliance with Colonel Umar Jess's militia against Morgan, who, in turn, joined forces loosely with another of Siyad's former generals, General Adan Gabio and his militia. With the two factions in Mogadishu, these were the most heavily armed and aggressive militias fighting for control of what was left of Somalia, or key regions in the south. All were based primarily on traditional clan groupings held together by the attractions of the spoils of war. The main leaders, the so-called warlords, were all dubious figures from the Siyad regime.

In addition to this relatively organized violence but on a smaller scale, trigger-happy gangs of *qat*-chewing youths spread mayhem, looting and killing randomly in Mogadishu.[12] With agricultural production devastated and livestock herding also severely affected, famine spread, particularly among those who could not protect themselves against the ravages of the warlord's attacks. The UN estimated a death toll of 300,000 from starvation, and 700,000 Somalis sought refuge in Kenya, Ethiopia, and, on a smaller scale, in parts of Europe, including Scandinavia, and North America. The death toll in the north in the earlier conflict between the Somali clansmen there and Siyad's army of occupation added further to the terrible human cost of the Somali tragedy associated with the dictator, Siyad.[13]

In this woeful picture there were, however, two rays of hope. In marked contrast to the chaos in the south, in the northeast and northwest the reversion to clan structures shows the positive side of traditional politics—all the more striking in the absence of significant UN or other external intervention. In the northeast in the organization of the locally based Somali Salvation Democratic Front (SSDF), traditional clan and modern political leadership combined to produce relatively effective local government. The northwest, the former British Somaliland, where the Somaliland National Movement (SNM) guerrillas had defeated Siyad's forces in 1990, faced with the chaos in the south, declared unilateral independence from what was left of Somalia in May 1991. Although the region is more heterogeneous in clan structure than the northeast, its clan elders proved remarkably persistent and successful in establishing and maintaining peace, to such an extent indeed, that they forced the SNM government effectively to disband and reconstitute itself through their traditional clan assemblies.[14] By 2009 this had led to the formation of a flourishing democratic state (the Somaliland Republic) with an elected government and the gradual restoration of functioning social services.

International Intervention

The pervasive conflict and absence of any recognizable successor government to Siyad's in the south discouraged humanitarian intervention. Foreign embassies were withdrawn (or fled) and UN organizations followed suit, virtually abandoning Somalia to its fate. Only the Red Cross and a handful of nongovernmental organizations (NGOs), including Save the Children and Médecins Sans Frontiéres, continued to work heroically in appalling conditions, having to employ armed guards to protect their houses, offices, stores, and hospitals. Even the International Commission for the Red Cross (ICRC), for the first time in its history, found it necessary to hire armed escorts for its vehicles. Following much criticism and pressure and several false starts, aborted through attacks on UN Staff, UNICEF reopened its offices in Mogadishu at the end of 1991. In early March 1992, Ali Mahdi and Aideed agreed to a cease-fire in Mogadishu, which reduced the heavy artillery shelling that caused such terrible civilian casualties. This lull lasted for several months, with only sporadic outbreaks of fighting.

Although humanitarian aid was still far from adequate, it began to increase, highlighting the growing problem of looting. Much of the subsequent fighting in 1992 resulted from attempts by different factions to obtain or maintain control over the ports and distribution routes through which food and other supplies passed. Control of relief food was very lucrative for the warlords and their merchant allies. A faction that controlled a port (above all Mogadishu, as Aideed did) levied exorbitant taxes on cargoes, as well as taking direct cuts of 10 percent or 20 percent of the incoming food aid (some of which was sold outside Somalia) and also providing trucks with machine guns (the Somali technical) to "protect" food deliveries. To add insult to injury, as we have seen, convoys were frequently robbed by those hired to defend them. Expatriate humanitarian organizations, despite the support of local Somali NGOs, thus found themselves caught up in a web of clan protection rackets and became part of the warlords' political economy. They were inevitably contributing to the problem whose most compelling symptoms they sought to assuage.

Relief agencies had already begun to warn that over a million Somalis were at risk of dying of hunger. From July onward, the media took up the story and television relentlessly presented gruesome images of starvation and death in Somalia. It was yet another African "famine" in which Somalis featured as helpless victims and objects of inexorable natural forces over which they had no control. This extremely powerful but misleading media coverage had the positive effect of catapulting the Somali crisis dramatically up the international political agenda to join Yugoslavia at the top. This even jolted the British foreign secretary and his EEC colleagues into making a hasty visit to Mogadishu to get some impression of the devastation at first hand, thus joining the throng of international dignitaries and film stars who touched down briefly on photo-opportunity missions.

Some of those who knew that Somalia was in the grip of a desperate man-made disaster, considering that since part of the fighting was over access to food, felt the solution was to flood the country with food and therefore added their voices to the demand for massive food aid. Responding to a great deal of pressure for action, President George H.W. Bush, in August, assigned U.S. military aircraft to transport bulk food relief for distribution to the interior where the devastated farmers were dying of starvation. Grain was also auctioned at reduced prices on the open market in Mogadishu in an unsuccessful effort to bypass looters. Abundant food was certainly now available to Somalia: the problem was to get it to the hungry and dying, particularly in the agricultural villages between the Juba and Shebelle Rivers. More and more NGOs were active in the country.

The UN had now begun, in a faltering way, to play a stronger role that began inauspiciously with an inept attempt at mediation in January 1992 by Assistant Secretary-General James Jonah. Security Council Resolution 751 of April 24, 1992, agreed in principle to the deployment of a UN Security force to enable aid workers to operate effectively and safely. But this was sabotaged by the white House, which did not want to raise the profile of foreign policy issues in an election year,[15] and it was only with Resolution 767 of July 27 that the deployment of a peacekeeping force of 3,000 was authorized. It was not actually until the end of September 1992 that a contingent of 500 lightly armed Pakistani blue helmets arrived in Mogadishu, and it was two months later before they were able to assume guard duties at Mogadishu airport. The only really positive development in this dismal saga was the short-lived appointment (April-October) as the UN secretary-general's special envoy, of Ambassador Mohamed Sahnoun, an energetic and shrewd Algerian diplomat with first-hand knowledge and understanding of the Horn of Africa. In the six months that he held the post, he showed skill and initiative in negotiating with all sections of Somali society—not just the military leders—and successfully persuaded them to agree to the deployment of UN troops to safeguard food delivery and distribution. Failing to receive the military support that the Security Council had authorized and extremely frustrated at the long delays and bureaucratic muddles involved in reactivating the various UN relief agencies in Somalia, Ambassador Sahnoun became strongly and publicly critical of the UN. He was forced to resign in October,[16] ironically in the same month in which the UN launched a vast "100-day Action Program for Somalia, which was a tribute to his efforts.[17]

Lacking adequate protection, of the kind requested by Sahnoun, the increased flow of humanitarian aid and the greatly expanded NGO presence were inevitably accompanied by a general upsurge of looting and protection rackets. CARE, the agency responsible for bulk delivery of food supplies, was apparently spending $100,000 per month on bodyguards.[18] Some agencies claimed that the level of looting and organized pilfering was such that 70 percent to 80 percent of relief food did not reach its destination.[19] ICRC ships delivering aid were often shot at by militia gangs. With wide media coverage and continuing reports of militarily weak

Somali groups starving to death in the hinterland, calls for some form of UN military intervention became compelling. Boutros-Ghali reported to the Security council in November 1992 that the UN Somalia policy had become "untenable" and that fundamental UN principles might need to be reconsidered to find a solution. The outgoing U.S. President George H.W. Bush, began to review U.S. options with his security advisers. Now that the elections were over, Bush evidently felt that he had nothing further to lose by a foreign policy initiative that might add to his international esteem. On November 25, 1992, he proposed that U.S. troops should lead a UN operation in Somalia. This was quickly accepted by Boutros-Ghali and endorsed by the Security Council on December 3 by Resolution 794, approving UN intervention with the use of "all necessary means to establish as soon as possible a secure environment for humanitarian relief operations in Somalia". For the first time in its history, the international community had approved unilateral UN intervention, with offensive military force, in a (theoretically) sovereign state. A few days later, the advance parties of Operation Restore Hope, which was to involve over 30,000 U.S. and other troops, were landing in Mogadishu in a carefully staged photo-opportunity exercise before the eyes of the world.[20]

From Operation Restore Hope to UNOSOM II

The Americans saw their primary objective as being to distribute food and humanitarian supplies securely to the worst affected areas of southern Somalia. They were, understandably, extremely anxious to avoid casualties (especially in the run-up to Christmas) and thus proceeded cautiously and with maximum (though often ill-conceived) publicity,[21] relying on their sheer numbers and technical superiority to overawe the Somali population. In this spirit, the operation was directed by an experienced diplomat, Robert Oakley, who had served as ambassador in Mogadishu and knew some of the protagonists personally. He also had the delicate task of coordinating the work of UNITAF (UNOSOM), which was now led by the Iraqi diplomat, Ismat Kittani, who had replaced Mohamed Sahnoun as Boutros-Ghali's special representative. One of the main tensions here arose from UN pressure for UNITAF to enlarge its role to include disarmament, and thus aid the process of negotiation and reconciliation among the main armed groups. The Americans for their part were apt to raise the specter of Vietnam and stressed the limited and short-term character of their intervention, which included an expanding circle of contingents from other countries—notably France <u>but</u> not Britain.

Most observers concluded that after a few weeks with a minimum of incidents UNITAF had succeeded in opening up the supply routes and getting food through to most of the needy areas in southern Somalia. This entailed establishing military garrisons in key regions to quell oppressive militias, impose peace, and control conflict—not always completely successfully. It also meant trying to reestablish a Somali police force in the war-torn capital, Mogadishu, where relations between the two local warlords, Ali Mahdi and Aideed, remained tense despite the truce negotiated by ambassador Oakley as a precursor to the American intervention. Both sides hastened to welcome the powerful new force and to take as much advantage of it as possible. Heavy weapons and military trucks (technicals) disappeared from the streets—some were hidden locally, others were moved into the interior. While many of the desperate citizens of Mogadishu and elsewhere unrealistically saw the Americans as saviors who would restore normal life and rebuild their country, others felt that the tyranny of the warlords was now sufficiently curtailed to allow them to voice independent views. Outside Mogadishu also, the U.S. military presence enabled local elders, previously terrorized by the militias of the rival warlords, to regain some of their traditional authority as community leaders.

The importance of reempowering traditional community leaders, which had been consistently urged on UNOSOM by the Uppsala advisory group,[22] had been initiated by

Mohamed Sahnoun, but was pursued only in a token fashion by his successor. With the usual Eurocentric preoccupation with hierarchical political structures totally different to the Somali system, the UN leadership in Mogadishu was more inclined to concentrate on the high-profile warlords who, though their military strength was now held in check, had gained in legitimacy through their extensive dealings with Ambassador Oakley, despite his efforts to prevent that.

Taking advantage of the precarious lull in the fighting, produced by the huge but transitory military presence, Boutros-Ghali pressed ahead with his conception of the reconciliation process and, despite a hostile reception when he briefly visited Mogadishu, opened a peace conference of the faction leaders and their henchmen in Addis Ababa in early January 1993. Agreement in principle on a cease-fire was reached, although the terms remained to be settled. Aideed and his allies wanted an immediate cease-fire to consolidate their territorial gains, with reconciliation postponed to a later date. The other groups wanted the militias to return to their traditional clan areas and then proceed immediately to reconciliation. Eventually, formal cease-fire and disarmament agreements were signed, with the handing over of heavy weaponry to a "cease-fire monitoring group" to be completed by March when a further and more comprehensive reconciliation conference would be held.

Clearly, the expectation was that UNITAF would not be involved in disarmament in one way or another. In fact, the uneasy calm that had been the initial reaction to the American intervention, had already begun to break down with renewed and sometimes sustained outbreaks of fighting in Mogadishu as well as in the southern port of Kismayu. The deteriorating security situation jolted the UNITAF troops into patrolling more aggressively, disarming townsmen openly carrying weapons, and raiding one of the most notorious arms markets in Mogadishu, where they seized quantities of weapons. One of Aideed's encampments was destroyed and a contingent of General Morgan's was attacked to prevent it gaining control of Kismayu. Given the vast quantities of weapons in the country and their constant replenishment from Kenya and Ethiopia, such action hardly constituted disarmament, although this was what Ambassador Oakley now vividly described as his policy of "bird-plucking" disarmament feather by feather. There were similar erratic shifts in dealing with the tricky question of the employment by NGOs of privately recruited armed guards—theoretically these free-lance security agents were supposed to be unnecessary with the presence of UNITAF. In practice arms permits were issued to various categories of NGO guards, as well as NGO personnel, but the rules kept changing.

Thus, although Somalia was far from fully sanitized, the twin organizations of UNITAF and UNOSOM had established an unprecedented level of UN intervention in a previously sovereign state. The terms "peacemaking" and "peacekeeping" hardly adequately covered the wide range of activities undertaken. Efforts were being made, especially by UNITAF, to involve local traditional community leaders—the elders—in aid distribution and preparations at local levels for reconstruction. Embryonic police forces were being recruited, and while the UN prepared for the march Addis Ababa meeting of warlords, some symbolic disarmament was taking place.

At the UN, preparations were similarly in train for the establishment of UNOSOM II, which would take over when UNITAF was withdrawn at the beginning of May 1993. Security council resolution 814 of March 26, 1993, provided for a multinational force of 20,000 peacekeeping troops, 8,000 logistical support staff and some 3,000 civilian personnel. The US undertook to make available, in addition, a tactical "quick-reaction force" as required. The whole operation was to be directed by Admiral Jonathan Howe, the new UN special representative, who had been a security adviser to President Bush. The armed forces would be under the command of a Turkish general with an American second-in-command, obviously an important appointment in view of the continuing U.S. tactical support facility.

On the Somali political front, the UN was continuing to maintain its pressure on the leaders of the movements. The third UN coordination meeting in Addis Ababa in March on humanitarian assistance, which received donor pledges of $142 million for relief and rehabilitation, was attended by a wide range of Somali peace groups who stressed the upsurge in violence in Somalia and the urgent need for improved security. This was highlighted by the brazen incursion of Morgan's forces into Kismayu—under the noses of the UN peacekeepers—which occurred during the national reconciliation conference that followed. The agreement signed on March 27, by the leading warlords and representatives of sundry clan movements (some of dubious status) committed the parties to "complete" disarmament, with the help of UNITAF/UNOSOM, urging that the latter should apply "strong and effective sanctions against those responsible for any violation of the cease-fire agreement of January 1993."

In a new departure, very much in line with the UN's understandable but misguided desire to cobble together a Somali government as soon as possible, the agreement also provided for the establishment over two years of a "transitional system of governance." This included a Transitional National Council (TNC) with representatives from the eighteen regions that had existed during Siyad's regime, where Regional and District Councils would be established—a concession to the "bottom up" approach advocated by the Uppsala advisory group and others. The TNC was also to be "a repository of Somali sovereignty," a particularly unfortunate reference, since the delegation from the self-proclaimed Somaliland Republic in the relatively untroubled northwest, who had attended the Addis Ababa conference, had left before the agreement was signed and quickly disassociated themselves from these provisions. This insensitive approach to the achievements and aspirations of the people of the northwest was unfortunately characteristic of UN policy since the departure of Sahnoun, and critics quickly warned Ambassador Howe to be cautious, because a heavy-handed UN troop deployment in the northwest would risk importing the chaos of the south into a region which had managed to control its own affairs surprisingly successfully. More generally, the agreement in Addis Ababa, that UNOSOM II forces should deal firmly with infractions of the reiterated cease-fire provisions, accorded well with the robust terms of Security Council Resolution 814.

UNOSOM II took over formally from UNITAF/ UNOSOM I on May 1, 1993. With initially a considerably reduced compliment of UN troops, drawn from a large number of countries, and with Aideed and the other militia leaders showing little sign of laying down their arms or disbanding their followers, it seemed likely that the resolve of the new UN force would soon be tested. This happened on June 5 when twenty four Pakistani blue helments were killed as their contingent prepared to inspect some of Aideed's ammunition stores in Mogadishu. The Pakistanis were despised by the arrogant Somalis, largely because the original UN detachment, which had neither the resources nor authority to do much more than ceremonial escort duties, had been Pakistani.) This incident, significantly, occurred near Aideed's radio station, which some of his militia apparently thought the United Nations was about to seize. It was in fact wastefully destroyed a few days later in the course of the powerful UN retaliation, which included aerial rocket attacks on Aideed's bases, producing civilian as well as militia casualties. Aideed, who had gone to ground in Mogadishu but still gave press conferences, was proclaimed a wanted outlaw who had committed serious war crimes.[23] Despite the many errors that were made in handling the situation, while it may have made tactical sense to deal with Aideed first, Somalis were naturally waiting to see what would happen to the remaining warlords if they continued to fail to implement the disarmament agreements.

Sudanese support for Aideed, who suddenly became a champion of Islam, and the subliminal Muslim xenophobia of Somalis, encouraged commentators to opine that the United Nations risked inadvertently igniting a *jihad* against Western Imperialism. The specter of Aideed as a new "mad mullah" seemed, however, a rather unlikely development. What was much more predictable was that Aideed's clansmen would close ranks behind him and, unless and until UNOSOM reached agreement with their elders, engage in guerrilla attacks on UN troops. Meanwhile, UNOSOM had embarked on more constructive action, responding in early July to the invitation of the SSDF (Majeerteen) clan leadership in the northeast region, where their help was sought in rebuilding wells and communications as well as demilitarization.

Their next step, which was likely to be more complicated, would be to initiate similar projects in the northwest (Somaliland Republic) where the newly elected president, Mohamed Haji Ibrahim Egal (Somalia's last civilian prime minister), had indicated that he would welcome UN help in establishing police forces, demobilizing irregular militia groups, and removing the hundreds of thousands of mines left behind by Siyad's forces in 1988-89. The problem for the northwestern Somalis was to obtain this help in such a way that it did not upset the delicate balance of relative tranquility that the clan elders had worked so hard to achieve. Nor could it be allowed to jeopardize their aspirations to retain their self-declared, separate status as the Somaliland Republic.

The Wider Political Economy of Conflict

There is an Islamic fundamentalist interest in events in Somalia, which in the Sudan, Iran, and to a lesser extent Saudi Arabia were seen as encouraging Western penetration of a Muslim region—a view promoted by Somali factions seeking Islamic military aid. Sudan, particularly, supported proselytizing fundamentalist groups—with food and, by all accounts, military aid—which had exerted a destabilizing influence in the northwest and northeast. The Sudanese appear to have given Aideed a portable radio transmitter and other comforts. Various Gulf States supported Aideed's rivals, as had until recently the Italians, who were always eager to regain influence in their former colony.

More immediately, the neighboring states of Djibouti (with its aging Somali president), Ethiopia, and Kenya (both with substantial ethnic Somali populations), had very direct political and economic interests in Somalia. Following earlier Djibouti initiatives, the new Ethiopian government, which included several Somali ministers, had played a leading role in peace negotiations as had also, more informally, the Eritreans. Both Ethiopia and Kenya had received huge influxes of Somali refugees, and associated skirmishes between rival militias had spilled over the ethnically porous frontiers. Kenya had not, as far as I know, engaged in any high-level peacemaking activity. And certainly neither country had taken any serious action to enforce the international arms embargo and reduce the continuing flow of weapons into Somalia. This would not have been easy, but with the sophisticated U.S. equipment available, something could have been done. Any fruitful initiatives here would have had to take account of the fact that the Kenyan chief of staff was a Somali with clan connections to some of the leading protagonists in Somalia. Of course, both Kenya and Ethiopia had experienced all too acutely the destabilizing impact of irredentist Somali nationalism in the past. This tended to encourage them to feel that the present Somali tragedy was not an unmitigated disaster in terms of their national interests.

Supplying arms was closely linked to the other major cross-border trade, which brought daily cargoes of the Kenyan and Ethiopian-grown stimulant drug qat (*Catha edulis*) to the militia fighters, who chewed it to keep alert, and other consumers. Qat flights from Kenya had regularly landed in Somalia when it was impossible to get food relief into the country. It was believed by Somalis that the qat planes flew back into Kenya carrying illicit hard drugs and other contraband, which, given the chaos there, could be readily redistributed using Somalia as a staging post. With the links between former Italian governments involved in Somalia and the Mafia, this seemed not improbable. In any event, it has been estimated that the Kenya-Somalia qat trade yielded more that $100 million annually to wholesalers, transporters, and street dealers and that its import value exceeds that of any other imported commodity, including food and arms.[24] One of the main merchants was a close associate of General Aideed and acted as his finance minister.

Thus the *qat* trade (which is not immune to subtle pressures) was one of the mainstays of the political economy of the warlords and their militias. Other important contributions came from clansmen overseas and, as we have seen, interested foreign governments. Ironically, an important element, which was hard to quantify, derived, as noted above, from stealing humanitarian supplies and from protection money directly or indirectly paid by NGOs. The provision of transport and accommodation to NGOs and the various branches of UNOSOM was also a very lucrative trade that had been cleverly exploited, largely by entrepreneurs with close clan links to the principal warlords. In many cases, this involved the rent of property stolen from the legitimate owners by warlords, and exorbitant rents were also paid to some of the most notorious ex-ministers of the Siyad regime. It would have been much better, obviously, to have paid such rents into a national fund to be utilized in the future reconstruction of Somalia. But here, as in the other respects in which it acted unwisely and carelessly, UNOSOM seemed unconcerned.

International Intervention in Somalia: Retrospect and Prospect

In the 1980s Somalia had ceased to be a banana republic and had become virtually dependent on refugee aid. The withdrawal of aid as human rights criticism increased paved the way for the collapse of the Somali state that finally disintegrated into its traditional clan components with the downfall of the dictator Siyad. The struggle for survival in this nation of opportunists then became particularly acute. A heroic band of well-intentioned, but not necessarily well-informed, NGOs entered the field and helped the media alert the world to the Somali calamity, presented as essentially a natural rather than man-made famine. The United Nations was gradually cajoled into following suit and, spearheaded by President Bush's publicity-seeking Operation Restore Hope (after his unsuccessful election campaign) had become more and more involved and now acted, to an unprecedented degree, as administering authority.

Unlike the earlier (1950-60) UN trusteeship, which was to prepare Somalia for self-government, now the aim was to enable Somalia (plus or minus the northwest) to become self-governing again. By any calculation based in reality, this would be a long and uphill task in which the primary condition of civil order had still to be established. As the erratic course of UN involvement to date showed clearly, there was a fundamental mismatch between the slow cradling, which Somalia ideally needed, and the short-term stop-go lurches that characterized UN policy formation and budgeting, through ad hoc Security Council resolutions whose outcome depended on the interests or disinterests of member states.

There is nothing surprising about this. The United Nations is at present simply not constituted to assume such a complex and costly role in a lapsed state pushed to the forefront of the world's conscience by the suffering of its people in a crisis that is, in terms of military technology, more amenable to treatment than Yugoslavia. There is, of course, at present no UN standing army, let alone an effective military command structure with its own appropriate logistical support. Moreover, member nations, which are prepared to contribute to UN multinational forces, always do so on an ad hoc basis and subject ultimately to their own publics' views of their involvement in a particular crisis, views that naturally may change over time and in the event of UN casualties. As the much publicized Italian attempt to make political capital out of their traditional association with Somalia illustrates, states that commit troops to UN operations may have their own private agendas and, at the very least, are apt to feel that committing troops entitles them to influence UN policy itself. On the other hand, governments that like Britain in the case of Somalia, do not contribute military personnel, lack direct access to, and forfeit influence over the daily conduct of operations. To that extent they are left out in the cold even, if, as in the case of the United Kingdom, they are members of the Security Council and paid something like 10 percent of the total cost of UNOSOM.

Given these intrinsic failings if the United Nations were to continue to exercise its present role there (and elsewhere), it would seem to be more cost-effective to subcontract the task of tutelage to an appropriately qualified single country. This, after all, is what happened in Somalia before: but it would not have been advisable to award such a contract to Italy this time! Multinational administration and military forces, coupled with UN careerism, offer conditions that competing Somali interest groups will always mercilessly exploit to the full. By the same token, in situations such as Somalia—and perhaps even Yugoslavia—it might be cheaper and more effective to subcontract UN military operations to an appropriate state. (The ideal force in the Somali case, given their experience in neighboring Djibouti, would probably have been the Foreign Legion.)

Of Course, if these procedures had been followed it does not in any way guarantee that the glaring errors of U.S./UN action in Somalia would have been avoided. Still, it might have been easier for such an operation to have taken appropriate measures to be better informed about he cultural specifics of the Somali context, and correspondingly less naïve in its dealings with Somalis. It would certainly not have been difficult to have been better advised about the intricacies of rival Somali political interests in Mogadishu and elsewhere, and to have appreciated from the beginning the critical importance of radio broadcasting as the key to influencing Somali public opinion.[25] Here the bizarre image of American helicopters dropping leaflets, couched in pigeon Somali, over Mogadishu's primarily oral population fittingly encapsulates the style of an overgrandiose Western intervention that was high on technology but low on culturally appropriate human understanding.[26]

Conclusions

This critique of well-intentioned but poorly designed and executed UN intervention in Somalia highlights the mismatch between such high-tech humanitarian intervention and local social and cultural conditions. Although, from time to time, lip service had been paid to a bottom-up approach, enlisting the support of local community leaders (as in the formation of district and regional councils), greater effort was expended in negotiation with the warlords and faction leaders selected by UN officials, sometimes quite arbitrarily, as Somali representatives for expensive high-profile, international conferences in Addis Ababa and elsewhere. This partly reflected the structure of the United Nations, its budgeting organization and constraints, and its unsatisfactory short-term recruitment practices governing the employment of civilian personnel who were often poorly qualified and ill-prepared for effective service in countries such as Somalia.

The inherent complexity of operating such an enormous multinational military organization has already been sufficiently stressed. But it is perhaps worth emphasizing the exponentially increased complexity of a U.S.-dominated UN military enterprise. It is difficult not to conclude that the huge UN budget could have been better spent on a smaller, tighter controlled, and longer term operation, including some form of UN trusteeship, and more in accord with local Somali timetables and processes. An essential feature here would have been a really effective UN special envoy with the negotiating skills and patience all too briefly brought to UNOSOM by Mohamed Sahnooun. That, of course, might have meant risking more foreign lives to stop Somalis fighting each other.

Let us now leave the United Nations and turn to consider further the nature of the conflicts that destroyed the state of Somalia. These are not of course strictly ethnic conflicts—though sometimes are misleadingly so described. More accurately, these are conflicts mobilizing clan and lineage allegiances in a society where, as we have seen, fighting and feud are deeply entrenched and highly valued in this essentially martial culture. The systematic character of the blood feud is reflected in the institutionalized system of settling disputes by paying blood compensation collectively. Clan conflict, typically over resources—traditional or modern—is thus generally based not on linguistic, cultural, or other visible differences between people, but simply on invisible differences of ancestry. People's origins are crucial. Descent as recorded in the genealogies Somalis cherish (orally), is the primary determinant of identity and political loyalty. People feel different from and potentially hostile to those who do not share their ancestry. As we have seen, aggravated by the firepower of modern weapons, this can produce extremely bitter fighting, rape, and pillage, and modern-style clan-cleansing in settlements and towns.

Thus, in Somali society today, as in the past, communal identity based on kinship has the same explosive potential as identity based on religion, ideology, or culture (including language), or race elsewhere. In my view, all these group identities belong to the same genus as nationalism: call them micronationalisms if you wish. What is involved here is essentially collective solidarity, group cohesion. Whether or not one accepts Emile Durkheim's distinction between organic and mechanical solidarity,[27] it is beyond doubt that internal segmentary structures weaken national or ethnic cohesion at the highest level of grouping.

The Somali dictator Siyad Barre, while practicing clan politics, professed to be constructing organic nationalism, based on literacy and the destruction of the traditional segmentary system. But that is not what actually happened. So it is not surprising that ethnic Somali nationalism, reactively stimulated but not created by the experience of colonialism, in its most expansive phase, found expression in the 1977-78 Somali-Ethiopian War, which sought to achieve self-determination for the Ogaden region of Ethiopia (Western Somalia) to enable it to join the Somali state. In opposition to Ethiopian identity, Somali unity stressed cultural, linguistic, and religious cohesion—their ethnic identity in contrast to the (misleading) stereotype of Christian (Amhara-dominated) Ethiopia. At the outset of the twenty-first century, however, the Somalis were conspicuously no longer mobilized at this level, and had fallen apart into their component clans and lineages, with the Ogaden Somalis participating in the multinational state of contemporary Ethiopia which, following its earlier centralization under a succession of autocratic regimes, had many similarities with Yugoslavia—as Yugoslav political scientists recognized. With the pervasive distribution of modern automatic weapons, and the policy of ethnic regionalism, that could naturally be a fateful parallel.

Although all these identities and divisions of humanity—nations, ethnic groups, clans, and the rest—present themselves as natural categories, automatically determining and directing sociability, they are of course nothing of the kind. This is conveniently illustrated by the English term for acquiring British citizenship—naturalization—which clearly implies a natural, biological process. Although they have the appearance of genetic origin, Somali genealogies are as arbitrary and man-made as culturally constructed ethnic or national identity. They are social not natural products. What they offer are natural-seeming, and hence indisputable, bases for belonging and communal action, which are so easily manipulated by politicians and used by them for their own purposes to confuse and complicate social interaction by seeming to simplify it. While the British (or was he South African or Israeli?) social anthropologist Max Gluckman long-ago stressed, cross-cutting ties—economic, political, and religious—may provide some measure of restraint on nihilistic communal violence,[28] it would appear that social relations are likely to be most harmonious where material resources and opportunities are felt to be equitably distributed within a system of shared, pluralistic values.

As I have tried to emphasize, the nature of political culture—which can be modified—is an important consideration. The self-help segmentary political processes of the Somali are profoundly antagonistic to the stable and peaceful mobilization of wider national identity. On the other hand, despite the obvious tendency toward disintegration along ethnic lines, Ethiopia enjoys the positive factor of a long tradition of political centralization. The crucial aggravating factor of the ready supply of deadly weapons in Somalia, in ex-Yugoslavia and, for that matter in northern Ireland, it too obvious to require further mention here. More grandiosely, as I have suggested elsewhere,[29] at a global level modern mass society seems, by its scale and anonymity, to expand the bounds of patriotism beyond acceptable, viable limits. This appears to evoke alienation at the local level, so remote from the centre of real power, and promoting a renaissance of the little tradition of familiar communal identity—with all that implies.

Notes

1. For a detailed analysis, see I.M. Lewis, *A Pastoral Democracy* (Oxford: James Currey, 1999).

2. See B.W. Andrzejewski and I.M. Lewis, *Somali Poetry* (Oxford: Oxford University Press 1964).

3. See S.S. Samatar, *Oral Poetry and Somali Nationalism* (Cambridge: Cambridge University Press 1982).

4. The Somali language, which contains a number of Arabic loan-words associated with Islam, belongs to the Cushitic family, which includes other languages spoken in southeastern Ethiopia.

5. This is a famous account by the Muslim chronicler of the period, written in Arabic, between 1540 and 1560.

6. See I.M. Lewis, *A Modern History of the Somali* (Oxford: James Currey, 2002); and A.Sheik-Abdi, *Divine Madness: Mohamed Abdulla Hassan* (London: Zed Books 1993).

7. One of the most famous of the Sayyid's poems is a chilling polemic commemorating the killing of the camel constabulary leader, Richard Corfield, on August 9, 1913. See Andrzejewski and Lewis, *Somali Poetry*, pp. 70-74.

8. Siyad's mother came from the Ogaden and that clan came to play an important role in his regime.

9. Although Siyad's regime was officially based on scientific socialism ("wealth-sharing based on wisdom," in Somali), in reality the core of the power structure depended on his own clan (M), his mother's

clan (O), and the clan of his son-in-law (D) known by the acronym MOD. His rule was thus a family business as was well known to most people in Somalia. See also chapter Three for a more detailed explanation of MOD.

10. See Africa Watch, Somalia: A Government at War With Its Own People, Washington, The Africa Watch Committee. January 1990.

11. Africa Watch, Somalia: Beyond the Warlords, Washington. The Africa Watch Committee. March 1993, p. 5.

12. Qat leaves, which look like English privet, are chewed raw, traditionally on religious or social occasions, when a group of men meets to talk in the evening. They are now chewed much more widely by individuals during the day and generate a strong craving for this stimulant in which the active ingredients are Benzedrine-type compounds. The young urban gunmen who have adopted looting and killing, virtually as a way of life, are known as *moryan* in Mogadishu. One of their most popular role models was the movie character Rambo.

13. Africa Watch estimates that between 50,000 and 60,000 civilians were killed by Siyad's forces in the north.

14. A Somali anthropologist and I assessed the procedure and success of local-level peacemaking by the northern elders. This study was under the aegis of the British NGO Action Aid. See A.Y. Farah (with I.M. Lewis), *The Roots of Reconciliation* (London: Actionaid, 1993). See also Chapter Six of this book.

15. See Africa Watch, 1993, p. 12. My own contacts in the Defense Department in Washington, DC tended to corroborate this.

16. Mohamed Sahnoun was a personal friend of Boutros-Ghali and seems to have felt betrayed when the bureaucrats in New York sabotaged his efforts and Boutros-Ghali failed to support him. His successor was generally considered to have been a disaster in Somalia.

17. Donor countries pledged $150 million toward the estimated budget of $180 million to be spent on relief and development.

18. Peter Hillmore, The Observer, June 27, 1993. Other sources reported that, very reluctantly, the ICRC was spending £132,000 per month for the same purpose.

19. This was the figure reported to the UN Security Council on November 25, 1992.

20. See I.M. Lewis "Restoring Hope in a Future of Peace," *Cooperazione*, Rome, March 1993, pp. 43-45. "Somali Peacekeepers: Precedent, Altruism or Public Relations," *Crosslines*, April 1993, pp.

4-8; and for a very critical assessment, Somalia Operation Restore Hope: A Preliminary Assessment," *Africa Rights*, May 1993.

21. See I.M. Lewis, "Misunderstaning the Somali Crisis," *Anthropology Today*, August 1993.

22. Based at the Horn of Africa Centre at the Life and Peace Institute in Uppsala Sweden, this small group, which I helped to establish, consisted of social scientists with specialist expertise on Somalia drawn from a number of countries and included three social anthropologists. With aid from the Swedish government, which financed a number of peacemaking projects in Somalia, four meetings have so far been held jointly with the senior officials of the political division of UNOSOM. The first two meetings were attended by the UN Special Envoy, Ambassador Mohamed Sahnoun. The group had consistently advised UNOSOM to follow a bottom-up regionalist approach, with as much decentralization as possible. The response, in practice, has often seemed rather different. The Life and Peace Institute published the informative Horn of Africa Bulletin.

23. See Amnesty International, *Somalia: Update on a Disaster—Proposals for Human Rights* April 1993; and also Africa Watch, *Somalia Beyond the Warlords*, March 1993.

24. See Jonathan Stevenson, "Krazy Khat," *New Republic*, November 23, 1992.

25. Thus, most Somali nomads have transistor radios on which they listen to all stations broadcasting in Somali, local and international. Their favorite was the BBC Somali program, which they listened to every afternoon with at least the same attention they gave to their daily Muslim prayers. At the beginning of UN operations in August 1992, I and others urged the critical importance of effective broadcasting in the presentation of UN aims and policies. It took almost a year before UNOSOM did anything about this.

26. In the first leaflets dropped at the beginning of Operation Restore Hope, the words "United Nations" were unfortunately, rendered as "Slave Nation." According to U.S. military sources, much time and trouble went into the preparation of the leaflet and its printing at Fort Bragg. Apparently, the only Somali with the requisite military clearance for this delicate task was someone who had left Somalia for the United Nations when he was twelve years old and whose command of Somali was "a bit rusty"!

27. I. M. Lewis, *Social Anthropology in Perspective* (Cambridge: Cambridge University Press). Also compare M. Maffesoli, *Le Temps des Tribus* (Paris: Librarie des meridians Klincksieck, 1992, pp. 259 1988).

Six

MAKING PEACE FROM THE GRASS ROOTS: SOMALILAND'S SUCCESS

✦

"War and famine: peace and milk."
−Somali Saying

After the flight of President Siyad Barre from Mogadishu in January 1991 following his ouster, rival armed militias established clan fiefdoms in areas dominated by their descent groups. The dismemberment of Somalia was most pronounced in Mogadishu city where hostile warlords (Ali Mahdi and Aideed), belonging to opposed clans of the Hawiye clan-family and its then political wing the United Somalia Congress, divided the city into two halves, north and south. The first was controlled by Ali Mahdi and his Abgal clan and the second by General Aideed and his Habar Ghidir forces.

In contrast to the faction-ridden and highly unstable south, the Republic of Somaliland (the former British Protectorate, proclaimed in May 1991), until 1996 enjoyed relatively peaceful conditions in the turbulent era following Siyad's overthrow. Several factors seem to be involved here. The first is environmental: during this period, the pre-dominantly nomadic rural and localized dry-farming subsistence agriculture flourished, whereas in the south extensive drought triggered a massive relief program. The extortion of relief supplies, and income derived from a monopoly of the import of goods needed by the relief agencies, strengthened the firepower of heavily armed, power-crazy warlords in the south.

Second, the bulk of the comparatively limited relief assistance donated to Somaliland during the Somaliland National Movement's interim administration May 1991-May 1993, was largely looted by competing clan militias. This prompted the termination of relief assistance and the evacuation of most nongovernmental agencies. The cessation of aid removed a major source of clan contention, leading to a reduction in conflict.

Third, the social upheaval in the south degenerated into a war of attrition, mainly because the major contestants were more or less equal in firepower. No clan had the might to exert control over all the others and so impose terms of settlement, with or without the agreement of the defeated parties. In the north, in contrast, the Isaq clan-family, the numerically largest group, became militarily dominant. Although the SNM administration reproduced this demographic dominance in the interim government, to the chagrin of non-Isaq groups, nevertheless the subjugation of other hostile clans, associated with the previous government, did not take place.

Fourth, and perhaps most important, was the bottom-up approach followed in the restoration of peace and stability at the local level pioneered in Somaliland by genuine leaders of the hostile clans involved. This comprehensive peace movement was first initiated at the local level by traditional political leaders, using conventional methods of arbitration between neighboring and intermarrying clans.

Starting at the grassroots level, this elders' peace movement progressed to district and regional levels. It reached its height at the Borama conference (known as *gurti*), where 150 delegates, consisting of clan councilors representing all the groups in Somaliland, managed to agree on separate regional and national peace charters. Here, for the first time in the post independence period, the elders extended their peace-making functions by acting as an institutional framework for the formation of an executive interim national government.

While this national conference received international support (more than $100,000), the prior clan and regional reconciliation conferences were essentially financed by local community self-help: only token external aid was provided in some cases by NGOs. Moral backing came particularly from the British NGO Actionaid, which had considerable experience of collaborating with local clan elders in Erigavo district. The results in terms of preventing serious clan conflict are all the more impressive when contrasted with the much less effective, elaborate, high-cost peace and reconstruction conferences organized externally for Somalia as a whole by the United Nations and other international bodies. These, of course, were primarily concerned with the long-drawn-out civil war in southern Somalia, epitomized by the chaos in Mogadishu.

Traditional Social Organization

The evocative power of kinship as the axiomatic natural basis for social cooperation and as the ultimate guarantor of personal and collective security is deeply rooted in Somali society. For the weaker and less successful members of Somali lineage, kinship is an indispensable source of protection and safety, readily manipulated by stronger more politically ambitious clansmen for whom kinship is an elastic resource, conveniently accessible and infinitely negotiable. "Our kinsmen right or wrong" is in effect the implicit motto of Somali social life. As the cornerstone of social cooperation, kinship enters into all transactions between and amongst individuals. There is scarcely any significant area of Somali social activity where the influence of kinship is absent.[1]

This emphasis on kinship in the formation of Somali political units can be seen at all levels of grouping. The highest level among the predominantly pastoral Somali may be designated as clan-family.[2] Widely distributed in space across the Somali region in the Horn of Africa and with populations sometimes in excess of 1 million (e.g., the Darod), clan-families are generally too large to act traditionally as corporate political units. The Isaq clans joined forces against the military regime (largely Darod) during the civil war, but fragmented into rival clan factions after the downfall of the regime in 1991.

The symbolic link binding members of the clan-family together mainly derives from links to a common remote ancestor, who is usually depicted as the central figure in the creation myth of the group. Those members of the clan-family who are able to participate, occasionally reinforce social solidarity by organizing large memorial feasts at the tomb of their common ancestor. The loose ties that obtain at this level of social formation are established by an elaborate and extensive genealogy (extending over 20-30 generations), in which the living generation counts back to the founding eponym. This elaborate genealogical reckoning, which acts as a device defining social relations in the widely segmented patrilineal system of the Somali, is learned by rote by each Somali child in early life under the instruction of his dutiful mother. Additionally, the extensive genealogy of the clan-family is sometimes recorded for posterity in venerated texts by religious men literate in Arabic, and today also in written Somali by educated clansmen.

The total Somali nation whose remarkable homogeneity (despite local variations) is founded upon common language (Somali—written in the Latin script since 1992), religion (Islam), and predominantly pastoral economy, is divided into six clan-families: Isaq, Dir, Darod, Hawiye, Digil, and Rahanwin. The first four clan-families, making up the bulk of the total Somali population, are primarily pastoral and widely dispersed, while the last two are largely agricultural, concentrated in the riverine region of southern Somalia and speak a separate, Somali related language, *af-May*. This tongue is not fully mutually intelligible with standard Somali, which is also known to many of this group.

Within the clan-family, the next most important social unit can be distinguished as the clan. This traditionally marks the upper limit of practical political solidarity. Hence when the situation demands, and the common interests of its members are at risk, a clan unites its constituent forces against rival and often hostile clans. Its political importance is further enhanced by the clan's territorial tendency, with each clan associated with a particular area frequented by its members. Also the dry-season corporate deep wells and trading centers dominated by clan members occur in its sphere of influence that is delineated by reference to local place-names. These territorial interests of clan members are defended collectively if threatened by antagonistic rival units. They are further distinguished by the titular office of clan leader with, in the late twentieth century, an inflationary tendency to multiply such positions.

Below and within the clan, the next distinctive kinship group has been defined as "primary lineage."[3] The sanctioned alliance-seeking tendency among kinsmen who belong to this unit, and also the predisposition among its members to identify with this lineage in ordinary kinship discourse, are its essential sociological features.

Within this system of groups that are always mobilized the basic political and jural unit is the *diya*-paying group (from the Arabic *diya*, blood money). Its strongly bound agnatic members commonly count from four to six generations to a common ancestor. The group has a strength ranging from a few hundred to a few thousand persons, conceptualized as male warriors. Apart from the principle of close agnation that binds its members, the group's social solidarity is also further cemented by the collective obligation to pay and receive blood compensation, and compensatory payments in respect of other acknowledged delicts. Here both principles that define social solidarity and political action, agnation (in Somali *tol*) and contract (*her* in Somali), supplement each other to produce a cohesive and relatively stable unit that provides the basic security and protection of the pastoral Somali. The crucial importance of this unit led past colonial and successive independent governments to appoint stipended *diya*-paying lineage leaders as chiefs or local authorities known as *aqils* (literally headmen) and finally, in the Siyad regime, as *nabad-dons* (literally), peace-seekers). These elders were supposed to maintain law and order among their kinsmen, and sometimes did, and to act as emissaries between their group and the government.[4]

This short review highlights only the structurally and functionally important points of cleavage within an all-pervasive agnatic context built of elaborate segments. Thus it must not be considered that clan, primary lineage, and *diya*-paying group constitute the only possible levels of active segmentation of the major Somali clan-families. In practice the actual levels of division are much more extensive. This ordered but outwardly intricate segmentary social system has the capacity to place every citizen in a corporate *diya*-paying lineage, where his basic rights are guaranteed and obligations clearly defined. Moreover it establishes social relations between *diya*-paying groups and other levels of political action, in a turbulent social environment where alliances need to be created and re-created to defend pastoral resources and retrieve access to pasturage and water usurped by enemies.

The eternal search for adequate pasturage and water in a semiarid nomadic environment characterized by unevenly distributed and often inadequate resources, provides uncertainty and generates fierce competition among members of different lineage groups. In practice in this setting, clans fight clans, primary lineage groups of a particular clan and those of different neighboring clans get locked in battle, and in the same way the *diya*-paying lineages of the primary groups confront one another in armed conflict.

This fluid situation, which has been so ruthlessly manipulated by Somalia's power-mongering warlords, has been eloquently described by Said Samatar:

Stripped of the razzle-dazzle with which it is often presented, segmentation may be expressed in the Arab Bedouin saying 'my full brother against my half-brother, my brother and I against my father, my father's household against by uncle's household, our two households (my uncle's and mine) against the rest of the immediate kin, the immediate kin against non-immediate members of the clan, my clan against other clans, and finally, my nation against the world!' In lineage segmentation one literally does not have a permanent enemy or a permanent friend, only a permanent context. Depending upon a given context a man—or a group of men, or a state, for that matter—may be your friend or foe. Everything is fluid and ever-changing.[5]

The Structure of Contemporary Peace Conferences

Current peace forums are described in Somali as *shir*, generically the traditional council of elders that deliberates matters of common concern at all levels of grouping. In spite of the urban bias of elders at the end of the twentieth century, political leaders involved in modern peacemaking are built from a core of *diya*-paying leaders and other distinguished elders of the groups involved in reconciliation. The traditional informal method of conducting peacemaking and other socioeconomic activities has adopted modern conference techniques. Thus, most peace forums are chaired by a select committee assisted by a secretariat. A technical committee, which often includes professionals who worked in the disintegrated Somali state as well as military officials, is also appointed to prepare the agenda and a general framework for resolutions that is endorsed by the *gurti*, as the assembled body is nowadays usually called.

Commonly, conference resolutions are legitimized by the unanimous consensus of all the delegates of the reconciling clans. In addition to peacemaking, the famous Borama national conference tackled the building of an executive government for Somaliland. So it integrated both principles of legitimizing resolutions—traditional consensus and majority vote. Mostly headed by sultans, the nominal leaders of clans and large subclans, the *gurti* is described as the highest traditional authority. A perceptive elder of the Warsangeli clan described *gurti* as: *wa garad hul ah qabiil ama ummad laga so huley*, which translates roughly as "the most enlightened and judicious persons found in the group or nation at large." This term[6] is not recorded in Lewis who, however, describes a similar institution that was reported to have occurred in traditions of the past dynasties of the Gadabursi and Isa clans. Lewis (1961, pp. 207-209) reports: echoes of a slightly more developed institution than that typical today, occur in the traditions of the Gadabursi and Isa. When a new Ugas (clan leader) was appointed among the Gadabursi, a hundred elders, representative of all the lineages of the clan, assembled to form a parliament to promulgate new *her* agreements, and to decide what legislation they wished to retain from the reign of the previous Ugas. The compensation rates for delicts within the clan were revised if necessary, and a corpus of Gadabursi law, as it were placed on the statutes for the duration of the new Ugas's reign. This was called the "law of the Ugas and his hundred men" (*herka ugaska iyo boqolka nin*). This council acted as a central legal court (*guddi*) to which all disputes that could not otherwise be settled should be taken. The Ugas and his court toured the country, moving amongst the various clan segments settling disputes, and receiving gifts of tribute and hospitality. There is said to have been no standing army or specialized functionaries to enforce decisions of the Ugas's court, other than men of the Midgan occupational caste, attached to the royal lineage, who acted as emissaries. Traditionally, the Ise clan had a similar arrangement with a permanent court of forty-four men attached to their Ugas. In both cases the Sultans were leaders on the egalitarian Somali pattern, dispute settlers and arbitrators vaguely responsible for the prosperity and fortune of their clans, not heads of a Muslim state.[7]

Today the *gurti* is sometimes referred to as *ergo*. However this latter term usually designates a group (or party) of negotiating elders appointed to settle an important problem with another group. It commonly consists of influential members of the *gurti* of a particular group, but not exclusively of it. As delegates assemble as the situation arises, the *ergo* can be distinguished from the standing clan council of elders. The *gurti* not only participates in interclan affairs, but also acts as the highest political and jural council of clans and large subclans. Elders' arbitrating panels (*herbegti*) acting within or between patrilineal segments, are selected on the basis of their knowledge of traditional customary law, rather than Islamic Shariah or modern Western law. They, like the *ergo*, have retained their traditional functions into modern times; but the gurti seems to be an obsolete institution that has regained use on account of the increased role of lineage elders in peacemaking.

Gurti Composition

To illustrate the actual composition of a particular *gurti*, we take the example of the Habar Yunis and Habar Jalo clans' joint *gurti* in Erigavo district. At the time of our research, of the forty-two members, thirty-three were Habar Yunis. These comprised a core of eleven headmen, representing the eleven *diya*-paying lineages of the Habar Yunis found in Erigavo district. Table 2 illustrates the proportion of councilors with reference to their main economic activities.

Table 2

Herding	19
Trade	8
Agriculture	6
Total	33

Of the eight *gurti* members who identified themselves as traders, one was an ex-civil servant, while three were employees of the former military government. The majority of these members of the conference gave their permanent address as Erigavo town or surrounding villages. Although these data refer only to one *gurti,* they suggest several significant features. There is first an overwhelming tendency of the lineage elders in the major district town and associated villages; a very small number lived in agricultural areas. However, the majority of the urbanized elders still depend primarily upon income derived from livestock herded by kinsmen in the interior. The continuation of economic and social links between urban and rural kinsmen exemplifies a widespread strategy of diversification through which extended families benefit from the economies of both domains.

The urbanization of the lineage leaders and other important social groups (e.g., traders) has certainly moved the center of power from the rural nomadic populace to important centers of trade and administration. However it is erroneous to consider the *gurti* as an urban clique lacking the interest and expertise to be able to offer a credible leadership service to their rural subjects. Despite the vital economic, agnatic, and contractual ties that bind the urban *gurti* and their rural kinsmen, the traditional leaders are recent migrants who are familiar with the pastoral tradition.

It is interesting to note that the Habar Yunis *gurti* in Erigavo district consisted of a core of eleven *diya*-paying group leaders. These represent the corresponding eleven *diya*-paying lineage divisions of the clan. This just representation satisfies the Somali egalitarian segmentary political principles. The remaining twenty-two members of the *gurti* are distinguished elders selected to assist the lineage leaders. Supported by two assigned members, each headman has primary responsibility in the affairs of his *diya*-paying group. In external matters that are of common interest to the clan such as arbitration and disputes with other clans, the whole *gurti* acts together to defend its collective interests.

Of course, despite the equitable distribution of political offices and other resources among the group, in practice strong lineages tend to dominate clan affairs. So, to take another example from the Gadabursi clan, the twenty-one seats on the council were distributed among the clan's three major divisions according to their relative strengths. The largest subclan, the Makahil, was allocated nine members, while each of the remaining two, the smaller Mahad Ase and Habar Afan, were each allocated six members. The attachment of the *gurti* to the corporate and stable jural and political *diya*-paying group certainly affords a certain permanency. Nevertheless, in its normal functions, the *gurti* of a clan or subclan often changes in its membership. At most *gurti* meetings some members fail to attend due to personal reasons, engagement in more serious duties, and so on. In such cases kinsmen of absentees take their place.

A comparison between *gurti* signatures of the successive peace treaties that act as legal contracts, which tend to promote harmonious coexistence between estranged neighboring clans in Somaliland, illustrates significant divergence between the signatories of the accords. Moreover, the existence of the formal clan *gurti* does not prevent a clan, or clans, from appointing a special committee for special purposes. So in the on-going preparations for the Erigavo regional meeting, the host Habar Yunis and Habar Tol Jalo clans found it fitting to appoint a new joint committee to attend to security despite the existence of the formal *gurti*. This can be seen as an attempt to bury their differences and work harmoniously together to guarantee the safety of the guest *gurti* representatives of formerly hostile clans.

As the highest legal authority, the council of clan elders deliberates on and arbitrates major conflicts between clans. The Erigavo regional meeting was given the mandate to resolve outstanding complex property rights, affecting land and urban property rights, between regional clans. These contentious issues were judiciously postponed in the earlier meetings in order to build up confidence and trust between the hostile clans.

At the local level, particularly at the buffer zones between reconciling clans, joint security committees are established to solve minor disturbances and prevent opportunistic banditry. Such local committees are known locally as *guddi turahan*, literally, the "committee that weeds the field." Here the act of weeding a plot is a metaphor for the pernicious effects of violent breaches of the desired peace. Consisting of dominant local elders, these local committees respond rapidly to acts of violence and livestock plunder, and also see to the return of stray livestock between neighboring groups. Moreover, they endeavor to police the bilateral contracts that have been agreed.

Apart from the participation in the peace conferences of politicians, military officials and professionals who worked for past regimes, and the adoption of procedures used in modern conferences, these peace assemblies can be described as essentially traditional clan councils (*shir*). The organization and format of this traditional assembly was described by Lewis as follows: The informal council (*shir*) summoned as need arises, at every order of segmentation, and attended by all the adult men or their representatives, is the fundamental institution of government. It has no formal constitution except that of membership of the lineage concerned, no regular place or time of meeting, and there are no official positions on it. All men are councilors and all men politicians. Agreements are reached by majority decisions following the direction taken by the consensus of feeling at a meeting. Usually the participants sit in a rough circle in the shade of a tree, in the central clearing of a nomadic hamlet, or they may meet in a "coffee shop" in a village or town. Where a large lineage with a male strength of several thousand is concerned, delegates may be chosen to represent each of the component lineages and sent to a central meeting-place. Sometimes, however, all those concerned even if they number several thousand attend the council and form a large loose ring. Representatives may then be appointed for the smaller units and sent into the middle of the circle to thrash the matter out while their kinsmen sit listening in the outer ring. Men sit or squat on the ground at a *shir* and when they wish to speak often rise to their feet. Although there may be a great deal of argument and wrangling, all those present are expected to behave courteously and breaches of good manners may be punished. Thus at a large Habar Awal *shir* which had met to discuss the rights of cultivators and pastoralists in the west of the Somaliland Protectorate, two of the lineages represented insulted the elders of other groups present. The offenders were directed by the Sultan to pay insult damages (*hal*) to the affronted elders.[8]

Membership of a strong group and inherited status may increase the influence and status of some aspiring elders. However, factors that determine successful leadership are generally open and attainable by potential candidates. Personal qualities and fortunes, including wealth, political acumen, strength, and courage; expertise in traditional law and religious knowledge; generosity, fairness and impartiality, probity, seniority, and skill in oral poetry and in oral discourse in general—all constitute ideals that are associated with distinguished traditional leaders. These qualities, possessed in various combinations by outstanding lineage leaders, cause the opinions of more successful figures to carry weight and command attention among rebellious kinsmen and the public at large. Nevertheless, as Lewis observed, it is difficult to rank leadership qualities in terms of their importance.[9]

Notwithstanding the effects of natural demographic growth, this study found a further proliferation of political offices among the clans of Somaliland. Most probably, this is mainly fostered by the need of clans and subclans to assert independence in a situation of turmoil and uncertainty; and moreover by the explicit tendency to search for solutions in the traditional lineage structure, given the paucity of effective modern law and authoritative administrative mechanisms. Table 3 shows past and present distribution of sultans among the clans of Somaliland and illustrates this point.

Table 3
Distribution of the Office of Sultan
among the Somaliland Clans

	Prior to Independence (pre-1960)	In 1993-94
Gadabursi	0	5
Iisa	1	1
Habar Awal	1	4
Arab	1	1
Iidagalle	1	1
Habar Yunis	0	2
Habar Jalo	1	1
Dulbahante	2	4
Warsangeli	1	1

Finally, it is worthwhile to briefly consider the motivations of elders who are active in peacemaking. First it is a truism that the maintenance of peace has always been the moral obligation of lineage elders, despite the fact that the existence of centralized authority has in modern times to some extent reduced this function. Second the authority of the clan elders started to gain increasing significance during the civil war. The defeat of the massive SNM offensive launched against the government forces in 1988 led to the formation of an Isaq *gurti* of fifty-three members that assumed responsibility for providing clan militias and logistical support to the impaired war effort. Held at Adarosh near the Ethiopian border, this important conference was organized by elders. Because of the vital collaboration between the elders, who had influence on Isaq lineages and the military leaders, the Isaq *gurti* was given recognition in the constitution of the SNM. In the same year the Gadabursi clan conducted a general conference at Qunujed that discussed the defense of its land and people.

The elders are certainly delighted by their increased peacemaking role and its attendant benefits. For instance, the host group lavishly entertains the members of the visiting *gurti* during a conference. The Borama conference, which was generously supported, continued for four months, throughout which the elders were sumptuously fed. This led the meeting to be dubbed *bulo*, "the nursing care provided for a sick person." Thus the elders involved were able to recuperate their strength after the lean period of the civil war.

Causes of War

Disputes over Land and Pasture

Conflict is accentuated by the multiclan composition of settled districts where land disputes are most pronounced. This is the case, for instance, where Isaq and Harti (Darod) lineages live together in disputed, sedentarized areas of Erigavo district, while Isaq and various Gadabursi lineages live in Gabiley district. In general, at the height of the civil war, in those locations the Isaq became displaced from their settled homelands that were usurped by rival residents. This process was reversed at the end of the civil war, which enabled the Isaq to return to these mixed sedentary areas. Consequently, the non-Isaq groups became displaced in their turn. Disputes over fixed agricultural land are more difficult to resolve than those over nomadic grazing reserves. Two factors seem to be responsible for this. First, pastoral land is little developed, and the available pastoral resources are determined by environmental factors beyond human control. Apart from trading centers, valuable long-term developments are confined to the construction of underground water tanks (*barkado*). These are mainly built by wealthy nomadic families who undertake such ventures in order to secure a reliable supply of water for their herds, and sell any surplus to supplement the income gained by animal husbandry.

The unpredictable distribution of pastoral resources necessitates the sharing of basic pastoral resources across areas controlled by different clans. If a particular clan or lineage refuses other rival groups access to pasture and water within its sphere of influence, it will face similar treatment at a time of hardship when it is indispensable to have access to grazing controlled by other groups. Second, investments made by those who hold arable land make this fixed property valuable. Furthermore, this type of property is regularly scarce, particularly in such districts as Borama and Gabiley that have a relatively prolonged history of settlement and cultivation.[10] The farming of sorghum and maize developed spontaneously in these two districts at the turn of the century. This highly significant economic transformation has been adapted from the neighboring sedentary Oromo in Ethiopia. The herding of cattle, sheep, and goats is an important supplementary element in the agricultural economy of Borama and Gabiley districts.

In the northeast of the country, Erigavo district is also a relatively sedentarized zone. Here, regulated smallholder dry farming and small-scale family irrigation agriculture, concentrated along perennial streams in the precipitous mountain complex, started during British colonial rule. In spite of this controlled agriculture, this district remained largely nomadic prior to the 1970s. Hence, Erigavo district became one of the troubled areas in the north. In addition to disputes over arable land, conflict over pasture is also pronounced— mainly because of the transformation of traditional pastoral land to grazing reserves and cultivated fields. An additional and far from negligible ingredient is the presence in the district of groups belonging to different clan-families (Isaq and Darod).

Politically Motivated Conflict in Burao

From February until September 1991, the euphoria generated by the downfall of Siyad Barre's tyrannical regime, led to a short period of tranquility in Somaliland. The Isaq thought that the change of government would bring them quick advantages, in which they would be well placed to benefit at the expense of others. Non-Isaq clans were wary about what the victorious Isaq might do to them. Some clans feared reprisals after the "liberation." In January 1992, deep suspicion between clan militias in the mixed Burao district degenerated into open conflict. The ensuing hasty war that continued for a few days displaced the returnees in the town who were striving to rebuild their lives. Since the combatants were the two rival militias based in Burao itself, their strife did not immediately spread to their kinsmen outside. However, the ability of the Isaq *gurti* to resolve internal differences was undermined by the polarization of the Isaq into the two main political factions (military and civilian). Thus the non-Isaq Gadabursi *gurti* elders and others played a significant role in the settlement of this conflict and subsequent internal Isaq wars. The neutral status of the Gadabursi and the embarrassment of the Isaq's failure to resolve its differences facilitated a successful reconciliation.

Berbera Conflict

The Burao conflict set a precedent for the second major clan conflict of the Isaq, which took place at Berbera, between the Habar Yunis and Ise Muse, and erupted in March 1992. Initiatives by the president's faction to centralize power led the administration to try to place the regional port of Berbera under its control. The local Ise Muse clan opposed this move. So the government organized a combined force to establish its control at Berbera. The resident Ise Muse opposed this move, which they saw as an attempt of the Garhajis-dominated government to appropriate the revenue from this important town and its resources.

The interim SNM administration disappointed the Isaq people and other clans who considered that they were not fairly represented. In 1991 the SNM had obtained some external assistance and their share of the newly printed national currency from Mogadishu. But such limited resources were not invested in urgent tasks, such as disarmament and demobilization of armed guerrillas, or the creation of embryonic national security forces. Limited though they were, such acquired resources were mainly appropriated by the corrupt civilian and military officials of the administration. Competition for political dominance and control over limited resources led to hostility between the Isaq clans. This also antagonized non-Isaq clans who felt that they were being marginalized. This competition intensified the power struggle between civilian and military factions in the SNM administration, widening this longstanding division within the organization. The new SNM administration was portrayed as being dominated by the civilian faction headed by the president and supported by his clan (Habar Yunis) and the related ldagalle. The association of the SNM interim administration with Habar Yunis led the rival Habar Jalo to become the major Isaq clan that pioneered opposition to the fragmented administration. The traditional rivalry between the Habar Yunis and Habar Jalo, which appears to have been suppressed during the civil war by the common Isaq cause, surfaced after the initial euphoria of victory over the detested Siyad regime.

As soon as the loose collective campaign to establish central government rule in Berbera started, the constituent clan militias—other than the Habar Yunis—withdrew their cooperation and left the joint force. This led to a war between the loyal Habar Yunis clan, which supported the president and his civilian faction, and the local Ise Muse. Compared to the limited upheaval in Burao, this flared into a widely spreading conflagration, which raged from March to October 1992, causing extensive human loss and damage to property. The firing by the president of five opposing ministers augmented the power struggle between the civilian and military factions. Many disenchanted members of the administration left the country. This aggravated the security situation in Isaq-dominated areas of Somaliland. The raging civil war and security crisis that engulfed the country shattered Isaq expectations, particularly the struggle to achieve international recognition for the embryonic state.

Public disgust and the elders' relentless endeavor to restore peace led to a conference in Djibouti between the political factions in the administration. This was followed by a return to Hargeisa where they formed a thirty-one-man reconciliation committee, comprising sixteen representatives of the dominant civilian faction and fifteen from the rival military faction. This joint committee was chaired by the distinguished religious leader, Sheikh Ibrahim Sheikh Yusuf Sheikh Maddar of Hargeisa. Unfortunately, the committee failed to stem hostilities between the Habar Yunis and Isa Muse clans, let alone tackle the urgent security crisis in Hargeisa and other areas. Worse still, the conflict between the political and military leaders weakened and indeed undermined the sustained conciliation effort of the Isaq *gurti*. The *gurti* visited Berbera six times in the course of the clan strife there. On each occasion the peace settlement arranged by the elders between the warring factions faltered, mainly as a result of sinister maneuvers by the hostile political and military factions.

The withdrawal of support by the other clans in response to the government's bungled attempt to establish control over Berbera was considered by the Habar Yunis as a betrayal. The ensuring disenchantment was further aggravated by the checkered fortunes of the strife. The initial assault by the Habar Yunis led to the capture of Berbera, but this short-lived victory was later reversed by a counterattack that established control of the town by the regrouped Isa Muse forces. On their part the Isa Muse regarded this as a government-orchestrated attempt, whose ultimate aim was to rob them of their valuable resource and impose Habar Yunis hegemony—a section of whom live in the Berbera area. Thus, they refused conciliation efforts arranged by Isaq reconciliation groups. The victims of the Habar Yunis and Isa Muse conflict rejected an article in a peace agreement devised by the Isaq peace groups. This relates to the control of Berbera by the government that was associated with the Habar Yunis.

Techniques of Peacemaking: The Role of Women

One of the conundrums of Somalia's civil strife is that the protagonists are usually neighboring clans related by marriage. In addition to Islamic law, which condemns fighting between neighbors who are also related, kinship morality also discourages fighting between affins. Thus the Somalis practice warfare that is contrary to strongly held Muslim beliefs and important principles of social formation. Traditionally, and to a significant degree still among the pastoralists, the need for access to basic resources at times of stress, controlled by rival groups, encourages corporate groups to marry outsiders. However this preferred pattern of alliance seeking exogamy does not transfer women's birthrights from their natal groups to those of their husbands. A woman after marriage retains her kinship and property rights in her father's group. The latter rights are often disregarded due to the Shariah inheritance bias in favor of men and also because of patrilineal ideology that mystifies primary community properties as lineage wealth (camels and agricultural land).

As members of patrilineal corporate descent groups and as affinally related foes, women were more distressed than men by Somalia's tragic civil war. With their dual kinship role, they were the only immediate means of communication between belligerent clans at the height of the civil war. Material assistance and information between hostile affinal groups were carried by women who were allowed to cross clan boundaries. This led them in Somaliland to be labeled "clan ambassadors." This title also reflects the reputation that they tended to acquire as "secret agents," on behalf of their natal lineages. They were frequently charged with passing military secrets from their husbands' to their fathers' groups. In appealing to unifying cultural bonds, reconciling elders emphasized these connections as they sought to soften and persuade antagonistic groups to make peace. To break a deadlock in the negotiations where one group refused to join the peace forum, distinguished elders who were affines with the defaulting group were sent in to win their support. For twenty-four days the Dulbahante *gurti* failed to appear at the site of the first major peace forum with the Habar Yunis at Dabarweyne. This led the Habar Yunis to send a delegation comprised of kinsmen born by Dulbahante women. They succeeded in persuading suspicious maternal relatives to come to participate in the forum.

To seal a peace treaty between warring parties, women were traditionally exchanged. This practice was followed in some of the major Somaliland peace settlements. So the reconciling Habar Yunis and Isa Muse agreed to exchange fifty wives from each group at the sheikh conference. Marriage as a symbolic union has individual and corporate symbolic significance and indicates a serious commitment by both parties. You give a daughter to someone you trust and with whom you desire to maintain a relationship. Particularly, where blood has been shed, Somalis regard the giving of a marriage partner as a mechanism for alleviating the loss of life. As the Somali proverb says: "the stains of blood (spilled) should be cleansed with a fertile virgin lady." As well as the reproductive function of wives that may be said to compensate for the lives of lost kinsmen, the symbolic significance of the practice is significant as a gesture of reconciliation.

Customary contracts are usually honored by Somali clans. They can, of course, be rescinded, amended, or abrogated as the situation demands. However, deliberate violation without a formal indication of the intention to rescind an agreement is regarded as a treacherous act and will blacken the name of the perpetrator.

In July 1992 while the Habar Toljalo and Dulbahante clans were busy making peace, ten armed militiamen of the latter were found to have been surreptitiously sent out to raid stock from the former. At the time it was still not safe to cross clan borders. So the Dulbahante took two of their wives of Habar Toljalo origin in a military vehicle and transported them to the border area. The women were sent to warn their kinsmen of the anticipated raid. The Dulbahante raiding party seized camels and killed a Habar Toljalo man in the process. However, the seized stock were retrieved because the timely information passed on by the Habar Toljalo women to their kinsmen alerted both groups. This flagrant breach of the peace was immediately corrected by the Dulbahante paying one hundred and ten camels in homicide compensation and a wife. The additional ten camels (100 plus 10) and the woman represented a public acknowledgement and offer of appeasement to restore relations between the clans that had been seriously jeopardized by this brazen act of aggression.

Notwithstanding these gender-based peacemaking contributions that derive mainly from their dual kinship status, women did not take a direct role in the successive reconciliation conferences in Somaliland. Although in the high profile Borama conference, and in the much-publicized southern conferences organized by the United Nations, women's delegations participated as separate groups, local Somaliland peace forums remained largely male activities. Nevertheless, northern women enthusiastically supported the local forums, and, most importantly, provided traditional domestic services. They prepared food for the assembled peace delegates and attended to the cleaning and public hygene requirements of the meetings.

Settling Outstanding Issues

The grassroots peacemaking activities in Somaliland can be described as a collective business. Certainly the arbitrating clan councils assume a central role, but they also make effective use of the services of the other traditional leaders, the most important of whom are religious men and poets. Other than the central *gurti*, participating elders, ex-professionals, politicians, military officials, religious figures, and poets are described as distinguished guests. They may offer advice and make suggestions in open bilateral peace talks, but the endorsement of the agreements is carried out by the *gurti*. To supplement the moral authority of the elders, with religious sanctions, many of the peace treaties also bear the signatures of religious elders.

To avoid futile and protracted opposing litigation, arbitrating *gurti* strive to encourage direct negotiations between the parties. Given the *gurti's* lack of instituted authority, which undermines any ability to enforce agreed decisions, it is also prudent to encourage disputing parties to reach bilateral agreements. This is important since the reconciling groups are ultimately responsible for the implementation of the agreements they have reached through consensus.

The national *gurti*, comprising delegates from all the major clans of Somaliland, offered its services in the serious Habar Yunis and Isa Muse conflict at Berbera. The latter group claimed to be the victims of brazen aggression and accordingly sought adjudication on the actual culprit. However, the national *gurti* repeatedly entreated the two parties to resolve their differences through direct negotiation. To the delight of the *gurti* this was finally accepted on the third day of the conference. However, the *gurti* also selected a special arbitration committee assigned to pronounce on any issues the two sides failed to resolve. Fortunately, all issues were resolved through direct negotiation. The general *gurti* assumed the supervisory role of assessing accord. To give weight and legitimacy to the agreements, they added their signatures to the bilateral contract.

Sympathetic attention is given to conflicting grievances held by the parties. Mutural interest and areas of consensus are emphasized in order to build trust and a wholesome atmosphere that can facilitate agreement on contentious issues. Judicious consideration is given to not upsetting the view of one party or the other, and the difficult side must be handled diplomatically. In effect, an informal and conciliatory tone is preferred to the investigation and examination procedures that place blame upon one party.

167

Traditional elders possess extensive endurance and the patience that is necessary to tackle delicate, unpredictable, and tardy peace business. The Habar Yunis *gurti* anxiously waited twenty-four days for their Dulbahante counterparts to attend the first joint meeting at Dabarweyne. The opening meeting in Eil Qohle, a pastoral area between Habar Jalo and Warsangeli lands, started with a prolonged elders' discourse under a tree that lasted almost a month. In a situation tense with hostility and deep suspicion, this delicate initiative had to continue seeking a breakthrough for such a long time in order to find an opportunity that gave hope of finding a peaceful outcome. If an irreconcilable difficulty arises in the course of a peace session, the proceedings are directly suspended until such time as a consensus is reached informally.

If a contentious issue is found difficult to resolve in a particular forum, it is usually deferred so as to prevent disruption of the peace process. Given the scope of the matters adjudicated by the elders and their lack of instituted authority, in the absence of the machinery of centralized government, it is usually the case that outstanding issues between the groups (especially disputes over property) fail to be resolved at the time specified in the accords. However, this does not disrupt a buoyant peace effort. Therefore the next scheduled forum is not cancelled due to the failure of one party or the other to resolve outstanding issues that were agreed to be settled in the preceding conference. Current forums rearrange the settlement of accumulated outstanding issues.

Redefining Responsibility for Penalities

From the very beginning, local clans in Somaliland made a significant concession that led to the unfolding of the peace process. In a conciliatory spirit, embattled clans agreed to bury the past and concentrate on the present and future issues of mutual concern: the restoration of peace and stability. This was achieved by a common agreement that annulled past events. Otherwise their inclusion would have led to massive and futile litigation and recrimination, complicated by the practical difficulties in the actual computation of the losses in people and property sustained by rival groups during the protracted civil war involving clans and the military regime.

Faced with the immense security task in an explosive situation, the *gurti* discerningly introduced harsh provisions that were designed to contain the endless cycle of plundering livestock. To dissuade armed militias from seizing herds, the elders decreed that the responsibility to pay damages should be narrowed to involve only the immediate families of the offender (his father, brothers, and uncles). This unprecedented decision, which placed responsibility for acts of violence firmly upon the family and immediate kin of the aggressor, undoubtedly discouraged blatant and opportunistic raiding. Instances of inveterate looters being killed by their own kin are cited by many clans in the region. The Warsangeli and Dulbahante clans further decreed that traffic accidents should remain the responsibility of the drivers, with the possible assistance of close kin. A Dulbahante informant explained this development as a response to reckless driving by the qat trucks that frequented the region. In addition, the introduction of capital punishment appeared to be gaining currency as an effective measure to curtail homicide. The Habar Tol Jalo and Habar Yunis sections in Burao, and the ldagala and Warsangeli all practice this punishment. In early 1992, the internal homicide rate reached an alarmingly high figure of thirty-six people murdered in one month. This led the ldagala to impose capital punishment, which reduced murder to nil.

Constraints on Effective Peacemaking: The Limited and Diffuse Authority of the Elders

In the highly democratic, uncentralized political system of the northern Somali, political institutions are invested with remarkably limited authority. Despite this, traditional political leaders at the various levels of grouping often managed, as they now do, to establish precarious law and order in the pastoral world and in recently sedentarized areas. In the absence of effective, centrally directed law and order, northern Somali elders braced themselves to attend to an expanded peacekeeping role that covers both rural and urban security requirements.

A widespread desire for peace and stability among the northern clans, mainly resulting from war-weariness, enhanced the peace efforts of the elders. This dispensation and appeal for fairness and justice that because of disillusion with past and contemporary political leaders, appears to have facilitated the peace effort of the elders. This helped the *gurti* to effect contractual legal accords between opposed clans. However the practical application of the contents of the extensive treaties proved a daunting task for the elders. The following case illustrates the difficulty encountered by clan elders in enforcing unpopular decisions upon their kinsmen. The arbitrating *gurti* of Somaliland decided to witness the exchange of prisoners between the successfully reconciled Habar Yunis and Isa Muse clans at Sheikh. The exchange was agreed to take place in Burao town. The Habar Yunis failed to deliver on time the eight prisoners they held at Gorgor near the Ethiopian border. These captives had been seized by a Habar Yunis man because his truck was lost in the clan war!

It took the Habar Yunis nine days to deliver the prisoners. The delay was caused by the clansman who held them and was demanding compensation for the loss of his truck and for his expenses in feeding the Isa Muse prisoners for five months during their captivity. The Habar Yunis finally managed to convince their kinsman to accept compensation, but only for his expenditure on the prisoners. Compensation for the truck was rejected because much equipment was lost during the conflict and had to be written off. When, as last, the Habar Yunis delivered the captives they were exchanged, under the supervision of the Somaliland *gurti*, for thirty prisoners held by the other side at Berbera.

The traditional system of governance that relies primarily on the moral authority of lineage leaders and the goodwill of their kinsmen has a limited capacity to prevent crime and violence. Thus the northern elders aptly describe their role in dealing with violence as *dab damin*, literally, "fire extinguishing," restricting the explosion of social upheaval. The colonial and successive independent Somali governments employed this traditional system in maintaining rural law and order. In the past, local political leaders, especially recognized local authority elders, were supplemented by modern security forces and institutions. During the period of British administration, written contractual agreements between the clans were recognized as a source of law. Copies of clan treaties were kept at the office of the local district commissioner and used in settling disputes and payment of blood compensation.

Freelance Militias: The "Dayday"

The Somali term *dayday* means literally a "thorough and avaricious search." In the present context, it refers to the ransacking that the *dayday* usually carry out after opportunistically plundering people's property. As some local authorities suggest, the word appears to have been borrowed from a "Dalaley" poem composed by one of Somalia's most distinguished artists, Hadrawi. The poem in question depicts the free-lance plunder and relentless terror launched against the public by some regular soldiers of the military regime that became habitual at the final stages of its existence.

The *dayday* in northern Somalia are portrayed as prototype miscreants and villains. Isaq informants are quick to retort that normal SNM militias relinquished military service after the liberation of Somaliland. It is assumed that people, who were disappointed by the failure of a nationalist victory to provide the employment opportunities they anticipated, returned to their areas of origin and resumed their previous activities. This widely held assumption implies that armed official clan militias contain a significant number of voluntarily dispersed ex-militias.

Mostly teenage boys and unmarried adult men, the *dayday* despise the older generation in general and the *gurti* in particular. They call elders *kofiyad bacle*, a derogatory term that means literally "wearers of plastic hats." Traditionally, elders wear hats as a symbol of moral authority. The negative implication here appears to derive from the fact that urban Somalis carry cash in plastic bags. So it is implied they have become corrupt by making money out of their peacemaking and other mediatory activities.

To disarm and demobilize the clan-based and heavily armed militias was the expressed wish of virtually everyone in Somaliland. Without the restoration of peace, it was realized that the illusive international recognition of Somaliland as a sovereign state would remain wishful thinking, a remote dream. This made urgent the demobilization and disarmament of the militias who posed the biggest threat to peace and stability. Yet, despite the improved relations between clans that reduced the risk of warfare, interclan suspicion still lingered. Obviously, each clan preferred to see its enemy disarmed first, and would wish to be the last to surrender its weapons.

The armed militias commonly operate in the areas controlled by their clan groups. At the time of our survey, fourteen militia-manned checkpoints were found on the Hargeisa-Borama road, and twenty-six along the Burao-Las Anod route. Each of the fourteen checkpoints on the former road is manned by a local lineage, or group of lineages, so that the overall pattern provides a sketch map of lineage distribution.

Acts of banditry perpetrated by opportunistic free-lance militias are constant threats to peace and stability in rural and urban areas. The organized plundering of trade goods, private property, and nomadic stock, which are apparently decreasing in this region, are not only committed by militias that are loosely recognized as clan armies, but occasionally also by armed kinsmen operating in the areas controlled by their lineages. In a sense armed militias look after the general interests of their own groups. If a member or members of a particular clan seize property of another clan, armed kinsmen of the victim launch a counter raid. This often leads to a cycle of violence.

Checkpoints manned by clan militias are concentrated along trade routes frequented by qat trucks (Nabadadis-Hargeisa, Burao-Las Anod, etc.). Driven at a frightening pace, these trucks are notorious for reckless driving and epitomize madness associated with drug operations in the West. Militia gun-mounted trucks (*tiknika*: English "technical's") have now overtaken the reckless driving of the *qat* drivers. The trigger-happy militias that ride the dreaded technicals menace both the *qat* merchants and the public at large. Clan militia squadrons, scattered along major roads, extort cash from passing private trade trucks, and a tax in kind from *qat* trucks. Since the checkpoints run through different lineage territories controlled by various militias, traders are forced to pay each militia they encounter for safe passage. Thus Berbera *qat* traders actually found it more economical and profitable to transport their goods in light aircraft from the Ethiopian border to Berbera town. However, the bulk of the trade is still transported over land with the traders forging agreements with the checkpoint militias, sometimes by recruiting militia escorts.

Militias themselves refer to the levy they exact on trade as a legitimate form of taxation compensating them for their services. Sometimes unruly militias fight over the spoils, especially the highly prized drug *qat*. In June 1993 the Somaliland government succeeded in its first step of centralizing important centers of revenue by placing Berbera town under the control of the state. This measure has since been expanded throughout the country, ending the former system of extortion and replacing it with general taxation. These militias constituted the first major obstacle that had to be overcome in the establishment of national security forces. Many young militiamen were thus absorbed into Somaliland's new army.

Size, Time, Protocol, and other Constraints

The strength and relatively effective nature of the Somaliland peace effort by the traditional leaders lies in its anchorage in the basic, segmentary structure of society. Representation in the interclan peace forums was based on the actual lineages of the the clans involved. Additionally, the organization and conduct of peace conferences mainly depended on local resources and facilities provided by the groups concerned.

Their organization and conduct similarly followed the pattern of traditional assemblies: slow, unwieldy, difficult to organize and manage, and massive in manpower. Despite prior agreement on the size of the essential delegations, peace conferences often expanded into large assemblies, swollen by the inclusion of uninvited kinsmen of all the parties. The Borama peace conference planned for the participation of 150 elders. The actual number of delegates who regularly feasted and mainly slept at the venue (Sheikh Ali Jowhar secondary school) was estimated at some 700 people. The participants at the Garadag and Daarweyne conferences were, respectively, 720and 500. Modeled on the traditional ad hoc council of elders, where all adult males had the right to attend, many men not included in the official *gurti* of the reconciling parties participated in the peace conferences.

The duration and starting dates of the meetings often defied fixed schedules. The need to attend to important matters affecting the interest of one party or another, failure to complete the required preparations on time, and so on hindered the prompt commencement of proceedings. Once started, the conference continued, rather slowly, until a satisfactory consensus was reached. The Borama conference was scheduled to start in January but was delayed until late February when, in order to discredit the government that opposed it, it was suddenly started with incomplete preparation. In the event, it was opened with seven days devoted to reading the Quran, which allowed time to make essential preliminaries. The actual business started on March 3. The regional Erigavo meeting was delayed for several months.

Disagreements between the Warsangeli and Habar Yunis clans over the chairmanship of the Jidali conference delayed its opening. Since the Warsangeli had chaired the preceding Yube conference, the Habar Yunis insisted that it was their turn. For their part, the Warasangeli argued that their sultan was the only available formally instituted clan leader and thus automatically qualified for the role. Agreement to lower the level of the meeting from that of clan level to *diya*-paying group level broke the deadlock over status. After eight days of discord on this issue, the conference finally started under the chairmancy of an eastern Habar Yunis elder.

Peacemaking Results

The formidable constraints of the traditional peacemaking process that spontaneously unfolded in Somaliland certainly delayed the establishment of a general peace in the country. These factors also hindered the practical implementation of many useful conclusions formally agreed to. However and rather surprisingly, these constraints failed to derail the impetus for reconciliation and peaceful coexistence among local communities. Driven by nationalistic endeavor to salvage the self-proclaimed state of Somaliland from unprecedented and senseless ruinous turmoil, and to escape the shame and disgrace that ensures from a cause supported by the public at large, traditional elders strove to maintain the peace under considerable pressure and against arduous difficulties.

This grass roots local-level approach to peace started with a series of interclan reconciliation conferences as early as 1991, immediately after the overthrow of the dictator, Mohamed Siyad Barre. Then it gradually progressed to district, regional, and national levels in which the collective service of the *gurti* of the major clans reconciled particularly difficult cases that failed to be resolved by the parties concerned. The Sheikh reconciliation conference represented the turning point of the elders' peace effort, which reached its height at the Borama conference. In the latter, a national peace charter was formulated that incorporated the provisions of the series of compacts between the local clans. Realizing that their peace functions could not effectively succeed without the effective support of a modern administration, the elders expanded their peace functions to tackle the complex task of building an executive interim government and a national charter—an unprecedented event in modern Somali history. Given these laudable achievements it is no wonder that the elders installed themselves in the structure of the interim government, which consists of three councils: council of elders, constituent (elected) assembly, and council of ministers.

The sustained effort of lineage and clan elders has thus firmly established an encouraging tendency in which peaceful dialogue is favored as a means to settle legitimate grievances in lieu of the use of force. Individual acts of violence are constrained not only by the legal ruling that places responsibility on the offender, but also by the predictable condemnation of agnatic kinsmen and opposition from other affected social groups. Legal contracts promulgated by a series of peace conferences define political and socioeconomic relations between local clans in Somaliland. Some tangible achievements of this process, already apparent in 1993, included:

1. The exchange of stray animals.
2. The exchange of looted livestock, trucks, and trade goods.
3. The gradual return to harmonious relations between clans. This reduced the traumatic pressures of the war situation such as vigilant preparedness to defend livestock and human lives in a situation of perpetual conflict.

4. The effective exploitation of scarce, widely distributed pasturage and water. This enhanced migration and mobility.

5. Dispersion of herds and herdsmen, reducing the spread of infectious animal and human diseases that afflicted locally concentrated nomadic encampments during the course of the civil war.

6. Increased trade and social interaction across clan boundaries.

7. Coordination and the prevention of acts of violence through the exchange of information relating to the activities of freelance banditry.

Over the period 1990 to 2005, high-profile peacemaking initiatives in southern Somalia, involving costs running into millions of dollars, produced few positive results. In Somalialand in contrast, between 1991 and 1993, the local clan elders organized a series of remarkably successful peace conferences, using traditional procedures, to secure a level of interclan understanding that surpasses anything yet achieved in the south. Except for a little assistance with logistics and conference food costs, foreign intervention was extremely limited.

Our conclusions suggest that the slow, local, traditionally based Somali process is the most effective process of peacemaking and that external conflict-resolving techniques should be tried on a pilot basis before being widely applied in Somalia. The ethnocentric assumptions that underlie these exotic procedures manifestly make them much less effective than existing local techniques. To facilitate and strengthen the expanding circle of interclan understanding, it may be helpful to extend the range of existing local facilities. Assisting local-level communications (through for instance local broadcasting) might be beneficial. Our conclusions also point to the danger that aid resources, unless restricted in such a way that local groups consider equitable, are apt to stimulate conflict.

Our study for the British agency Actionaid was limited by time and budgetary considerations to a short field survey and literature review. Using the same anthropological techniques that we consider essential for understanding rural Somali society, it would be worthwhile to extend our research to include the northeast, now called Puntland, where local elders seem to have achieved comparable results.

Notes

1.   I.M. Lewis, *Blood and Bone: The Call of Kinship in Somali Culture* (Red Sea Press 1994), p. vii.

2.   I.M. Lewis, *A Pastoral Democracy* (London, Oxford University Press 1991).

3.   Ibid, p. 127.

4.   Ibid, pp. 200.

5.   S.S. Samatar, *Somalia: a Nation in Turmoil*, (Minority Rights Group Report 1991), p. 25.

6.   It seems likely that this word is derived from the verb *gur*, to move, by the addition of the ending *ti*, this pattern of word formation of substantives being common in Somali. It would thus suggest a peripatetic council.

7.   I.M. Lewis, *A Pastoral Democracy* pp. 207 – 209.

8.   Lewis, Ibid pp. 189-99.

9.   Ibid, pp. 196-98.

10. Ibid, pp. 90-126.

Seven

MOGADISHU SCRAP MERCHANTS FORM A GANGSTER GOVERNMENT: AN EU CONTRIBUTION

✦

Yet another "last chance reconciliation" conference to restore Somalia was mounted in Kenya in autumn 2002 and staggered on for over two years. To understand what appears to have happened there and how it compares with so many earlier grand Somali peace conferences, we need to look at the background and especially the failure of the Transitional National Government, established in August 2000 with such optimism at the end of the exhausting Arta Conference in Djibouti.[1]

The Djibouti project, launched by the enterprising Djiboutian President Ismail Umar Geelle, with Arab and UN support, involved (at various times) as many as 2,000 Somali participants. These were reported to be "representatives" (and certainly many so claimed) of various clans and lineages, many of whom styled themselves as members of civil society (always a problematic concept in Somalia),[2] and included a fair selection of more or less notorious warlords from southern Somalia. The original idea, laudable in theory, was to exclude those warlords with the worst human rights records, and form a provisional government that could bypass their endless rivalry and conflict.

The main figures, whom I call the "scrap merchants" of Mogadishu, did not initially receive important ministerial positions in the resulting Traditional National government (TNG). These major "big men" had built up their economic and political status essentially by successfully exploiting the UN presence up until March 1995. Thereafter, they stole and then sold what residual UN equipment and assets they could seize, subsequently demolishing buildings and other resources to create a flourishing industry providing all manner of building materials. Typical of these new Hawiye entrepreneurs was strongman Muse Sodi Yalahow, who became a most successful scrap merchant and wholesaler of stone and other building material excavated from the ruins of Mogadishu. As with other warlords, these stolen resources included water pipes, copper lines, roof tops, and even telephone poles, as well as military hardware, farmland, and public and private property of all kinds. You could call this recycling, I suppose. Building up his circle of protected clients and kinsmen, who paid tax to him, not only at road checkpoints but even on improvements to their houses (often also stolen from the previous inhabitants), he soon eclipsed Ali Mahdi as the major Abgal bigman.

Still within the Hawiye but on the opposing Habar Ghiddir side, a similarly self-made man, with a more complex personality, was Osman Ali Atto whose father had been a camel herder. He had achieved economic prosperity through trading in metal and organizing mechanical and armaments work and, as is well known, became General Mohamed Farah Aideed's financier—although they later quarreled.

Many other lesser figures, in the same entrepreneurial mode, rose to prominence during and after the UN presence in Mogadishu where, it was claimed in the early 2000s there were hundreds of "dollar millionaires"—many of whom were also currency speculators. These scrap merchant warlords have appropriated profitable public and private resources, and turned the dwindling tree and bush cover around Mogadishu into charcoal for export to Arab countries, as well as producing drugs on stolen farmland. Large or small in following, these figures exercise an impressive hold on their protected clients (kin and non-kin). The latter are strongly attached to their protectors to whom, as indicated, they pay regular tithes, and with whom they identify in opposition to other warlords and their followers. Those who have found a haven as refugees in Western Europe and other countries, especially when they are also kinsmen, send regular remittances to the bosses back home. Their attitudes are revealing. I have been particularly struck by the vehemence with which, at meetings and on the Internet, these southerners have responded defensively to what they evidently take as negative assessments of the warlords as a category. Although the description scrap merchant is not particularly defamatory in England, refugee kin and clients here seem upset when it is applied to their warlord connections.

Thus although UNOSOM II failed to restore a durable peace in Somalia, it played a major, if inadvertent, part in shaping the future political economy of the south. Habar Ghiddir forces, led by General Aideed into Mogadishu in alliance with the Abgal and other Hawiye already in the area, soon established their dominance. Although frequently contested, their hegemony quickly spread along the coast to such places as Merca and Brava, and even Kismayu, where they wrestled for control with general Morgan and his Darod forces.

So, while Admiral Howe and his UN forces were obsessively pursuing General Aideed. The Habar Ghiddir (partly in alliance with other Hawiye) were busy endeavoring to consolidate their position—in southern Somalia where their opponents had come to identify them as "invaders." This new process of clan colonization, in Mogadishu and southern Somalia generally, took advantage of technical superiority in military equipment, but was otherwise, of course, not a new phenomenon. In a wider historical perspective, successive waves of different colonizers had, over the centuries, settled in the south, dislodging earlier inhabitants, seizing their lands, and imposing their authority. Although in the modern world, ideally, the former owners had rights that they sought to claim, ultimately, as in the past, legitimacy depended on superior force. In the contemporary context, the resulting warlords, and clan-affiliated militias, carved up amongst themselves what was left of Mogadishu and the Benadir Coast.

The result was a series of imprecisely defined territories, each dominated by one or more warlord bosses, with constant rivalry over the extent of their respective authority. Thus, southern Somalia's political economy is not greatly dissimilar to that of Mafia-dominated southern Italy. It is true that the Italian Mafia does not perhaps possess such an extensive and ramifying clan structure, and the poverty and uncertainties of life are obviously more acute in southern Somalia today than in contemporary Italy. However, the parallel is sufficiently close to assist us in understanding the sad state of southern Somalia today. The new Habar Ghiddir colonizers showed great skill in exploiting the UN presence, both in renting out their new stolen property (houses and vehicles) to UN staff, as well as finding local employment within the organization itself. This included securing key positions in the UN Somali information Service (IRIN) in Nairobi and in London in the famous BBC Somali program itself.

The Arta Conference and Its Aftermath

In the squabbling and wheeling and dealing to choose an interim president, competition was naturally fierce and, not unexpectedly, dominated by former ministers from the disgraced regime of Siyad Barre and his senior officials. The retired American ambassador, Robert Oakley, who dropped into Djibouti to see what was going on there, was so struck by the prominence of this group of ancient Siyadists, that he jokingly turned to a group of them, and enquired "Where is Siyad?" Siyad's ghost certainly hovered over the gathering at Arta: some 60 percent of the 245 participants were estimated to be former members of his parliament. Siyad's ex-minister of the Interior, Abdulqasim Salad Hassan, emerged as the favorite candidate. This choice reflected his standing as a Habar Ghiddir elder, and his earlier initiatives in trying to unite the Hawiye in Mogadishu during the war between the United Nations and General Aideed. Since Mogadishu was now dominated by the Hawiye, and especially by the Habar Ghiddir, it was argued by many that he was the right person to deal with the powerful warlords who belonged to the same clan that had ruined Mogadishu and the Benadir.

This argument, however, did not take account of Somali clan dynamics. The divisions between rival Habar Ghiddir mobsters were heightened, rather than diminished, by the injection of another competing leader from the powerful 'Ayr lineage. Far from healing divisions, the selection of the new president increased tension and inflamed conflict to the point where, eventually, all the principal warlords who had not become ministers in the TNG banded together to form a loose alliance called the Somali Reconciliation and Restoration Council. The formation of this powerful opposition group was a tribute to the energetic politicking of the forceful Puntland leader, Colonel Abdillahi Yusuf.

The Fate of the Transitional National Government

Despite the naïve enthusiasm of UN bureaucrats in Nairobi and New York, and the remarkably persistent support of the Italians, the TNG was doomed from the start. Overwhelmed by the confidence radiated by the president of Djibouti, the United Nations agreed immediately to officially recognize Abdulqasim's regime as the legitimate government of Somalia (including Somaliland, despite its determination to stay independent), and welcomed its representative in New York at the UN General Assembly. Despite Italy's similar enthusiasm, the EU more prudently declined to do the same, and decided to wait upon future developments. This was obviously the sensible course to follow. It would clearly have been wiser for the United Nations to do the same and withhold recognition until Abdulqasim's government had demonstrated, through national elections, that it had a popular mandate.

Instead, the UN relied on the problematic mandate afforded by the Arta Conference, claiming that it was genuinely representative of the Somalia nation when the reality was much less clear-cut. It was equally ill-advised of the United Nations to support the unitary, highly centralized state constitution that had issued from the Arta Conference. This obviously inappropriate formula was another direct legacy of Siyad's rule.

These factors immediately further alienated the peoples and governments of Somaliland and Puntland (who had shunned Arta), stimulating the determination of the latter to develop its own form of local autonomy in northeastern Somalia. Adding insult to injury, Abdulqasim and his ministers, ably assisted by their friends and relatives in the media, went out of their way to belittle and insult the remarkable achievements in both territories. Later, they resorted to direct attempts to destabilize both.

The TNG president also made a major political (as well as moral) error in failing to honor the undertaking made in Arta that the capital of his government would be in Baidoa and not Mogadishu. This act of bad faith alienated the crucial support of the Digil Mirifleh, (Rahanwin) whose capital is Baidoa. They consequently proceeded to consolidate their struggle for local autonomy led by the Rahanwin Resistance Army commander, Hassan Mohamed Nur, "Red Shirt," the local Garibaldi.

In retrospect, Abdulqasim's bad faith and inept tactics benefited the Digil Mirifleh (Rehanwin) considerably. With the help of the Ethiopians they proceeded to develop and strengthen their local independence within Somalia. The involvement of Ethiopia—interpreted in terms of age-old rivalry for control of the Nile—probably encouraged the Egyptians and some Arab states to support the TNG, even in some cases to the extent of recognizing it diplomatically. The TNG leaders proceeded to put more effort into soliciting Arab financial aid than into implementing their official policy of reconciliation and peacemaking with the Bendadiri warlords. Their wider efforts at nation-building seem to have amounted to little more than turning a blind eye to further penetration by Abdulqasim's clan (the Habar Ghiddir) in southern Somalia. Of course, given the uncentralized nature of traditional Somali politics, Abdulqasim probably exercised little real control over the Habar Ghiddir invaders. At the same time, TNG leaders continued to refer to Somaliland and Puntland as though they were colonies of Mogadishu, a policy also followed by insensitive and arrogant UN and Italian officials.

With their first prime minister, Ali Khalif (Darod: Dulbahante, thrown out after a familiar financial scandal in October 2002), the TNG had sought to undermine Somaliland through his ties with the Darod clans in the east of the country. This stragegy was not particularly successful, and after Ali's dismissal, the appointment of a Mijerteyn successor in the same spirit sought to turn the heat on Puntland. The campaign against Puntland was, no doubt, also directly fuelled by the policies of the Mijerteyn leader, Colonel Abdillahi Yusuf. He played a major role in organizing the alliance of anti-TNG warlords (including the Rahanwin leader "Red Shirt") that formed the Somali Reconciliation and Restoration Council, a loose coalition posing an increasing threat to the transitional government.

Thus the TNG was more strenuously engaged in negative than in positive nation-building. Through their clan solidarity with president Abdulqasim, his Somali clansmen in the UN information service IRIN and the BBC Somali service presented a very different picture, essentially concealing Somalia's political deficiencies at this time and doing their best to give listeners the impression that the TNG actually existed as a viable government. Such clan loyalty is to be expected; indeed those journalists concerned would have been open to serious criticism from their own clansmen had they adopted a genuinely neutral policy in their media reporting. Regrettably, and less excusably, the UN bureaucracy in Nairobi (and New York) was equally biased in its reports on the unfolding Somali drama. The UN secretary-general's special representative was personally committed to the TNG enterprise and clearly determined, whatever the reality, to present it as a great success. His former career in public relations may have assisted him in producing reports pleasing his UN employers in New York. Of course, through telephone links, radio, and the Internet (where each major clan group has at least one Web site), the globally dispersed Somali refugee communities knew the real picture, and spent much energy correcting what they saw as misleading UN and BBC propaganda. Those who were not TNG supporters complained bitterly and stridently to the BBC in London.

This situation was intriguing. From an objective perspective, the TNG's public relations were in effect run for free by the UN and BBC with an expertise and cachet they could not have managed themselves. The role of the BBC here is especially ironic. Financed by the British Foreign Office, the BBC Somali language program had been originally established in the 1950s to counteract the Egyptian leader Nasser's anti-Western propaganda in the Horn of Africa. That this program should have been hijacked by sectarian Somali interests is remarkable to say the least, and a testament to Somali ingenuity. To have become, as some Somali listeners called it, the "Voice of Arta," is thus an interesting example of what the distinguished African political scientist, Ali Mazrui, calls—with reference to reactions to European colonial penetration— "counter penetration."[3]

Al-Qaeda and Somalia

For the most part, however, the wider outside world ignored this media war and left Somalia to its own devices, paying little attention to the continuing struggle for supremacy among the competing forces in Mogadishu and the Benadir. The notorious terrorist attacks on the World Trade Center twin towers in New York City on September 11, 2001, changed all this. In pursuit of Osama bin Laden and his followers, international attention returned to the political and religious situation in the ungoverned southern region of Somalia. Particularly by the Americans, this was seen as affording a possible haven for Al-Qaeda fugitives, although how they would get there was not clear. Perhaps it was imagined that, as the founding ancestors of the main Somali clans are supposed to have done, Osama (if still alive) and his men would have sailed across the Indian Ocean on their prayer mats!

World attention consequently focused on reported fundamentalist tendencies in Somali Islam. In response, Abdulqasim and his warlord opponents professed their hostility to fundamentalism, and fell over each other in their eagerness to denounce their enemies as harboring Al-Qaeda supporters. Charge and countercharge flew back and forth, with a balance of credibility attaching to those who pointed to the TNG's links with fundamentalist Islamic states. Here, of course, the leading center of Islamic fundamentalism was the Wahhabi state of Saudi Arabia, the principal financier of fundamentalist missionary activity and mosque construction throughout Africa. With its ramifying economic interests in Saudi Arabia, this awkward fact had only recently begun to be acknowledged in the West, but was far from being effectively addressed. As is well known, we were left with what the majority of Muslims regarded as the "evil empire" of Western capitalism, led by the United States confronting what President George W. Bush and his allies denounced in parallel terms, and the consequent dangerous rekindling of ancient "holy wars."

Bush's crusade against terrorism made southern Somalia's continuing political crisis a matter of international concern. Action was taken against the Islamic banks alleged to be involved in contributing money to fundamentalist activities, and Western patrol units were established in the area (based in Djibouti and coastal waters). The United States and its allies were prompted to review current Somali political realities: the existence of the functioning state of Somaliland, and the absence of effective government in southern Somalia. This new focus of attention on Somalia highlighted the locally well-known fact that the TNG was far from constituting a real government, leaving Abdulqasim clinging forlornly to the wreckage, and his UN supporters with a lot of egg on their faces.

Kenya to the Rescue?

The latest international peace conference (the fourteenth in the long series since 1991), began with some promise in Kenya on October 15, 2002, under the patronage of IGAD (the intergovernmental authority composed of Djibouti, Ethiopia, Sudan, Kenya, and Uganda), and in the final months of Kenya's President David arap Moi's long reign.[4] This initiative enjoyed considerable international support (including European Union (EU) and U.S. backing), and involved realistic (if not uncontested) acknowledgment of the crucial interest of Ethiopia as the local superpower. Somaliland declined to participate, which helped to focus attention on southern Somalia, the septic center of what has been aptly dubbed by some Somali commentators the "Somali tropical ulcer." Various delegates who excelled in raising irrelevancies and what their critics attacked as "road blocks" to progress, tried to insist on the inclusion of Somaliland (without specifying how this might actually be achieved).

It has to be explained that the hostility of some southern Somali intellectuals to Somaliland's independence resembled the well-known medical phenomenon of a person who has had an arm amputated, but believes it is still part of his body. This phantom-limb syndrome was especially strongly developed among the remaining supporters of the phantom TNG. But by the spring of 2003 it seemed to have been generally accepted by the organizers that this unrealistic aspiration was pointless. Rather, for the foreseeable future, the emphasis should be on restoring peace and governance to the south. Thus the recognition that Somaliland had achieved peace by its own efforts and was fully engaged in democratic politics (underlined by the April 2003 presidential elections there), seemed a sensible step forward. Similarly, the belated recognition by external parties that the TNG was a faction like any other was helpful in clearing the way to a better understanding of current Somali problems.

At the start of the conference, six technical committees were envisioned to deal respectively with: the future constitution, demobilization, land disputes, economic recovery and institution building, international and regional relations, and conflict resolution. It took almost a month for the well over 400 Somali participants (distributed equally between the main clan-families—Dir, Darod, Hawiye and Digil Mirifleh (Rahanwin)—with quotas of eighty four seats each, with forty two allocated to minorities, and twenty two held in reserve)—to reach agreement on the representation of the constiturent clans on these working committees. A declaration on the Cessation of Hostilities was nevertheless quickly signed (by the TNG representatives and twenty one other factions), but armed conflict continued as usual in Mogadishu, which raised questions about the actual power held by different warlords at the conference. By April 2003, after many interruptions and a change of location and chairman, the conference was still limping along in Kenya, but few participants seemed to feel that much had been achieved.

Early on, in addition to the theoretical cease-fire, agreement seemed to have been reached in favor of a federal constitution as advocated by the Puntland leader, Col. Abdillahi Yusuf, who appeared to be presenting himself as a potential candidate for the presidency. However, in the months that had passed since the conference started, the security situation in Putland had deteriorated markedly with an unpsurge of political violence and accusations, by his opponents, that Abdullahi Yusuf was behaving like Mohamed Siyad Barre of unlamented memory. With important clan communities in both Kismayu and eastern Somaliland, the Putlanders had never of course proposed to withdraw from Somalia. But, whatever its causes, the unsettled political situation now obtaining in Puntland was adding to the general destabilization of southern Somalia, where there seemed no significant new movement toward the formation of peaceful, locally autonomous units.

Grasping at straws, some participants claimed in April 2003 that the bitter arguments that had marked the long weeks of debate in Kenya had at least produced a wider understanding, which justified the continuance of the proceedings. There was now a new and apparently more popular chairman in the shape of the Kenyan special envoy, Ambassador Bethuel Kiplagat. Obviously, the success or failure of the whole enterprise depended to a crucial extent on the developing pattern of events in southern Somalia. The scrap merchants who—in contrast to Arta—had been deliberately included here, seemed to play a particularly negative role at the conference. According to some optimistic commentators, they were running out of resources to exploit and declining in power. An unusually serious UN committee established to monitor arms supplies to the southern Somali factions also reported in April 2003. If its recommendations actually had been applied, this would obviously have helped to discourage violence in southern Somalia.

Realistically, however, short of some form of external intervention, it was difficult to see how the southern Somali warlords, with their limited, self-centered interests and short-term outlook, could be induced to adopt a wider sense of social responsibility. They were, after all, engaged in the traditional Somali system of social control based on localized self-help, which could be expected to decline only when a wider system of law and order developed or was imposed. Without this transformation, it would appear impossible to envisage the formation of a viable administration capable of meeting the needs of the local population. Evidently, the warlords all felt they had too much to lose by giving up the individual systems of local extortion that were the basis of their present survival. No wonder those few leaders with wider aspirations issued appeals for an external peacekeeping force. Such an intervention would almost certainly have to be prepared to first establish a peaceful environment. It would also now have required a longer and much more intrusive (as well as better-informed) intervention than Operation Restore hope's ill-fated UN/U.S. successors. What would have been required, presumably, would have been a very intricate and far-reaching exercise in multiple regime change for which there seemed few, if any, precedents, and no enthusiasm on the part of the international community (principally the EU).

Having acted as patrons and financiers of the protracted Kenya negotiations (which they imaginatively represented as a "peace process"), the latter were of course desperate to present a positive outcome, and even when, after over two years the conference disbanded and the assembly it had fathered fell apart, went on paying the salaries of the assembly members! It was more than six months before the interim president and prime minister with about half the assemblymen moved to Somalia, setting up their operations under the protection of an initially friendly warlord (a patron of the prime minister) at Jowhar, a safe distance from Mogadishu. The former capital was still far too dangerous for this core of the government to contemplate as a viable base. (When the prime minister made an exploratory visit to the capital in November 2005 he narrowly escaped assassination).

Accordingly, when, after a few months, their relations with their Jowhar protector soured, instead of trying to move to Mogadishu, the new leaders moved to Baidoa among the Rahanwin. With three major rival local militias, the security situation there was by no means uncomplicated. Nevertheless, with a more direct supply line from Baidoa to munition suppliers in Ethiopia, Abdillahi Yusuf evidently felt able to make peace with some of his adversaries in Mogadishu and, for the first time, to open what was hoped to be a full session of parliament on Somali soil. This was held in Baidoa on February 26, 2006, but seventy members failed to turn up. The most conspicuous absentees were the major Mogadishu warlords who, however, were now in the grip of a major internal local conflict between a growing Islamist faction and more secularly oriented warlords.

It was very difficult to foresee how this new schism would develop and how it would affect the efforts of Abdillahi Yusuf and his prime minister to establish a functioning government capable of actually ruling Somalia. With this political impasse, and the absence of all the means of actual governance—police, civil servants, judiciary, social services—as well as the relative isolation of Baidoa, it was hard to exaggerate the plight of southern Somalia, which, to cap everything, was also at this time (April 2006) in the grip of an excruciatingly severe famine. A measure of the hopelessness of the situation was the uncontrollable pillage of aid convoys that seriously hampered relief efforts, the growing prevalence of armed piracy along the Somali coastline, and increasingly ferocious faction-fighting in Mogadishu. The country's desperate straits now strongly recalled those that fifteen years previously had prompted the unprecedented UN/U.S. intervention known as Operation Restore Hope.

Although all independent observers agreed that southern Somalia had once again no effective government, EU President Jose Manuel Barroso nevertheless judged this an appropriate moment to urge European member states to recognize the new Somali "government"! Evidently nothing had been learned from the United Nation's premature recognition of the short-lived Arta government, which had reduced the subsequent ability of the international community to effectively influence events in Somalia. The Alice in Wonderland nature of EU diplomacy here was thrown into sharp relief by the contrasting situation in the north, where the democratic and fully functional state of Somaliland remained without diplomatic recognition.

It seemed that none of the external organizations that had taken it upon themselves to participate in restoring government in southern Somalia had any realistic idea of the difficulties inherent in this project. How could a people whose last experience of state rule was the Siyad dictatorship, who had been without centralized government for over fifteen years, and whose indigenous political traditions were in any case inimical to centralized government, suddenly revert to this style of governance? That southern Somali politicians seemed to assume this was hardly an any more reliable guide than the ethnocentric assumptions of poorly informed Western politicians and officials. The transitional federal government project, totally misrepresented as a "peace process" by the inadequately informed United Nations and various bilateral aid agencies, had deliberately included the warlords, officially excluded from the previous Arta exercise, in the hope of neutralizing their Mafia-type activities by making them government ministers. The failure of the TFG to launch itself as a viable decision-making body of ministers, with shared policies and responsibilities, demonstrated the enormity of the task of transforming self-employed Mafia bosses into effective cabinet ministers.

In retrospect one can only marvel at the ethnocentric naivete of the Western advisers who had encouraged this enterprise. Their basic error was to assume that the only difficulty in restoring centralized governance in southern Somalia was that of recruiting the right category of political leaders. Arta had not worked with traditional leaders and now, manifestly, warlords were not proving the answer either. No one seemed to have asked if it was sensible to move so directly from Mafia boss local anarchy to centralized governance instead of building up a hierarchy of increasingly more inclusive local groups. No one seemingly wanted to follow the bottom-up pattern successfully applied in Somaliland. That would have required a genuine peace process rather than the purely rhetorical exercise followed in southern Somalia.

In considering the lack of such radical social engineering we should also note the remarkable Somali tolerance for such anarchic conditions as those existing in Mogadishu and its hinterland throughout this period. With their traditional experience of uncentralized politics, it is nevertheless little short of amazing how successfully people have managed to survive, and even create new commercial enterprises ranging from Coca-Cola plants to universities and hospitals, and most recently a highly successful mobile phone and telecom company that is claimed to be the most advanced in Africa.

Notes

1. I.M. Lewis, *A Modern History of the Somali*, pp. 290.

2. In traditional society, strictly the only noncombatants, are "men of religion" and women generally. In modern Somali society, this term has been invoked to refer to the self-styled "intellectuals" (males or females with some degree of Western education), often also referred to more accurately as "professionals." Since everyone belongs to a clan and its segments, very few people stand outside clanship, capable of acting independently of clan loyalties. At the same time, I would argue that there are as many true intellectuals among the pastoral nomads as among the Westernized elite. Thus, across the whole of Somali society, it is questionable whether civil society actually exists here. Indeed, the term has only come into use (like many others) as a consequence of the influence of Western aid agencies and the United Nations, who are very Eurocentric and profoundly ignorant of Somali institutions and culture.

3. Ali Mazrui, 'Africa's wisdom has Two parents and one Guardian: Africanity, Islam and the west,' *Horn of Africa*, v & xxiii, 2005, pp. 1-29.

4. There was even some talk at the beginning of instituting a "truth committee" to deal with human rights issues on the South African model.

5. Commentators attending the conference described the unedifying spectacle of British Foreign Office Officials desperately trying to persuade such notorious warlords as "General" Morgan, who had walked out of the conference to return to participate in the final sessions. This man is widely regarded by Somalis as an outstanding war criminal!

Eight

VISIBLE AND INVISIBLE DIFFERENCES: THE SOMALI PARADOX

+

I

The Colonial and Postcolonial Framework for Ethnicity in Africa

Generally, Africa's colonial and postcolonial states share two striking structural features that are often insufficiently emphasized in discussions about their stability. First, as is well-known, these "new nations" were typically accidental aggregates of peoples and tribes thrown together within a single political framework by the colonial process itself. Second, they were created by conquest ("pacification") or the threat of conquest. Consequently they bear the marks of what I call the "conquest mode of state formation" to a degree that is rarely fully appreciated by those who, Eurocentrically, seek to impose a uniform style of democracy in Africa.[1] Political scientists and politicians, particularly grossly underestimate the difficulties this legacy poses for the development of what they understand as "democracy" in contemporary postcolonial states.

As a result, that most states are cultural (and ethnic) patchworks does not facilitate harmonious governance even under imaginative pluralist formulae. It is obviously much more difficult for one of the elements in the ethnic mosaic to establish its authority than it was for a group of foreign origin, blessed with technological superiority (the colonizing Europeans).

Thus, the ethnic diversity characteristic of most colonial and postcolonial states compounds the problems of maintaining political solidarity—just at in the past it may often have facilitated external European control, on a divide-and –rule basis. At the same time, ethnic pluralism in the composition of states usually further encourages hierarchical rule and discourages egalitarian democracy. (Unfortunately, contrary to the opinion of the nineteenth-century political philosopher J.S. Mill, the reverse does not necessarily promote democracy.) Hierarchical forms of tribe and state were, moreover, general (though not universal) in pre-colonial Africa. (As will be emphasized, the Somalis were a striking exception.[2])

In general, the prevailing pre- and postcolonial political traditions in Africa favored hierarchically organized states in which force, or its threat, played a crucial role in governance. In these circumstances, it is not difficult to see how the paradigm of ethnic divisions (usually denounced as "tribalism") has come to play a dominant role in political discourse about African problems. Ethnicity in this context is typically seen as divisive (neglecting its lower-level, integrative function), the implacable enemy of African nationalism. However, as is equally obvious all over the contemporary world, ethnicity is also an ideal basis for nationalism. The celebration (and cultivation) of visible cultural differences in language, behavior, dress, custom, and cuisine, frequently associated with in-marriage, are readily seen as linked to biology and hence to the (often overlapping) idea of "race." However spurious its biological claims, ethnicity is essentially a form of materially and visibly distinctive communal identity providing a ready basis for solidarity for those who, in its name, distinguish themselves from others.

Precolonial Nationalism: The Somali Case

African nationalists in most colonial states, because of their multiethnic character, did not have the luxury of a ready-made, countrywide local foundation for nationalism.[3] They had to rely almost exclusively on opposition to colonial rule. In the mid-twentieth century, well-known for their vigorous ethnic nationalism extending into neighboring states, the Somalis appeared in this respect unusually fortunate. They did not have to invent a suitable ethnic identity to sustain their nationalist aims, which were naturally reactively strengthened by the colonial experience of division and fragmentation.

Yet, this tailor-made national ethnicity, which arose from their traditional culture, rather than vice-versa, came at a high price. It was accompanied by a pervasive system of internal divisions based on the ideology of kinship, and hence invisible, which carried the same emotional and subjective charge as visible ethnic distinctions elsewhere. Indeed, as we shall see, these kinship divisions, as they are formulated in Somali ideology, have many of the characteristics of race.

Family trees (genealogies) were, and are, not simply quasihistorical documents, but essentially the fundamental principle of personal and social identity. From a European perspective, this is perhaps most readily understood in terms of aristocratic dynasties, or more generally, in terms of the Mediterranean blood feud with its axiomatic evocation of kinship solidarity. The notion of genetically based political identity is also, of course, etymologically the foundation of Western understanding of the term "nation" and of acquiring (adopted) nationality by a process of "naturalization"—implying (totally falsely) that this acculturation is actually biological, conferring a "natural" status.

Similarly, the kinship groups or lineages that are, as we shall see, the basic building blocks of Somali society, have a biological form, although they are entirely cultural products, the results, over a long time span, of Somali "social engineering".[4] The sociologically significant point about this form of social division is that it produces what appear to be axiomatic, natural distinctions, with the same ontological status as botanical species or zoological breeds. Despite its lack of any significant visible markers, this is, consequently, a very powerful cultural construction of sociopolitical identity since, by definition, it flows in the blood and must be taken for granted. In this respect, as a number of Somalis now recognize, it is similar to scientific understanding of the biological concept "race." In popular thought, of course, races are assumed to be observably distinct and so treated as what are properly ethnic groups. (Ethnicity, which may also aspire to present itself as a natural force, relies, in contrast, on the accentuation of *external* markers—language, custom, costume, cuisine etc.)

Whether conserved orally or in writing, the genealogies embodying the invisible force of clanship are, therefore, in effect genetic blueprints governing the social and political interactions of those whose descent they record. The genetic assumptions implied here are further exemplified in the case of lineages of holy men, whose hereditary mystical powers are conceived to be a direct consequence of their shared descent from a famous saint.[5] Religious blessing here is assumed to be a genetic endowment.

Casting this demon in the atavistic role of out-of-date loyalties, unfitting for the modern age and hostile to progress, Somali nationalists gravely underestimated the catastrophically disintegrative forces that could be evoked in its name. Beating the drum of ethnic unity, modern Somali nationalists thus seriously miscalculated the divisive power of their traditional political heritage—as was so cruelly brought home to them by the collapse of the Somali state in 1990. They were not alone in this wildly inaccurate assessment. Others, including the present writer, attributed greater resilience and adaptability to Somali ethnicity as a political force than it has turned out to possess.

Despite their different foundations, I also tended to see traditional Somali democracy and egalitarianism as likely to contribute to the effectiveness of modern democratic structures in Somalia. This assumed, optimistically, that the Somalis would be able to arrive at a distribution of power among the major kinship groupings, based on consensus. In the event, alas, on the contrary, major lineage blocs sought to monopolize power and included others only on a token basis, or when they could be usefully employed to carry out awkward, unpopular coercive tasks.

Somali Ethnicity in Historical Context

As a single ethnic group in the Horn of Africa, with only one major internal division (that of the Digil Mirifle clans speaking a distinctive language/dialect),[6] the majority of Somali people considered themselves bound together by common language, by an essentially nomadic pastoral culture, and by the shared profession of Islam. Their common faith had made its appearance in the ninth century along the coast and thereafter gradually spread inland. The importance of religion was reflected in a pervasive distinction in Somali society and culture between two basic traditional male roles (or kinds of men): "men of religion" (*wadad*, pl. *wadaddo*), and lay "warriors" (*waranleh*—literally "spear-bearers"), the latter laiety being in the majority. Only the former could be considered to constitute a kind of traditional civil society. Both categories were equally prominent in the pastoral society and in the trading centers that, over the centuries, gradually developed along the coast and at watering places inland. These developments introduced the new category "merchant", a role often combined with that of religious specialist—partly because both utilized Arabic. The high value attached to religion was also reflected in the practice of tracing Somali genealogies ultimately to noble Arabian origins connected with the family of the Prophet, Muhammad. This can at the same time be seen as an expression of Somali Islamic identity, in the normal Somali currency of descent and genealogy that ultimately underwrite all relationships.

The first known occurrence of the ethnic name "Somali" is in the fifteenth century, in an Ethiopian hymn celebrating the victories of the Abyssinian king, Negus Yeshaq (1414-29), at the time of the holy wars against surrounding Islamic principalities. The Somalis played an important military role here as expert "cutters of roads"—a specialization for which in its modern form they are especially well-known today. Later sources chronicling the course of these long-drawn-out wars between Christian Ethiopia and the encroaching Muslim centers of power have occasion to mention Somali militiamen frequently, and even to record the involvement of individual clans who are still prominent today.

It is, however, only in the nineteenth century that we begin to have more detailed accounts, by European explorers, of Somali society and culture. These make it clear that, despite the internal clan and lineage divisions of the nation, there was already a sharp sense of Somali cultural identity. An important element in this was the extraordinary egalitariansm, and (except to some extent in the southern inter-riverine region) a marked absence of hierarchical political structures comparable to those elsewhere in Africa. The remarkable Arabist explorer Richard Burton, who understood their culture well and particularly appreciated their oral poetry, memorialized the Somalis appropriately as a "fierce and turbulent race of republicans." Later witnesses, including an outspoken sergeant in the kings African Rifles, deployed against the Dervish forces in the period 1900-20, made the same judgment, complaining, "Somalis no good, every man his own chief." More analytically the Somali historian A.A. Hersi succinctly judged that in traditional Somali society, "central political authority meant nothing….and does not even today" (Hersi, 1977, p. 177).

The Concept of Somali identity, based on an awareness of common culture and language, thus *preceded* the development of modern nationalism. This long-standing sense of cultural uniqueness, it may be conjectured, developed in the interaction with neighboring peoples over the centuries, and with increasingly cosmopolitan trade. Hence, as I have argued elsewhere (Lewis, 1958, 1961, 1983, 2002), what modern nationalism did was to politicize an existing cultural phenomenon: cultural nationalism became political nationalism in the modern sense and not vice-versa. There was previously no tradition of political unity at this level of the transcendent nation and, *a fortiori*, no tradition of statehood based on Somali culture. This project became a modern aspiration in the context of the independence movement.

So in the Somali context, as I have always stressed, the movement was from nation to state rather than, as mostly elsewhere in Africa, from state to nation. Consequently, in the Somali case it is not the nation that is artificial but the state, indeed doubly so in that hierarchical governance is foreign to the major Somali political tradition. Without going into all the details (recorded and analyzed elsewhere), we may usefully distinguish the phases in the next section in the growth and decline (or better, waxing and waning) of Somali nationalism. This is a force, I believe, that, like the inner workings of component clans and lineages, also tends to be segmentary in character, as the clan divisions of the nation tend to unify reactively in response to external pressures, and to disassociate when these disappear. At this ultimate level of solidarity—which is modern—this is not strictly phrased, however, in genealogical terms.

Stages of Modern Somali Nationalism

As elsewhere, colonialism naturally provided the frame in which modern Somali nationalism developed. Given the fragmentation of the nation, colonialism here, however, was an unusually varied experience. Over the period 1860-1900, the Somali nation was divided into five regional groupings. From north to south these were: French Somaliland (also containing the Afar, a related pastoral people), the British Somaliland Protectorate (with no colonial settlers), the Italian colony of Somalia, the Ethiopian Ogaden (named after that local clan), and British northern Kenya. The experience of these artificial divisions—involving, different administrative traditions and languages—had a formative impact on the growing politicization of Somali culture that ensued.

To understand how this multiple partition cut across internal Somali clan divisions, we need to refer to the Somali national genealogy, an ethnic family tree that I hasten to stress existed before the birth of modern nationalism. Within this, the Somali as a whole are divided by family trees based on descent traced patrilineally in the male line, and named after their (eponymous) founding ancestors from whom each group takes its collective name. This system of grouping is not, as some misinformed commentators have supposed, a colonial artifact devised for administrative convenience. It existed long before colonial partition and baffled most colonial officials in its complexity.

The highest level distinction between Samale and Sab refers to the cultural and linguistic cleavage between the mainly nomadic pastoralists (Samale) and the agropastoralists (Sab), which, as we have mentioned, is the deepest division within the nation. The latter occupy the relatively fertile area between the Shebelle and Juba Rivers in southern Somalia and speak May, a Somali-related, separate language. It seems likely that the genealogization of this cleavage is more recent than that which locates the Samale groups in the national genealogy. However, since it is reported by nineteenth century travelers, it clearly antedates modern Somali nationalism and is not a direct product of that movement. Of the six main groups which for convenience I refer to as clan-families—Dir, Isaq, Darod, Hawiye, and Digil and Rahanwin (Sab)—the Darod are the most widely distributed and this is consistently reflected in their political aspirations and behavior. After the Digil and Rahanwin, the Isaq, who formed the backbone of what became British Somaliland (today the Somaliland Republic) are the most localized (see map). The Darod and Hawiye share what became successively Italian Somalia independent Somalia (including

Somaliland), the Democratic Republic of Somalia (under military rule), and its residue today (excluding Somaliland, but tenuously including Puntland, based on an alliance of Darod clans).

National Genealogy of Somali Clan-Families

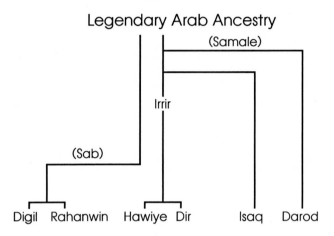

Source: Lewis 1994, pp. 95-112.

Foreign Influence and the Rise of nationalism

Contrary to the picture presented by some recent writers of Marxist or "Rococo Marxist" orientation,[7] who ethnocentrically seek to promote the virtues of primitive precolonial Somali culture, which they associate with supposed geographical isolation, Somalis have for centuries been involved in a lively entrepot trade. This traffic has extended from their neighbors in the Ethiopian highlands on the one hand, to the Arabian peninsula and more remote eastern ports on the other. Down the centuries, men of religion traveled both to inland centers of religion (such as Harar), and overseas to famous Islamic cities—not least Mecca.

These travels naturally sharpened Somali self-awareness and their sense of the distinctiveness of their culture, language, and religion—perhaps most fully in the period before European colonization in their involvement in the medieval religious wars in Ethiopia—between Christian and Muslim. This exposure to other cultures and traditions was intensified by alien colonial rule, which included the opportunity for significant numbers of Somali men to serve as merchant seamen all over the world. They then returned to retire to the traditional nomadic life, often bringing home a fund of exotic knowledge and rich store of memories.

The Second World War, in which they served in the forces of their colonial masters, was another important source of new experience. The defeat of the Italians, in which Somalis played a significant part, certainly had an eye-opening impact (to use a phrase common to both Somali and English), as had the British Military Administration, which governed the former British, Italian, and Ethiopian Somali territories from 1941 to 1949. About this time also, there was a significant development of other channels of foreign influence through the ever-expanding rise of radio and the press, with programs in Somali as well as Arabic beamed to the Somali area from stations around the world. The establishment of local schools, and later of scholarships for study abroad, consolidated all these modernizing influences.

Following the protonationalist jihad of the famous Somali sheikh and poet Mohamed Abdille Hassan, the first recorded stirrings of modern political activity occurred.[8] Nevertheless, by 1935 most Somaliland towns had embryonic political associations founded by local merchants, and the Somaliland National Society was founded shortly afterwards. Further south, explicit political aspirations appear to date back to the last days of Italian fascist rule in Somalia, between 1937 and 1940, when the pioneer modern politicians were a handful of government employees mainly drawn from the Rahanwin and Digil clans.

These trends received direct encouragement from the British military administrators (most of them civilians on war service, rather than career colonial office officials) who succeeded the Italians. The new authorities not only promoted

Somali trade and business but also removed previous (fascist) restrictions on social and political activities. In Mogadishu particularly, between 1941 and 1943 numerous Italian societies formed, covering all shades of political opinion and held meetings that were sometimes also attended by Somalis. The Italian Communist Club, which stressed racial equality and progress achieved in the Soviet Union, attracted some Somali interest. At the same time, the British political officer (district commissioner) in Mogadishu was holding weekly meetings and discussions on current affairs (cf. Lewis, 2002, pp. 120ff). He emphasized how the Allies (in whose forces Somalis had served) were liberating the world from fascist oppression and that, after the war, all races and peoples would enjoy freedom. These pronouncements reinforced the growing aspirations of progressive Somalis and their nationalist interests, encouraging the proud sense of Somali cultural identity and exclusiveness that, to some extent, had been earlier expressed in the Islamic *jihad* waged by Muhamad Abdille Hassan (1900-1920) against the Christian colonial authorities.

Bringing these currents of opinion together with the blessing and assistance of the British, the Somali Youth Club was formally launched on May 15, 1943—coincidentally the date when German and Italian forces in Africa were finally defeated. At its foundation, the Club had thirteen members representing the major groups and the ancient Benadiri population of Mogadishu. Members shared aspirations for self-government, literacy and education, and the eradication of divisive clan schisms. In the years immediately after, as the question of the future status of Italy's former colony, Somalia, became a general public as well as international issue, the Club spread its wings and attracted wider support. By 1948, when the Four Power Commission (representing Britain, France, the United States and the Soviet Union) visited Somalia to ascertain Somali concerns for their future status, the Club had changed its name to the Somali Youth League (SYL). With over 25,000 estimated members throughout the country, it was now well-established as a political organization, appealing in principle to young nationalists irrespective of clan allegiance (Lewis, *A Pastoral Democracy*, pp. 285ff). An important element in its initial success, however, reflected its heavy Darod support, which was similarly strong in the new Somali police force (the Somalia Gendarmerie), established by the British Military Administration.

The SYL now had a four-point program:

To unite all Somalis generally, and the youth especially with the consequent repudiation of all harmful old prejudices (such, for example, as tribal and clan distinctions); To take an interest in and assist in eliminating by constitutional and legal means any existing or future situations which might be prejudicial to the interests of the Somali people; And finally, to develop the Somali language and to assist in putting into use among Somalis the "Osmaniya Somali script." (See Lewis, 1958.)

In this initial period some ephemeral smaller political groups formed, the most significant being that calling itself originally the Patriotic Benefit Union or Jumiya, and mainly representing southern Rahanwin and Digil, the Bantu riverines, and some local Arabs. This association originally benefited from Italian settler financial support and favored more conservative policies than the SYL, aiming especially to protect the southern agropastoralists from the dominant northern nomads, who generally supported League. In 1947, the *Jumiya* changed its name to the Hizbia (party) Digil Mirifle) (HDMS). In the heated public debates about the future status of Somalia, the SYL meanwhile campaigned on a wider front to bring all the Somali territories together under a single government, and to work toward full autonomy after a ten-year period of trusteeship under the Four Power Administration. This program excluded the return of Italian rule.

With Italian support, most of the non-SYL Somali groups formed a consortium under the name Somalia Conference, proposing a thirty-year trusteeship under Italian administration. The HDM however, broke away from this alliance and, like the SYL, advocated a Four Power Trusteeship—but for the longer period of thirty years. In the event, although recognizing that the SYL had the widest public support, in an effort to satisfy their own competing political interests, the Four Powers eventually decided in favor of an Italian trusteeship, under UN mandate, with ten years (1950-60) to prepare the country for independence.[9] Following this, the British Somaliland Protectorate was reestablished and, despite strong Somali opposition, the Haud and Ogaden regions were returned to Ethiopian authority. In the event, Somalia accepted its new status under Italian administration without serious incident and in 1954, the first municipal elections were held on a basis of male suffrage. The SYL won over half the available 281 seats.

In 1956 (when I first carried out field research in the south), as Somalis were replacing Italians in senior administrative posts, the earlier Territorial Council was transformed into a legislative council composed of seventy seats. Ten were reserved for ethnic minorities: the Italian and Arab communities (four seats each), and one each for Indian and Pakistani immigrant groups. The SYL won forty-three seats, the HDMS, which campaigned only in its clan area, gained thirteen seats, and four others were won by two smaller parties, one (the Marehan Union) a frankly clan-based organization. Thus, although the SYL claimed that it enjoyed significant support from the Digil Mirifle clans, the traditional division between this agropastoral May-speaking community and the Samale pastoralist clans was strongly reflected in the emerging modern party politics. The HDMS alleged that the SYL government (in which at this stage it held no ministerial posts) discriminated against its clansmen in the public service (where it was certainly under represented).

In the discussions that followed on a constitution for Somalia, which would enable it to unite easily with neighboring ethnic communities as these became independent, the HDMS favored a federal state while the SYL insisted on a unitary structure. Indeed, at this time, the HDMS went even further to advocate the formation of a separate state (for a detailed study of party politics in this period, see

Lewis, 1958). The SYL for its part, was held together by a precarious alliance of Darod and Hawiye (some of the latter supporting their own clan party). In this first Somali government, with responsibility for internal affairs, there were three Hawiye ministers (including the prime minister), two Darod, and one Dir—no Digil Mirifle. In this first phase of modern political experience, if the HDMS was actually a clan coalition party (like the SYL), there were still unashamedly clan (or in the case of some minority groups) ethnic parties.[10]

However, with the rising tide of nationalism, the SYL government introduced legislation making it an offense for political parties to bear tribal names. This may have been directly aimed at the opposition HDMS, which, adroitly, retained its existing acronym by adopting the Arabic title Hizbia Dastur Mustaqil Somali (HDMS). Legislation promulgated in 1959, to abolish the traditional status of client-tenant farmers, appears also to have been aimed at the HDMS, since clientship was a fundamental building brick in their mixed-clan composition. The effect, if not the motive, was to encourage divisive tendencies among Digil Mirifle clients, who belonged originally to other clans (as the majority did) to reassert their original identity. This move tended to discourage sentiments of Digil Mirifle identity, and hence paved the way for further SYL penetration.[11]

In the same year, in the last national elections in Somalia prior to independence, now with universal suffrage the SYL won decisively and formed a new government of fifteen ministers and undersecretaries, evenly distributed among the Darod, Hawiye, and Digil and Rahanwin. This implementation of the implicit principle of clan-family balance did not, of course, represent a final resolution of the problem of competing clan allegiances, or "tribalismo", as it was known in the Italian tradition. Equally, the ingenious invention of the Somalized neologism "ex" (clan), which enabled the clan discourse to be conducted as though it existed only in the past, perpetuated rather than, as had been hoped, discouraged continuing clan loyalties.

This precarious clan balance was immediately disturbed by the union, at independence in 1960, of Somalia with the former British Somaliland (on party politics in the latter country prior to independence, see Lewis, 2002, pp. 148ff; and for an excellent documentary history, Jama Mohamed, 2002). In that embryonic state, party politics tended to follow the genealogical split between the Isaq clans of the center of the country who supported the Somaliland National Party, and the United Somali Party (USP), the bulk of whose support came from the non-Isaq clans on their eastern and western flanks (who belonged to the Darod and Dir clan-families). Since these two parties gained the majority of votes in the Protectorate's last elections, held a few months before independence and union in 1960, they were allocated two ministries each in the new government of the enlarged Somalia, formed in July 1960.

The parameters of the clan equation at the national level had widened, and the struggle for power had become more complex. Traditional kinship ties encouraged USP Darod to ally with their clansmen in the SYL, while for the Dir USP tradition suggested alliance either with the Hawiye within or outside the SYL, or with the Isaq. In addition to traditional clan loyalties and cleavages, a significant new interface was that between the diverse British and Italian colonial experiences. This differentiation fostered a persistent sense among (British) northerners that they had lost power, and were marginalized in the new, united, Somalia. The most dramatic early symptom of disaffection here was the short-lived and abortive military coup launched, at the end of 1961, in the former Somaliland by a group of British-trained officers.

Somalia's politics were thus essentially now divided internally by clan, and the tension between the ex-British and ex-Italian traditions (all the "exes" one might say), but united externally by pan-Somali nationalist irredentism and the corresponding opposition of neighboring states (especially Ethiopia, with whom there was a long-standing and intractable border dispute).[12] Such external pressures, however, did not end the continuing rivalry for power between leading

Somali politicians who, within their parties, relied ultimately on clan support. The initial north-south rivalry was thrust into the background by the developments that followed the 1964 national assembly elections, won decisively by the SYL.

Now intense competition broke out within the Darod leadership of the SYL and led to the election of a new president, a former Darod premier, with the appointment of his ally, a prominent Isaq figure, as prime minister. This effectively consummated the union of north and south and brought Isaq politics center stage on a par with the other major clan blocs. The new premier soon judged it prudent to make peace with Kenya and Ethiopia, thus reducing external pressures, and in 1969 held what turned out to be Somalia's last civilian elections. Over 1,000 candidates representing sixty-two parties (i.e., clan and sub-clan groups) contended but, with allegations of widespread corruption, the scene was set for considerable instability. The SYL as usual won, and at the first session of the new Assembly, with the exception only of a single assemblyman, all the members of the other parties crossed the floor to join the SYL government. Somalia had finally become a one-party state.

This meant that the SYL was now a cumbersome umbrella organization effectively for all the clan interests in the country. The National Assembly, itself, was widely recognized as a chamber of commerce where deputies cynically traded votes for money—as they had done with their electors in the election. The next step was the move to a one-person state and this followed more quickly than many had anticipated.

Siyad Barre's Rise to Power

The assassination of the Darod president, while the premier was out of the country, provided a convenient opportunity for the military to seize power. Led by the head of the army (also Darod), General Mohamed Siyad Barre, whose ruthless ambition and tyrannous rule surprised many who did not know him, the army quickly established their authority, ominously changing Somalia's name to the Somali Democratic Republic. This was a sure sign that Somalia's chaotic democracy was judged to have gone too far, and was now gone for good: parliament and all constitutional provisions were suspended (i.e., abolished). While quickly consolidating his grasp of the reins of power, General Siyad launched Somalia into a new era of rhetoric where the only actual policies that mattered were those that controlled and punished disobedience and dissent. The coup became retrospectively a bloodless revolution, and with East European support, was dedicated to the cause of "scientific socialism" (literally in Somali, "wealth-sharing based on wisdom"). Socialism, Siyad and his apparatchiks endlessly intoned, unites while tribalism divides. Of the various (largely theoretical) measures invoked in the fight against tribal (i.e., clan) loyalties, undoubtedly the most colorful was a national campaign that included the burning of effigies representing tribalism, corruption, nepotism, and misrule. The term "comrade" (*jalle*) was introduced to replace kinsman, and even the circumlocutory term *ex* was outlawed as the "victorious father of the nation" (also known as "the good conductor") boldly led his people forward.

This elevated political discourse convinced some young officials with leftist aspirations; others saw it as a convenient vehicle for autocracy. As a Somali friend exclaimed, in a heated exchange on the nature of scientific socialism, with a French Marxist anthropologist (Claude Meillasoux): "We don't need Marx; he needs us!" This imposing ideology was actually however no more than a rhetorical facade, while Siyad got on with the serious business of consolidating his power base, consisting of his own and related clansmen and carefully selected members of coopted marginal groups. Siyad possessed an unrivaled knowledge of the Somali clan system, partly based on his earlier experience as a police officer.

As I found during my regular visits to Somalia throughout his reign, Siyad's government was still evaluated by ordinary people in terms of clan inclusiveness, although it was a serious offense to say so publicly. Within this typical clan rainbow, three groups in particular exercised special power, a trinity known sotto voce as MOD after the initial letters of the corresponding clan names. M (Marrehan) represented the president's own clan, O (Ogaden) that of his mother, and D (Dulbahante) that of his most prominent son-in-law, head of the sinister national security service (NSS) established, with East European advisers, shortly after Siyad's coup. Although officially dedicated to "scientific socialism," it is more accurate to regard this phase of Somalia's existence as "scientific siyadism" (as I dubbed it).[13]

Two innovations of Siyad's did, however, enjoy wide public popularity: the introduction in 1975 of a national Latin script for the Somali language (hitherto almost exclusively unwritten), and the launching of the 1977 war against Ethiopia, which sought to liberate his mother's clansmen, the Ogaden.[14] Both initiatives had nationalist implications and capitalized on Siyad's official policy of national solidarity. This sought to include the less powerful lineages and marginal groups, whose assimilation within the nation was strongly encouraged—with members of these groups co-opted to hold formally impressive positions (e.g., as in the case of the ministers of Defense and Education). Discrimination against such minorities was quite strongly discouraged and this enlightened attitude, I found, made considerable headway among the educated elite.[15] Final authority, of course, was firmly centralized in the hands of the leader and his MOD clique; indeed, even leave and promotion applications by humble members of the police force and government officials were personally scrutinized by the head of state. Imagine how difficult it was to secure an exit permit or passport. Somalia was now a prison, presided over directly by the tireless tyrant Siyad, who had immense energy and by preference worked through the night, sustained by endless cups of black coffee. This batlike work pattern was especially irksome to foreign ambassadors who had to sacrifice their sleep if they wished to see the "old man" (as Somalis familiarly called him).

This two-dimensional political structure, with clandestine clan politics at the core and surface socialist nationalism for everyone else, became less clearly differentiated following Somalia's traumatic defeat in the Ogaden War of 1978. The military collapse brought hundreds of thousands of Ogadeni Somalis and Oromo refugees flooding into Somalia. These refugees were distributed around the country, in huge hastily assembled and poorly equipped camps (often 40,000 strong), which produced significant demographic changes in local clan composition, especially in the northwest (the former British Somaliland). Predominantly Ogadeni (Darod) refugees, strongly supported by the MOD government, were thus brought into direct competition with the local Isaq and Dir residents, who were already poorly served in the delivery of state services (expect that provided by the hated NSS).

Clan tensions were also inevitably heightened, as the causes of the bitter defeat were debated—of necessity clandestinely. Insurrection was in the air. The arbitrary execution of a group of critical officers, an abortive coup (led by Majerten officers) in April 1978, a train of government reshuffles, and the imprisonment of several high-profile former ministers, all indicated the level of divisive clan turbulence now confronting the regime. The predictable response was an attempt to turn the screw of MOD control even more tightly.[16]

But the writing was at last on the wall. The first formal opposition militia movements (both launched in the north in 1981) were the Majerten (Darod) SSDF, which developed out of the 1978 coup attempt, and the Isaq-based SNM, a direct response to Siyad's vicious Darod military dictatorship in Somaliland.[17] These pioneers in the armed struggle against the Siyad regime were soon joined by other groups (e.g., the Hawiye-based United Somali Congress) in a loose alliance. With the further blow to residual national solidarity delivered by Siyad's negotiated peace with Ethiopia, their combined efforts culminated in 1990-91 in the collapse of the dictator and his ignominious flight from Somalia. His pathetic appeals to his Darod clansmen to come to his rescue only resulted in their being singled out for vicious retaliation and clan-cleansing (as Somalis called it) in the ensuing chaos of Mogadishu.

The Reemergence of Naked Clan Loyalties

Taking appearances for realities, it is sometimes claimed—by apologists for Siyad and others—that the Ogadeni disaster brought clan factors into play for the first time, forcing Siyad to employ them also for his own survival. As indicated above, the evidence on the contrary shows clearly that, for all the frothy rhetoric of scientific socialism, the crucial political forces remained throughout the Siyad era those of clan loyalties. As time went on, in this segmentary society these traditional forces, with their modern elaborations, simply became increasingly important and conspicuous.

Throughout Somali society, and especially in the rural areas where the bulk of the population lived as pastoralists, the segmentary clan structure continued to provide an individual's primary identity and political loyalties. Scientific socialism was primary rhetorical, and at best patchy and superficial in its distribution. The substance of the nation's political diet remained that based on clan and kin ties, mobilized and exploited by entrepreneurs who were mainly urban-based. Despite superficial cultural differences in lifestyle, town and countryside remained closely linked by clan ties and mutual economic interests in livestock and land.

On the surface, townspeople lived differently, to some extent wore different clothes, and ate different foods, and lived in modern homes with domestic equipment rare in the interior. Yet, the principal security lines, safeguarding the individual's personal security and property, remained the kinship system that in rural areas, comprehensively held sway; whereas in urban contexts these were supplemented (variably) by the agencies of government (where they existed).

The backbone of economic cooperation and trust in town as in the countryside remained that founded on kin ties. As the national economy declined in the 1970s and 1980s, male labor migration (called by Somalis the "muscle drain") to the oil-rich Arab states became a vital source of additional income, much of which (in kind or cash) returned home along kinship lines. Somalis placed much greater trust in such connections than in deposit banks that were, in any case, running into financial difficulties.

The judicial and police systems collapsed into corruption and anarchy in the late 1980s, and the security function of kinship became as important in urban areas as it had been throughout Siyad's rule in the countryside. As we have seen, the final overthrow of Siyad was achieved through the clan-based militias and guerrilla organizations that with the addition of Islamic forces, have shaped the post-Siyad Somali political scene.[18] The resultant polities vary in size and scale and in their readiness to adopt civil forms of government—the most impressive and progressive so far being the Somaliland Republic (formed in 1991), and the so far less successful Puntland State of Somalia (proclaimed in 1998).

The first had grown out of the Somaliland National Movement, based on the Isaq clans, allying with the local Dir clans in the west (the Ise and Gadabursi) and the Darod (Dulbahante and Warsangeli) in the east, to reassume the shape and demography of the former Somaliland Protectorate. Puntland had developed from the Somali Salvation Democratic Front guerrilla movement and was, similarly, essentially based on a single clan, in this case the large, multi-segmented Majerten clan of the Darod clan-family (other Darod minorities are included), which was the last to fall under Italian rule in 1925.[19] Puntland has not yet claimed complete independence as Somaliland has done, and remains (at the time of writing i.e. 2008) committed to being part of a federally organized Somalia, on the assumption that this format will eventually be adopted.

Both states, which jointly must make up about a third of the total population of the former Somalia, are heavily engaged in the livestock export trade, with thriving ports, and are gradually establishing social services to levels that are in many respects already well above those achieved during Siyad's rule. Although there are deficiencies in hospitals, there are more medical doctors in practice in both territories than there ever were before. Electricity is widely available, and banking and telephone (and fax) services extend throughout the world. Somaliland has two universities, Puntland one. These developments have been achieved under democratically appointed governments with, in both cases, heads of state elected by a combination of traditional and Western procedures. That Puntland has so far opted for local, rather than full autonomy, is largely a consequence of the fact that thousands of Majerten clansmen also live in the Kismayu region of southern Somalia, which discourages it from breaking away completely.[20] Somaliland is subject to no such comparable constraint.

Since clanship remains the fundamental (but not unique) basis of security in Somali society, its prominence, as we have seen, waxes and wanes with the availability and adequacy of alternative agencies of social control. Another crucial factor, of course, is the volume and acuteness of threats to security in the broadest sense. In periods of tranquility and prosperity, and when government agencies provide an acceptable and trusted level of social control, the primacy of clanship diminishes. Under the reverse conditions it develops in importance correspondingly. So the forces that led to the collapse of Somalia, and that continued thereafter, promoted the influence of divisive clanship and reduced the strength of nationalist sentiments. Because clan and lineage ties are most crucially focused at the local level, this is the level at which peace has to be negotiated by traditional, populist procedures if progress is to be made. This is what was successfully achieved in Somaliland and, initially, in Puntland.[21] Its disregard elsewhere largely explains the continuing failure, over subsequent years, of (generally misconceived), high-profile international negotiations to produce a national government for Somalia.[22]

As I see it, what has happened until now can be regarded as the crystallization out of the Somali maelstrom of two effective states (Somaliland and Puntland), with a third state, containing the Digil Mirifle clans in the Bay region between the rivers, in the process of formation. Further developments in this process with the formation of additional regional polities are to be expected. It remains to be seen how such new entities will relate to each other, and whether they will eventually join together in a wider reinvented Somalia. This might, of course, take the form of a loose association of states.[23]

Toward a Reevaluation of Ethnicity and Clanship

The continuing power of clanship as an ongoing basic component of social cohesion (not a determinant) is obvious, even interestingly, at that shrine of modernity, the Internet, where each of the main Somali clan blocs has its own Web site (indeed often several). At a wider, more general level, the clan and lineage genealogies that underpin the clan political system provide the basic system of personal identification utilized by Somali refugees throughout the world to send remittances to their kin at home. This form of indirect aid from the countries where the refugees had found asylum was estimated to have an annual value of more than US$800 million and to constitute between 20 percent and 40 percent of per capita income in Somalia. The global process (known as *hawilad*), producing this huge volume of family aid, operates by telephone, fax, and radio. These modes of communication enable the sender to transfer funds instantly through his local office (which often also operates as a computer café), or bank, to his kin in Somalia, via one of the hundreds of informal remittance points scattered throughout the country. The sender specifies the genealogical identity of the addressee, and the recipient in Somalia has to identify himself in these terms to collect the funds transmitted. Trust here, as in other commercial arrangements, is based on kinship connections (cf. Lewis, 1963; Little, 2003).

The resilience of this social system in adopting, and adapting to, the forces of modernization is impressive, and quite baffling to those whose Eurocentric bias encourages them to regard kinship as an archaic, primordial relic incompatible with progress. The negative loading (also associated with its divisive role in a nationalist context) that this term has carried in the minds of poorly informed foreign commentators, and Westernized Somalis alike, has, as will now be evident, distracted Somali politicians from acknowledging its reality, and so facing up to its implications and seeking realistically to come to terms with them.

It is an interesting, though sad, commentary on the force of a widespread delusion that it has taken the tragic collapse of their state to bring home this conclusion to the majority of Westernized Somalis (who tend to call themselves intellectuals). More humble Somalis (i.e., the majority) never doubted the efficacy of this everyday aspect of their traditional heritage, nor, or course, in practice did politicians—although they professed hypocritically that clanship (which they lived by) had died. If the continuing force of clanship had been frankly recognized and acknowledged and means sought to accommodate it politically, rather than pretending it did not exist, things might have turned out differently for Somalia. There would still, of course, have been the handicap of no precolonial experience of centralized government.

Kinship Relations

Is the form of organization I am calling (segmentary) clanship here the same now as it was in precolonial times? Neo-Marxist and Rococo Marxist interpreters of Somali institutions do not think so. They paint a rosy picture of the pristine innocence of the precolonial world, and assert—without offering any evidence—that modern Somali clanship is a distinct, degenerate form, a mere tool for unscrupulous, self-serving urban politicians to employ in manipulating their ignorant countrymen. It is also, they assert, a malign legacy of the colonial presence that similarly in their eyes invented clan warfare.[24] As Bernhard Helander wryly remarked (1998), few writers in this vein exceed the tortuously contradictory logic of Besteman (1996a, 1998) that "clans do not exist; if they do they are constructs by a British anthropologist (i.e., the present writer) and CNN, which obscures real, class and regional issues!"

A.I. Samatar 1993 (a political economist) even goes so far as to claim that kinship relationships (*tol*) are to be distinguished conceptually, as well as linguistically, from this debased contemporary form of clan politics, which he identifies with the Somalized Arabic term *qabila*. Samatar does not cite any evidence for this alleged linguistic distinction between old-fashioned benign kinship (*tol*) and politically destructive new clanship (*qabila*). This is not surprising since in fact there is none: both terms are used interchangeably, and this is not a modern development.

I found both words used without distinction in my earliest field research (in the 1950s) among the northern pastoral nomads.[25] *Qabila* is, of course, an Arabic loanword. It is interesting, also, that the preference for the more authentically Somali term *tol* is reflected in the modern construction *tolnimmo*. This term may be used to translate nationalism (the opposite of tol in the narrow sense!), and, more generally, social cohesion at other levels.

From the earliest records we have of Somali political institutions, it is clear that elders of influence (based on family strength, livestock wealth, oratorical skills, shrewdness, etc.)—in short, pastoral big men—endeavored to manipulate their clansmen in traditional politics to their advantage. Given the extreme individualism and democracy of the nomads, very rarely, however, did such figures succeed in establishing hereditary power—except in exceptional circumstances where they were able to monopolize external resources (e.g., those obtained through trade or plunder).[26] Among the Digil Mirifle, with their mixed-clan composition and agropastoral economy, this trend toward hierarchical organization was, as we have seen, stronger, but it did not constitute a role model for pastoralists who affected to despise cultivation.[27]

Naturally, the development of towns, communications, and economic and technological change (including the availability of modern weapons), provides a wider range of resources and choices with which politically ambitious entrepreneurs today can accumulate influence and power. As I wrote several years ago, clanship is, of course, an elastic principle, differentially manipulated by ambitious power-hungry individuals. In the modern setting, with their privileged access to external sources of economic and political power, to sophisticated weapons and Swiss bank accounts, successful big-men like Siyad and his successors, the so-called "war-lords" can in this egalitarian society pluck the strings of clanship to their own advantage to an extent and on a scale beyond anything realized before. (Lewis, 1994, p. 233)

So, for those who have significant sources of wealth and power outside the traditional system, clanship falls into place as one resource among a number of facilities to be exploited to the full. It is striking how frequently it is invoked to mobilize support—either alone, or supplemented by money and payments in kind—and as a source of trust for economic and other purposes. Its salience throughout the decade following the collapse of the Somali state in 1990-91 is indeed remarkable. Clearly, when Siyad proclaimed that he had "buried" clanship he might well have added, "the clan is dead; long live the clan!" He meant, of course, all forms of lineage solidarity, but particularly that at the level we call clan-family.

This is the inescapable and paradoxical price of Somali cultural nationalism (ethnicity), which comes ready-made, off-the-peg, but with this deadly, divisive undertow. For the student of comparative social institutions, this might be seen as demonstrating the greater significance of sociological than cultural factors. Cultural cohesion here is undermined by social structure, by the centrifugal pressures of the Somali segmentary system, and the pervasive force of the call of clanship (literally). Unfortunately, despite the considerable impact of literacy,[28] Somali nationalism has not been transformed by modernization into the organic mode of social solidarity envisaged by Emile Durkheim. The extreme, not to say excessive, democracy of traditional Somali political culture with its acute emphasis on individual decision-making, is a further major impediment to the formation of stable, centralized political units. Ethnicity alone is not remotely enough.

Thus, the struggle for Somali social cohesion is a real and continuing battle, and even when achieved by remarkable efforts at regional levels (as, e.g., in the Somaliland Republic), is always menaced by the hazard of erratic centrifugal segmentary forces. This can to some extent be offset by developing a political structure with balanced representation and power sharing at the clan level (as in Somaliland and, initially, in Puntland), and a correspondingly more equitable distribution of state resources and services.

Above all, if further progress is to be achieved in state-formation, Somali politicians will surely have to come out of denial and start seriously exploring how clan and lineage ties can be utilized positively. Perhaps they could learn from their nomadic kinsmen who unashamedly celebrate these traditional institutions. Here a less Eurocentrically biased, and less evolutionary view of lineage institutions by Western commentators, social scientists, and bureaucrats might help to create a more productive environment for rethinking clanship (i.e., agnation) positively.[29] However ancient its origins, and historically "primordial" (to use a banal and generally misleading term), clanship, as we have seen over and over again, is no stranger to modernity: I is not that it is incompatible with modernity, but rather that it is all too compatible with it!

Recent Attempts to Re-establish Government

In line with this, and despite their earlier attempts to keep clanship at bay, at least officially, the most recent efforts to reestablish government in Somalia have indeed sought to base political representation on a clan basis. The main building blocks of the nation (the Dir,[30] Darod, Hawiye, and Digil and Rahanwin clan-families) have been allocated quotas of representatives to elect transitional government.

The first experiment along these lines was the Transitional National Government established under UN auspices at the Arta Conference in Djibouti in August 2000, after almost seven months of grueling debate and argument among the 2,000 or so people who attended. Under the stage management of the president of the host state, Djibouti, this remarkable event produced a "Transitional National Assembly, which, after the usual horse-trading, in turn elected a "transitional president" and under his aegis, a government. The person chosen as president was a well-known southerner who had been a minister under Siyad. Because, like so many of the Mogadishu warlords, he was a Hawiye of the Habar Ghiddir clan, it was assumed by some of his supporters that he would be able to establish his leadership in that conflict ridden city. This optimistic view, however, did not take adequate account of the internal, segmentary clan dynamics. The effect of the appointment, thus, was to promote a struggle for power among the various established Habar Ghiddir warlords and the transitional president and his followers.

With, additionally, constant controversy over how representative its members actually were, by 2003 the Transitional National Government had degenerated into being regarded and behaving) as simply another armed faction. It controlled only a few streets in Mogadishu, with a militia that could not contend effectively with the hostile forces of the other southern Somali warlords (cf. Lewis, 2002 pp. 302ff).

Racked by internal financial scandals, and without advancing the cause of reconciliation or being able to hold any of the public elections that would have been necessary to establish its bona fides, this doomed regime had virtually collapsed by late summer 2003,[31] when its mandate expired. At this juncture, Somali politicians, large and small, military and nonmilitary, were busily engaged in yet another exercise in their long-running saga of high-profile international peace conferences: the thirteenth major performance in a little over a decade!

This time the location was in Kenya, where the participants again decided that, in the future assembly, seats should be allocated by clan quotas. Clans had definitely come out of the closet, as had the warlords who had been officially discouraged from open participation in the Arta maneuvers. The problem was now to find a consensus on power sharing among the principal military figures. Proudly claimed as a major achievement was the adoption, after nine months of acrimonious and tortuous debate, of a complex and far from easily workable federal constitution (which was still being bitterly opposed by some factions long after it had been officially adopted).

The viability of this framework, and of any other positive conclusions reached, would obviously be severely tested by whether or not it proved possible to restore public security and order in Mogadishu and its hinterland. This would require the local warlords to agree to modify their claims to control those sections of the city that each sought to monopolize, and to surrender authority to some form of collective administration. Such a far from likely development would be required to pave the way for the reopening of major public facilities like the airports and sea ports that had been closed for over a decade.

Without this, no progress would be possible in the south. Disarmament would be the next challenge, and would certainly test to the full the patience and endurance of the force of African peacekeepers whom it was optimistically envisaged might be deployed.

Not surprisingly, many Somalis considered that, faced with such formidable obstacles (previously defying all attempts at practical resolution), the volumes of rhetoric and money disbursed in Kenya would, as in the past, soon disappear with little trace beyond the temporary enrichment of an army of conference hangers-on and cynical operators. But however little of the conference's official decisions would actually bear fruit, the invisible man of Somali clanship, enhanced in conspicuousness, as always in times of insecurity, was now openly dominating political discourse, and frankly accorded an official presence at the center of political life. What was not being adequately discussed was how the proposed new (federal) government structure would accommodate the traditional decentralized decision-making power of the elders within a modern government.

Southern Somalia was still a long way from developing political structures designed to include traditional leaders in the political process, along the lines pioneered in the bicameral system of representation followed with considerable success in Somaliland. Unfortunately, the external pressures on peacemaking exerted by the representatives of the European Union, the UN and other international organizations were too ethnocentric and lacking in cultural sensitivity to be helpful here.

For various reasons, all sides at the Kenyan peace conference preferred to ignore the demonstrably viable local model, combining traditional and modern government, in operation in Somaliland (see Drysdale, 2000, pp. 174ff; Bryden, 2003). While certainly not perfect, this offered a more locally appropriate form of democratic government than the structures envisaged by the southern Somali leaders and their foreign mentors.

Conclusions

On a more abstract level, this analysis of Somali politics at the beginning of the twenty-first century highlights the strength and persistence of clanship at the expense of ethnic nationalism. Somali identity, based on shared language, culture, and religion, still has widespread currency in the rhetoric of political leaders and those who define themselves as Somali intellectuals.

Ethnicity here, like clan identity, is also of course relational, vis-à-vis non-Somali peoples of other ethnic groups such as Ethiopians or Arabs. However, as we have seen, although it lacks comparably external markers and depends formally on orally recorded genealogical criteria, clanship remains a more comprehensively powerful focus of identity in Somali society. A Somali friend from southern Somalia recently expressed this succinctly: "There is only one loyalty all Somalis share. It is not Islam. It is not nationhood. It is not love of country, it is clanism—a phenomenon I like to call the Hidden Religion."

This incisive definition is true despite the fact that clan-family is the ultimate agnatic level of political identity in a cumulative system of seamless segmentary lineage divisions that make it always provisional and subject to schismatic centrifugal pressures. Solidarity is more commonly mobilized at the level of clan within the more widely encompassing clan-family. What is involved here is Durkheim's mechanical rather than organic solidarity.

In contrast, the formal aspects of ethnic identity (culture, religion, language, etc.), are not susceptible to comprehensive internal division and subdivision in the same consistent and seamless manner. Divisions within the ethnic group are based on characteristics other than those used in defining the ethnic group itself, which does not have a systematic segmentary structure. These differences between clanship and ethnicity are formal distinctions that have, however, a practical outcome: in the Somali case, solidarity at the level of the ethnic group (the nation) is less binding than that within the clan structure, segmented though that is.

Notes

1. In terms of indigenous precolonial political structures, colonization thus imposed, or superimposed, the conquest state (typified in Africa by Ethiopia) through a process I have called the "Ethiopianization of Africa" (see Lewis, *Arguments with Ethnography*, pp. 58-68).

2. Cf. Lewis *Nationalism and Self-determination*, pp. 67ff.

3. On the development of nationalism at the tribal level within African states, see Argyle, *Oedipus in Central Africa*. Much of the literature discussing the supposed differences between tribalism and nationalism n my opinion is vitiated by ethnocentric assumptions. For a refreshing recent discussion, see Vail, 1989; see also Lewis, *Arguments with Ethnography*, pp. 58-68.

4. For a full analysis of the Somali segmentary lineage system, see Lewis, *A Pastoral Democracy*.

5. See Lewis, *Saints and Somalis*, New Jersey, Red Sea Press, 1998.

6. The characteristic features of this division are discussed more fully below. Other, unrelated ethnic groups caught up in the wider Somali society, and hence in Somali nationalism, include the riverine cultivating Bantu groups in the south of the country (who are attached to Somali clans and have adopted Somali genealogies); the Bajuni coastal fishermen and merchants of Brava and Kismayu; and the various Somalized Arab communities in the southern coastal towns (e.g., the Reer Hamar of Mogadishu).

7. This useful, term, borrowed from Tom Wolfe, refers to the bizarre mélange of postmodernism and politically correct pseudo-Marxism that many social scientists currently affect (especially in America).

8. See Jama Mohamed, "Somali Diaspora Nationalism," ms, 2003 in press.

9. Somalia's fate was complicated by its inclusion in the disposal of Italy's other former colonies, Eritrea and Libya. Earlier British proposals, including Somali unification and independence (the Bevin Plan) foundered through the mistrust and competing interests at the end of the war of Britain, France, the Soviet Union and United States (see Becker, 1952).

10. For example, the Young Benadir (based on the Reer Hamar Arab settlers in Mogadishu), the Bajuni Fiqarini (for the Bajuni fisher folk on the coast ground Brava), and the Agoi/Wardegle based on the Geledi clan and their associates.

11. See Lewis, *A Modern History*, pp. 159-60.

12. See ibid, pp. 182-83

13. See ibid, pp. 223-25; Hassan, "Status of Human Rights," pp. 3-11; Haakonsen, *Scientific Socialism*; on Siyad's character, see Laitin and Samatar, *Somalia*, pp. 158ff; and Sheikh and Petrucci, *Arrivederci a Moganiscio*.

14. See Lewis, *A Modern History* pp. 213-41. As I have argued elsewhere there is abundant evidence that literacy is not, as has generally been supposed (even by such a well-informed comparativist as Gellner,

Nations and Nationalism) an indispensible condition for nationalism. It may, as here, nevertheless fortify orally based nationalism.

15. See Lewis, ibid, pp. 245ff.

16. See Prunier, A candid view... pp. 107-120; Lewis, pp. 177-220.

17. For a remarkable insight into how these were recruited, and how their formation literally changed the lives of young city sophisticates, see Osman's brilliant novel, *In the Name of Our Fathers*.

18. See Lewis, *A Modern History*, pp. 99-100.

19. See Helander, unpublished ms. "Rumours of Rain".

20. See Farah, "Roots of Reconciliation" (and chapter six above).

21. The UN and EU efforts in this regard at the Djibouti peace conference amounted to an outrageous farce.

22. See Lewis and Mayall, *Decentralized Sructures*.

23. This is claimed by the most intellectual former minister (in a modern sense) in Siyad's government (who belongs to Siyad's clan), Dr. Mohamed Aden Sheikh, *Arrivederci*, as well as by some American academics, Somali and non-Somali; see A.I. Samatar, Besteman, *Representing*, Kapteijns 2001

24. For a more realistic account of the bellicose character of traditional Somali institutions, and one less patronizing in its implications (since it does not deny Somali agency), see International Red Cross, 1997.

25. See Lewis, *A Pastoral Democracy* and S.S. Samatar Introduction ... p. xiii

26. The closest political formation to a more durable, hierarchical structure among the nomads occurred in the Majerten sultanate, controlling incense cropping, pearl fishing, and piracy along its coastline On a smaller scale, a similar pattern was found among the coastal Warsangeli clan. See Lewis, p. 208.

27. See Lewis, *Arguments with Ethnography* pp. 59-78, *Blood and Bone* pp. 133-48; Helander, pp. 195-204.

28. See Lewis, *Arguments*, chapter 5.

29. At the (May-August) 2000 Djibouti peace conference, designed to resurrect a unitary Somali government, this issue surfaced in a complex argument, as to whether the new national assembly should contain members on the basis of clan or regional representation. For what it is worth in relation to this highly hypothetical body, it is interesting to note that the advocates of clan representation won the argument. This example of distributing representation, by clan blocs (i.e., clan-families, Darod, Hawiye, etc.), was repeated

in the successor 2002/2003 peace conference (signaling the failure of Arta), which for the first time adopted a federal constitution for Somalia (excluding Somaliland). The Somalialanders strenuously refused to compromise their independence by sending any representatives. This did not stop some southerners pontificating about Somali unity and claiming that Somaliland was included by virtue of the clan-bloc name Dir, from which the Isaq clan-family which forms the backbone of Somaliland, is historically a breakaway group.

30. This category has caused sharp controversy; the Isaq no longer accept that they are included as Dir and no official representatives from the Isaqis in Somaliland attended Arta or the successor conference in Kenya. The only official Dir delegates were from the Dir of southern Somalia (i.e., Biamal)—the Ise and Gadabursi Dir of Somaliland did not send official representatives (nor of course did those from Djibouti).

31. See Lewis, pp. 296ff; and chapter seven, above

References

Ahmed, H.O. 1993. *Morire a Mogadiscio.* Rome:

Ahmed, I. 2000. "Remittances and their impact in Post-war Somaliland," *Disasters,* Vol. 24, no. 4, pp. 380-89.

Argyle, J. 1971. *Oedipus in Central Africa.* Natal: University Press.

Besteman, J. 1996. "Representing Violence and 'Othering' Somalia," *Cultural Anthropology*, Vol. 11, pp. 120-33.

_____. 1998. "Primordialist Blinders: A Reply to I.M. Lewis," *Cultural Anthropology,* 13 Vol. 1, pp. 109-20.

Bryden, M. 2003, "The Banana Test: Is Somaliland Ready for Recognition?" *Annales d'Ethiopie,* Vol. 19, pp. 341-64.

Compagnon, D. 1990, "The Somali Opposition Fronts," *Horn of Africa*, Vol. 13, nos.1 and 2.

Drysdale, J. 2000. *Stoics without Pillows.* London: Haan.

Farah, A.Y. (with I. M. Lewis) 1993. *The Roots of Reconciliation: Peacemaking Endeavours of Contemporary Lineage Elders.* London: ActionAid.

Ghalib, J. M. 1995. *The Cost of Dictatorship: The Somali Experience.* New York: Lilian Barber.

Gellner, E. 1983. *Nations and Nationalism.* Oxford: Basil Blackwell.

Haakonsen, J. M. 1984. *Scientific Socialism and Self-Reliance*. Bergen: Department of Social Anthropology, University of Bergen.

Hassan, M. 1980. "Status of Human Rights in Somalia," *Horn of Africa*, Vol. 3, No. 2, pp. 3-11

Helander, B. 1996. "Rahanweyn Sociability: A Model for Other Somalis?" In R.J. Hayward and I. M. Lewis (eds.), *Voice and Power: The Culture of Language in North East Africa: essays in Honour of B. W. Andrzejewski*. London: School of African and Oriental Studies.

_____. 1998. "The Emperor's New Clothes Removed: A Critique of Besteman's 'Violent Politics and the Politics of Violence'," *American Ethnologist*, Vol. 25, pp. 122-32.

_____. Unpublished ms. "Rumours of Rain: Ideas of Centralization, social Fragmentation and the Nature of Power in Post-Government Somalia."

_____. 2003. *The Slaughtered Camel: Coping with fictitious Descent among the Hubeer of Southern Somalia*, Uppsala: Studies in Cultural Anthropology, p. 34.

Hersi, A.A., 1977, *The Arab Factor in Somali History*, unpublished Ph. D. dissertation, University of California at Los Angelus.

International Red Cross (Somalia Delegation) 1997. *Spared from the Spear: Traditional Somali Behavior in Warfare*, Nairobi: International Committee of the Red Cross, Somali Delegation.

Issa-Salwe, Abdissalam, 1996. *The Collapse of the Somali State*. London: Haan.

Kapteijns, L. and Farah, M. 2001. "I. M. Lewis, A Pastoral Democracy", *Africa*, Vol. 71, no. pp. 719-22.

Laitin, D. D. and Samatar, S. 1987. *Somalia: Nation in Search of a State*, Boulder, Co: Westview Press.

Lewis, I. M. 1958. "Modern Political Movements in Somaliland," *Africa*, xviii, pp. 244-61, 344-64.

_____. 1991/1999. *A Pastoral Democracy*. Oxford: Oxford University Press/James Currey.

_____. 1963. "Lineage Continuity and Modern Commerce in Northern Somaliland," in P. Bohannan and G. Dalton (eds.) *Markets in Africa*. Evanston, IL: Northwestern University Press.

_____. (ed.) 1983. *Nationalism and Self-determination in the Horn of Africa*. London: Ithaca Press.

_____. 1994. *Blood and Bone: The Call of Kinship in Somali Society*. Lawrenceville, NJ: Red see Press.

_____. 1998. "Doing Violence to Ethnography: Some Comments on Catherine Besteman's Distorted Reporting on Somalia," *Cultural anthropology* Vol. 13, pp. 100-108.

_____. 1999. *Agruments with Ethnography.* London: Athlone Press.

_____. 2001. "Why the Warlords won," *Times Literary Supplement,* June, pp. 3-5.

_____. 2002. *A Modern History of the Somali,* Oxford: James Currey.

_____. and Mayall, J. (eds.) 1995. *A Study of decentralized Structures for Somalia.* London: London School of Economics.

Little, P.D. 2003. *Somalia: economy without State.* Oxford: James Currey.

Luling, V. 2002. *Somali Sultanate: The Geledi City-state over 150 Years.* London: Haan.

Mohamed, J. 2002. "Imperial Politics and Nationalism in the Decolonisation of Somaliland, 1954-1960," *English Historical Review,* Vol. 117, p. 494.

_____. in press. "Somali Diaspora Nationalism and Haji Farah Omar."

Mukhtar, M. H. 1996. "The Plight of the Agro-pastoral Society of Somalia," *Review of African Political Economy,* Vol. 32, pp. 543-53.

Nicolosi, G. 2002. *Imperialismo e Resistenza in Corno d'Africa, Mohammed Abdullah Hassan e il derviscicsmo somalo (1899-1920).* Rubbettino

Osman, A. Y. 1996. *In the Name of Our Fathers.* London: Haan.

Prunier, G. 1992. "A Candid View of the Somali National Movement," *Horn of Africa,* Vols. 13 and 14, pp. 107-20.

Samatar, A.I. 1989. *The State and Rural Transformation in Northern Somalia, 1884-1906.* Madison: University of Wisconsin Press.

Samatar, A. I. (ed.) 1993 (1994 p. 232. *The Somali Challenge: from Catastrophe to Renewal.* Boulder, Co: Lynne Rienner.

Samatar, S. S. 1996. "Somalia's Horse That Feeds His master," in R. J. Hayward and I. M. Lewis (eds.), *Voice and Power: the Culture of Language in North East Africa,* London: School of Oriental and African Studies.

_____. 1999. "Introduction," In I. M. Lewis, *A Pastoral Democracy.* Oxford: James Currey, 1999, pp. ix-xiv

Schlee, G. 2002. "Regularities dans le chaos: traits recurrents dans l'organisation politico-religieuse et militaries des Somali," *L' Homme, no. 161, pp. 17-50.*

Sheik-Abdi, A. 1993. *Divine Madness, Mohammed Abdulle Hassan (1856-1920).* Lonson: Zed Books.

Sheikh, Mohamed Aden with P. Petrucci 1991. *Arrivederci a Mogadiscio.* Rome: Editori Associati.

Vail, L. (ed.) 1989. *The Creation of Tribalism in Southern Africa,* London: James Currey

Nine

AN INTERVIEW WITH THE AUTHOR BY CHARLES GESCHEKTER

✦

Ioan Lewis Interviewed at his Home in London in 1999 by Charles Geshekter, Professor of African History, California State University, Chico.

CG: I wanted to start with basic things. I have your vita here with date of birth. Could you tell me where you were born?

IL: I was born in Scotland, in Glasgow. But I'm actually half Welsh, because my father, who was a journalist, was Welsh and we lived in London. In fact, curiously, the last place we lived in London when I was a child was near here. My father died when I was seven and we moved up to my mother's parents, to my maternal grandparents. I was brought up there from the age of seven until I left the University of Glasgow and came to study at Oxford.

CG: Is there anything in particular that you reflect on that began to move you toward social anthropology as a field when you were in secondary school and in the university?

IL: I didn't actually know either the word anthropology or social anthropology while I was at school, nor really while I was at Glasgow University until just about the point when I was graduating in chemistry. Strangely enough, I did some research on the synthesis of antimalarials, which was published with my supervisor in the Journal of the Chemical Society. At this time, I saw some advertisements of the Nuffield Foundation, offering conversion studentships to people trained in the natural sciences to move into the human sciences, and I applied. I thought they looked interesting. I was lucky because there was a very informative academic at the University of Glasgow whom I then met. He was actually a social anthropologist specializing in Burma who had recently been introduced to Glasgow University, as an exotic import, to set up a program of Third World social anthropological studies under a new government scheme. This was to develop in various university centers the teaching of social sciences.

My contact, Noel Stevenson, was a former British administrator in Burma and someone who had fought in the Burma campaign as a rather daring colonel. Apparently, he had happened to meet the vice chancellor of Glasgow University while traveling, and they got on very well. He was subsequently appointed to this new post at Glasgow University to set up social anthropology. He was a great proselytizer and that is, of course, a good thing, but his proselytization was rather undiplomatic. He told various senior figures in the Glasgow University establishment that the trouble with them was that they didn't know anthropology. If only they knew a little, their understanding of the classics and Old Testament would be greatly enhanced. This is no doubt true, but it didn't make him a very welcome colleague. He was gradually frozen out of the University of Glasgow and moved into Scottish television, as initially the presenter of a popular quiz show in what were the early days of Scottish television. He ended up as the managing director of Scottish television, a role that he regarded as a form of applied anthropology!

IL: I met this colorful personality who kindly explained to me a bit about social anthropology, and suggested some reading material and where I might apply to study for it through this Nuffield Scholarship Scheme. He suggested Oxford, where he had studied briefly with Edward Evans-Pritchard, and I applied for a Nuffield Studentship to study social anthropology there. I was very lucky because I was selected for an interview for this studentship, which was held in London. When I got to the interview panel, I discovered that the chairman of the panel was the vice chancellor of Glasgow University, my university, who was a well-known academic politician called Hector Hetherington. His son was the editor of the *Guardian* newspaper and he was at this time a major figure in academic politics in Britain. Rather typically, he said to me, "think we may have traveled down on the same train, but I of course traveled first class." He was just slightly off-putting.

There was a panel of people, none of whom I had the remotest idea who they were. They started asking me questions about "what have you read?" I had been advised that I should read a bit of Evans-Pritchard's works, which I had looked at as I traveled on buses and tramcars in Glasgow. They started asking me things like, "What do you think about Evans-Pritchard's book on Azande witchcraft?" which I hadn't read thoroughly at all. In fact I was very far from knowing enough to appreciate what a classic the book was.

Consequently I was guarded and rather unenthusiastic, so they asked me to declare an opinion. I said that I had not found it very exciting. Then all my inquisitors started laughing and I couldn't understand this. But unknown to me Evans-Pritchard himself was one of the interviewers, and his enemies on the panel relished my ignorant remarks. I had no idea who they were, but miraculously, it worked out well. Some weeks later I got a letter from Evans-Pritchard himself saying, "Although you were so rude about me, I'm pleased to tell you ...." And I soon found that he was an inspiring teacher, and a warm, and stimulating and altogether marvelous person to study under. He regarded my unfortunate interview gaffe as a kind of joke, which he often repeated when he introduced me to others. One of his most attractive features was his treatment of students as equals: in this egalitarian respect Evans-Pritchard was very Somali!

CG: It was when you were at Oxford that you began your interest in Somalia and Somali studies?

IL: Yes, that's right and it was an accident. Following my undergraduate degree in chemistry, I had completed a conversion course in anthropology, in the form of a postgraduate diploma. With this behind me, I was looking for a subject for writing a library thesis which was then called a "B. Lit."—more or less the equivalent of a master's degree in those days. The scholar, who had been one of my supervisors, when I was doing the diploma was Franz Steiner, famous for his work on taboo. He was a Czech refugee in Oxford. He had been given funds by the International African Institute to compile a bibliography on the Somalis, and to write an ethnographic survey of the Somalis and related peoples in the Horn of Africa. He hadn't actually written this. But he had complied an excellent bibliography, and he felt guilty about not using it to write the agreed book. He suggested that I should take this project on for my B. Lit. thesis. So, I wrote a thesis (a library, scissors, and paste job) on the Somalis, the Afar, and the Saho, in order to produce the ethnographic survey required for Daryll Forde's International African Institute, Survey of Africa. (Many years later, when I had become professor of anthropology at the London School of Economics, I succeeded Daryll as director of the Institute.)

IL: The resulting volume, Peoples of the Horn of Africa, published by the International African Institute came out in 1955. By then, unfortunately, Franz Steiner had died of a heart attack so I was left with his marvelous bibliography and the work that I had done through him more or less by accident. In the course of all that, I met various Somalis, notably the folklorist Musa Galaal. I also met an intriguing character, and he must have been the first Somali I actually met, called Abdi "Telephone" who was in charge of various security telephones in government offices in central London. I don't know if he was actually in charge, but he worked with the scrambling machines for various telephones in government offices in central London. He was an intriguing, flamboyant character. One thing led to another. Then I met Goosh Andrzejewski, the famous Polish linguistic specialist at the School of Oriental and African Studies, and I became a pupil of his as far as linguistic matters were concerned, and a lot of other things in Somali culture. We became close friends and his friendship certainly cemented my interest in Somali studies.

CG: It seems like by dint of circumstance or coincidence, you had contact with three rather enthusiastic individuals: Abdi "Telephone," Goosh Andrzejewksi, and Musa Galaal. It was probably hard for you to resist their kind of enthusiasm.

IL: Oh yes, of course, as a young, enthusiastic student of social anthropology, I wasn't really prone to resist. I was looking for fields that were interesting, exciting, and relatively unexplored from the point of view of the subject of social anthropology, which was the case with the Somali scene. I had met an archaeologist at Cambridge University who had done some work in Somalia during the Second World War. I came across other people who had been there in the British military administration, as well as some people who had served after the war in the Somaliland Scouts, as it was then called. I met a little caucus of people, a little network would perhaps be a more accurate description, who were either Somalis or concerned with Somali studies.

CG: And then you went up to Oxford for your PH. D. work?

IL: I was already in Oxford and I had this research grant from Nuffield and they extended it to cover the equivalent of what is today a master's degree. Then I applied for research funds to do research in Somalia among the Somali. I was very lucky. Surprisingly quickly, I secured a grant under the Colonial Development and Welfare Fund scheme for research in developing British protectorates, colonies, and dependent states. They had never allocated one of these before to Somaliland, so I got one. Before that, I had been working for a year with the great doyen of African administration and colonial rule in Africa, Lord Hailey, author of the famous African Survey. I had been his research assistant, which was an incredible experience because he was a demanding person who seemed to think he was still acting viceroy of India, and I was his sole research assistant!

CG: It was right at that time, in 1954, that Somaliland and Somali topics become the subject of a kind of political explosion. Can you comment on that? Because you came into Somaliland just after the transfer of the Haud back to Ethiopia.

IL: That's quite right. In fact, I met at that time a number of the members of Somali delegations who came to London to protest about the transfer to Ethiopia of the Haud. I got to know some of them rather superficially, and was attracted by their cause and eagerly wished to support them in my small way.

CG: Was this part of what you referred to as your "youthful idealism" at the time? Of course later, you became involved in giving speeches or talks and exhortations to some Somali groups.

IL: Yes, of a rather limited kind.

CG: Was this something that fired you further? There was a sudden contemporary political dimension to the study of the Somalis.

IL: Yes, indeed. I was very taken. I was attracted and impressed by the Somali nationalist cause, the desire of the Somalis to get independence and to get themselves together as a state, including the various territories that had been divided by colonial rule, by the African partition.

CG: Was this unusual for someone to be in Britain, studying social anthropology and then to adopt or embrace Somali nationalism, which had a strong component of declonization and anticolonialism as well?

IL: No. I would have thought that most of the students that I know and can think of now, my contemporaries who were doing anthropology, were probably leftist in political orientation and certainly very anticolonial. They were trained to be suspicious of colonialism and that was the overall ethos under which we were schooled. I think also it was a question of, as you said a moment ago, youthful romanticism, adventure, and political activism, if you like.

CG: I was intrigued by some of the things you have written about your relationship with the Protectorate Administration. You mentioned that the Protectorate Administration attracted a high proportion of people of "exceptional character, including many unusual individuals with eccentricities." Can you elaborate on that and explain where you fitted into this scheme of things? You have devoted nearly fifty years to the serious study of Somalia. How did you find these Protectorate people and where did you see yourself in terms of their characteristics?

IL: Well, first of all, officially, I was incorporated into the Somaliland Protectorate Administration as the lowest possible ranking expatriate. I came right at the end of the list of the expatriate officials. This seemed to me initially a big problem because I had been trained to avoid colonial officials in carrying out field research in Africa. I had the idea they would try to subvert my activities or co-opt me in some way that would not be productive for my intellectual, political independence. I had been led to assume that was the situation. So when I found that I had been incorporated into the Protectorate Administration I was troubled and worried. I wondered whether it would work out for me at all. The Protectorate Administration wouldn't allow any loose, unaffiliated social science researchers to mill around in Somaliland in the middle 1950s, unless they were part of the administration and theoretically subject to its control. They did not want any uncontrolled outsider coming to disturb the Somali peace. They saw the Somalis as lively, vivacious characters, with a tradition of active resistance to whatever seemed to smack of anything that they didn't like, particularly if it seemed to have some tinge of Christianity. They did not want the Somalis disturbed by those who did not understand their ways.

In other words, the memory of Sayyid Mohamed Abdille Hassan and his nationalist movement, rebellion, or whatever you like to call it was still very much alive. (I think myself that it was a protonationalist movement.) That memory was still quite vivid and strong in a curious sort of way. None of the officials I met ever had any direct contact with that period. But this sort of ghost was a kind of memory that haunted the political imagination, to a large degree, of the colonial office in its dealings with Somalis. And that affected the people who were sent to work in the Somaliland Protectorate. At least it affected them officially. What they did when they got there was another matter. But officially, it did. So there was an incredible anxiety not to disturb the Somalis. I would say the guiding motto of the Protectorate Administration was to do nothing that would upset Somali opinion. The aim was to do what the Somalis wanted, within the limited budgets available to the Protectorate Administration, which generated a very pro-Somali administration. In fact, people who didn't get on with Somalis were quickly weeded out and discouraged from continuing in the Colonial Service in Somaliland. They were advised to transfer to other territories.

CG: Can you comment on some of the characteristics, or the kinds of things that would predispose a non-Somali to "get on" with the Somalis? What would predispose someone to realize after a month that this wasn't a place he wanted to be?

IL: Obviously, they had to be adventurous characters who were attracted by the notion of a semidesert country, and nomadic movements of nomadic peoples, the sort of haughty dignity of people like the Somalis, and who were not simply interested in exerting their own authority over some local, subservient population. They had to be people who were interested in arguing democratically in an egalitarian fashion with a tough-minded local population. If they weren't like that, they couldn't possibly succeed with Somalis. They had to like that kind of environment, or be interested in its wildlife, as a number of them were. Generally, they should regard the Somalis as a development challenge to which they could perhaps contribute something useful. Certainly, for the most part, the people that I met in the administration were concerned to make some contribution to the walfare of the Somalis. Obviously there were some who were not so idealistic, but the major ethos was to contribute to the development of the Somali people in one way or another.

Following this train of thought, it wasn't surprising that they should have been so supportive of Somali efforts to get the Haud grazing land returned to Somaliland and taken away from Ethiopia and that they should be so pro-Somali and anti-Ethiopian. There was an interesting polarization between the Foreign office and the Colonial Office. The foreign Office, with its larger concerns, was pro-Ethiopia in this context, but the Colonial Office was pro-Somali. This was very evident "on the ground" in the behavior of Somaliland administrative officials. For instance, when the British ambassador from Addis Ababa came on a visit to Somaliland and met the governor of Somaliland and the senior officials, their relations were not particularly cordial. There was quite an impact of the Somali point of view versus the Ethiopian point of view. It was interesting to me, the extent to which these English, mainly British (some of them were Polish) colonial civil servants had been, as it were, brainwashed by the Somalis. I mean there was a notable extent to which Somali ideas and values were transferred to these expatriate officials. Those who got on better with the Somalis were those who made this transference best.

CG: Can you give me some examples of that?

IL: Certainly. This illustrates the character of this administration also. When I was there, from 1955 to 1957, was a crucial time, because it was the beginning of the transfer of power, the promotion of independence, and the preparation for independence, just the beginning of it, and a great step up in education and development activity. The hierarchy of this tiny little "Cinderella of the Empire," as it was well described, consisted of the governor at the top, then the chief secretary, and, under him, the next senior official was the commissioner of Somali Affairs.

The governor at the time [Theodore Ousley Pike] was a genial Irishman, interested in rugby and livestock; he used to travel around on treks in the interior with trucks filled with growing vegetables and two cows. Somalis knew him as "two cows." ("Two camels" would have been better!)

The man who was commissioner of Somali Affairs substantively was an interesting person indeed. He was a member of the British Communist Party and was exceedingly democratic in his activities and general ethos. At various points, he was acting chief secretary that is he would act for his senior when his senior was on leave. Sometimes, when the governor wasn't there and the chief secretary wasn't there, this particular individual was actually de facto in administrative charge of the whole Protectorate. He was a man of considerable experience in district-level Somaliland administration. For instance, he had demonstrated that bait that was distributed to kill locusts was harmless to livestock by eating it! He did things like that.

At one point, there was an unfortunate golfing accident where a golf ball struck a Somali. It was from a club wielded by somebody who was an administrative official. The Somali naturally sued for damages. There was a certain slowness in the pursuit of this legal matter and this "Communist" commissioner of Somali Affairs, who was personally quite wealthy, let it be known that, unless the matter was proceeded with quickly, he would fly out at his own expense a famous left-wing barrister from England (Dingle Foot—as it happened, someone whom I met later in life). That, of course, accelerated the legal process and the matter was brought to a speedy conclusion. There were people like that in this administration. He was the only one, as far as I know, who was a member of the Communist Party; but there were all sorts of people you would not expect. I suppose the most knowledgeable ones had had some experience with Somalis during the Second World War; for example, John Drysdale, who'd been with a Somali battalion in the Burma campaign. And various other people who had military experience with Somali units.

CG: Mr. Richard Darlington?

IL: Yes, that's right. And also a remarkable character who used to run the Anglo-Somali Society, Colonel Eric Wilson V.C., whose life was saved by Somalis in the war and who was forever grateful for that.

CG: That was apparently what convinced Richard Darlington to devote the rest of his life to education at Amud because he was left for dead, stabbed in the face by a bayonet in one of the Burmese campaigns, and his life was saved by the Somalis.

IL: Very interesting. Well, he wasn't the only one. Some expatriates had very strong bonds of personal loyalty as well as friendship with Somalis.

CG: I was recalling as you were saying this, there were some British officials, I don't know if you overlapped with them or not, who spent long periods of time in the Protectorate. I was thinking of John Hunt in geology, Edward Peck who did veterinary science, and Dudley Walsh.

IL: They'd all gone. Walsh was much earlier but John Hunt was just retiring when I went there. He had recently written that encyclopedic, but scatterbrained, survey of the Somaliland protectorate. But he left a legacy in the geology department of people going on long treks with camels, and expecting all his expatriate officials to follow this tradition to get to know the country at firsthand. I knew a number of young officials and their wives who went out into the bush on foot for weeks on end. A very interesting and often tough experience for them, as you can imagine.

CG: In the back of the first edition, and in all subsequent editions of Peoples of the Horn of Africa, was a carefully delineated map that folded out and opened up. I think the map was from about 1945 or 1946. As part of your research, did you have access to maps and other kinds of materials as part of the official Protectorate?

IL: Oh yes, I was given access to anything that I knew I wanted. I may have wanted things that I didn't know existed. I was treated very well by these officials. Despite my fears and worries about becoming a kind of an adopted client of the Somaliland expatriate administration, I was very much a beneficiary. What was really wonderful was that nobody tried to interfere with me at all. Let me be more accurate. When, on a rare occasion, an official tried to direct my researches, the governor, who knew something about social anthropology, told them to stop. I was absolutely given carte blanche. In retrospect, I could say that I got away with murder, metaphorically, of course, in the way I exploited this situation to the benefit of my own activities and research.

CG: From my recollection of your writings, it was during this time that you had interesting encounters with two rather different Somalis who seemed to have an impact on you. You talk about meetings with Mohamed Abshir and also the chance encounter with Aw Jama Umar Isa. Could you elaborate on your early contacts with them; after Musa Galaal and Goosh and Abdi "Telephone"? Having said this, could you identify the most memorable encounter or event that occurred to you during that period of field research and which Somali, for example, had the greatest impact on you at this time?

IL: If I could just respond to your question about Aw Jama Umar Isa. I met him first when he was a so-called bush *wadaad* near Las Anod, at a place called Wudwud, when I was trying to collect material about the clan history of the Dulbahante and material about Sayyid Mohamed Abdille Hassan. I met this man who covered his mouth with his cloth whenever he spoke to me because I was obviously a disgusting infidel, a potentially polluting infidel. He made cryptic responses to things that I asked him, and generally exuded a rather sinister, forbidding impression. I became actually frightened of him, and thought perhaps he would try to murder me as I lay in a camp bed in my tent. He didn't [try to murder me], as far as I know, and we had numerous conversations; but I never got very far with him at this stage, such was his obvious suspicion of me.

However, he turned up in my life much later in the south, on a subsequent visit to Mogadishu and the Benadir Coast. I met him in Mogadishu. By that time, he had turned himself into a self-taught oral historian, aided by the other man you mentioned, the police commander General Mohamed

Abshir, who lent or gave him a tape recorder because Mohamed Abshir was very interested in Somali nationalism, being a nationalist especially interested in the history of Sayyid Mohamed Abdille Hassan. Consequently, he was keen to encourage people to study that topic.

So, there was Aw Jama Umar Isa now doing research with a tape recorder. He told me that he had watched me and made inquiries about me in the bush, after we had first met. And that in the end he had come to the conclusion that I was a fairly harmless character, and was not some kind of spy, as he had first assumed, and that I was not doing anything that disadvantaged his kinsmen. He came to the conclusion that because my spoken Somali was rough and rudimentary, compared with his natural, flowing Somali, and his huge grasp of vocabulary and cultural context, he could do much better than I could on the kind of research I was trying to do. To a certain extent, this of couse was absolutely true. He had become an oral historian (also, of course, literate in Arabic), really self-taught apart from possibly the demonstration effect of an infidel at work in the interior on whose techniques he could obviously improve. He developed from that into a considerable figure, although he lacked a formal Western education. He produced wonderful work. I think he is now unquestionably one of the very best chroniclers of the Dervish period.

CG: Was there any incident that you recall during that period of twenty months of research in the Protectorate that was singular or that convinced you that you were doing the right thing in your field research? Or whether you were doing the wrong thing?

IL: At that time in a young researcher's life, one tends to be rather self-confident if he is doing research in such circumstances, and one is not likely to feel that he is doing the wrong thing. I was attracted by Somali nationalism and have not so far mentioned that I made a visit of about a month to Somalia in the south in 1956. That was at the point when internal self-government there was being handed over by the Italians to the Somalis. I toured all the main provinces of southern Somalia and most of the main districts. I was interested in finding out what was going on in this "Italian" region. I met the local district commissioners, provincial commissioners, and police chiefs.

It was at his point that for the first time I met Mohamed Abshir, who was then he regional police commander of Isha Baidoa. We met there and we got along personally very well. I met a number of other characters around that time, many people who subsequently became prominent politicians and government ministers. I knew the Mariano family from the north, and I had got to know various politicians in the north while I was up there. I attended many meetings of the Somali Youth League (SYL) (and also in the south of the Hizbia Dastur Mostaqil Somali (HDMS), often in the bush, which was interesting. When I went back to Somaliland, I arrogantly made some small interventions at local meetings of the National United Front, the NUF. I said in my rather inadequate Somali that the south seemed very advanced compared to the north, and it was time the northerners got themselves going politically—a very simplistic comment.

CG: In what sense was the south more advanced politically?

IL: It was impressive to go around the whole country and find that there was a Somali district or provincial commissioner everywhere, that the police chiefs were Somalis. There was a big educational program and the politicians were well organized in the Somali Youth League. They were obviously heading for imminent independence in 1960.

CG: At that time, six years on in terms of the UN's sponsorship, there was a timetable already for the former Italian Somalia's independence, which made all the difference in the world, I assume because of the money. But when did you first hear talk of a potential union between the Protectorate and the south? Was that on the agenda in 1956?

IL: Oh yes, because that was part of the original SYL manifesto, the union of all the Somali territories.

CG: What was the feeling about that in the north when you came back and talked about a rather different timetable. You said that a "new day is dawning in the south but it's still nighttime in the north." How did the Somalis in the Protectorate respond to that?

IL: I don't know how the Somalis as a whole responded because I didn't hear it. I can only say that probably some of the politicians that I knew were annoyed with me for being so cheeky as to make comments on the speed and success of their nationalist movement. But, obviously, the main nationalists in the north, as far as I knew anyhow, were committed to union with Somalia and to union with, as they then saw it, the Somalis in French Somaliland, the Ethiopian Ogaden, and northern Kenya. Obviously, there were nuances to the extent of their willingness, their eagerness, to pursue those goals, but I don't recall meeting anyone who was hostile to that project. The strategic aspects and the tactics of it were a different matter. But the general project, as far as I know, was widely endorsed by the leading politicians. Some of them probably had reservations and wanted to guard their own power bases. But that wasn't something I really knew about at that time.

CG: You mentioned several times that it was fairly easy (a) to do social anthropological field research in the mid-1950s, and (b) to identify with Somali interests and the Protectorate Administration government itself identified with Somali interests.

IL: That, of course, made it easy.

CG: This question of "Somali interests" interests me as they were defined in the 1950s. I want to ask you about Somali interests in 1999, but what would you say were Somali interests in the 1950s? Besides independence, what were the top concerns of the administration or of yourself when it came to defining Somali interests in the 1950s?

IL: I think that the Protectorate Administration would have wished to prepare Somalis to be in a position to govern themselves in a modern sense and, therefore, wanted to provide a sufficient degree of in-depth education to try to develop the limited, as they saw it, economic resources of the north, primarily the exports of livestock, and to get Somalis trained in civil administration. All those rather obvious things at a rather simple level I think. What happened was the pace of all this suddenly accelerated in a way that the protectorate people who were administering the territory in 1955-57 never envisioned. They thought there would be perhaps a period of ten years or that Somalia would be independent for quite a bit before Somaliland possibly joined with Somalia. And in this interval, Somaliland would get its act together in terms of the development of education, training, of possible economic resources to a higher pitch, which would enable the Somalilanders to be potentially an autonomous enterprise if they wished to be so. I don't know whether anyone seriously considered how autonomous Somaliland would be economically. But if they did, they probably saw this in terms of livestock exports. There was a big input of livestock health assistance through the veterinary department.

CG: You once claimed that the Somalis were "precapitalist capitalists." Can you elaborate?

IL: They obviously are in the literal sense in relation to their livestock and their interest in maximizing livestock holdings, but also being prepared to sell their livestock. Only recently I became aware, when speaking to some Afars in the hinterland of Djibouti, of the extent to which the Afar have a much more mystical symbolic attitude toward camel's milk: for instance, that it shouldn't be sold, that you should give it to people, if you dispose of it at all. I never came across anything like that in my dealings with Somalis. I can't remember meeting any Somalis who were not thoroughly commercialized, if we could use that expression, and who were unaware of and were not part of an economic order in which things were bought and sold. I don't think there are any, in that sense. I don't think there are any sort of precapitalist Somalis, or if there are, I haven't met them.

CG: This reminds me of something Gordon Waterfield commented on in his book *Morning Will Come* (London: Murray 1944) and I wondered how much you saw of this, obviously in the mid-1950s. That was the extent to which rural Somalis in the bush not only had a connection to urban Somaliland, but were conscious of the outside world. Can you comment on what you saw in the 1950s?

IL: I always found Somalis extremely cosmopolitan and this partly explains their interest in radio broadcasting and news broadcasting. That interest is reinforced by the availability of news programs in Somali around the world. I always think of an experience that I had much later on the Juba River in southern Somalia when I was doing some work with an NGO development agency, when we were looking at refugee settlements in Somalia and were trying to cross the river. We were waiting for the little ferryboat to come and there was a quite impressive Somali family with livestock standing, waiting for the ferry as well. The man was diverting himself, making good use of the time by frolicking in the river and he kept shouting to me "Why don't you come and join me?" I said, "Well, that's very kind of you but unfortunately I'm afraid of crocodiles. You obviously aren't but I am." I got talking to his wife, who had a huge transistor radio, a "ghetto blaster," whatever they call it, a huge one on the back of a burden camel. I asked her what were her favorite programs.

She said she liked Radio Ethiopia for music, the BBC for truth, and Radio Mogadishu for news. She was really very funny. This was a good illustration of the extent to which Somalis were tuned into the wider world. The examples she chose, apart from the BBC, were mainly local stations, but I've met many Somalis who listened to Peking or Soviet transmitters all over the place or any available broadcast in Somali and, to some extent, in Arabic. Obviously, these are people whose experience of the world is not limited to their locale. In that sense, they are locally bound in their lifestyle but their thoughts and awareness of the world are a great deal wider, it has always seemed to me.

CG: You finished your field research in 1957, then moved to take a university position in Rhodesia.

IL: That is right, in what is now Harare. I was one of the founding members of the University College of Rhodesia and Nyasaland as it was then called, now the University of Harare.

CG: This was where you essentially worked on *A Pastoral Democracy*? (Oxford University Press/James Currey, 1961/1999).

IL: Yes, I wrote it there.

CG: How did you spend your time and what were your main responsibilities when you were in Rhodesia?

IL: Teaching African studies and not teaching Somali studies at all. I had no scope for teaching Somali studies other than aspects of Somali life that were germane to some social anthropological work I was doing or writing. I had no opportunity to teach Somali studies as such. We didn't have a course in Somali studies or even in studies of the Horn of Africa.

CG: Since you had just come from a period of intense research in Somaliland, were you able to draw from your own personal experiences into your course work?

IL: Oh yes, of course. Yes, but not specifically within a Somali studies framework. In fact, I've never, except for a very brief period at University College, taught any course that was specifically on the Horn of Africa or on Somali social anthropology.

CG: Really?

IL: No, never.

CG: Is that unusual?

IL: It was just the way that we've carved up the pedagogics of teaching social anthropology in Britain. As I said, I did teach a course on the Horn of Africa when I was at University College, but that's a very exotic subject, or at least it was then in the late 1960s. There weren't many takers and it was a minor course in my teaching duties.

CG: I'm in a different situation than you are, but whenever I talk about Somali studies or Somalis or Somali history or culture and any of the incredibly interesting facets to it, my experience with students is they become drawn to Somalia, they want to learn much more about it because, I think you and I would agree, they are an intrinsically attractive and extremely important people to try to make sense of.

IL: Well, they've got an interesting set of social arrangements, which are certainly rather unusual and make good material for thinking about society and how social organization works. Somali concepts and elements of Somali social organization and politics have crept into all my teaching in social anthropology without exception.

I remember a rather witty professor of sociology at the London School of Economics saying that there was no aspect of general, comparative sociology that could not be illustrated with reference to the Somalis as far as my lectures were concerned. There was a lot of truth in that. For example, I wrote a standard textbook of social anthropology called *Social Anthropology in Perspective* (Penguin, 1976), a rather successful textbook that's filled with examples relating to Somali society and Somali culture, put in a comparative framework. I've never taught a solely Somali course or hardly ever, and rarely one on the Horn of Africa. I've used the material in a broader comparative framework in general social anthropology, political anthropology, or comparative religion teaching. A lot of the ideas that I have tried to develop in the study of religion have come from my experience in Somalia, as I directly acknowledge. The same is true in my theoretical contributions to kinship and comparative politics. On all these areas my theories were triggered by Somali examples. Thus, my contributions in books like *Ecstatic Religion* (first published by Penguin, 1971) can ultimately be traced back to Somali saar spirits. This is why I have repeatedly referred to anthropologists as "plagiarists." This basis of so many "theories" in social anthropology is a major theme in my most recent book, *Arguments with Ethnography* (Athlone Press, 1999).

CG: Did students ever come to you wanting to develop a graduate program, a graduate-level interest in Somali Studies.

IL: No, unfortunately they didn't. That would have happened if I'd been teaching at the School of Oriental and African Studies, which would have been a natural development, but it wouldn't develop in the way we organized teaching at the London School of Economics, which was not by area but by topic.

CG: What's the key difference between the two universities in that sense?

IL: The School of Oriental and African Studies is an area specialist school, as the name suggests, and so African Studies breaks down into parts of Africa, and there are, consequently, courses on these various components. Goosh Andrzejewski was very lucky because he could spend his life teaching the subject he was most interested in, namely the Somali language. But I couldn't get way with that in social anthropology, except by subterfuge, by using endless Somali examples in a more general context.

CG: You are arguably the most prolific scholar on Somali studies in the English language. No one has written more than you have on a wider range of topics.

IL: Perhaps not, but that's the way things have worked out.

CG: I remember you once said something to the effect that "when it comes to explaining who I am or what I have become, the Somalis have a lot to answer for."

IL: Oh yes, I did say something like that.

CG: Could you elaborate on that? What did you mean by that?

IL: I was thinking originally in terms of becoming slightly more politically cynical or slightly more cynical about political activity. I had learned a little bit about politicking from the Somalis and, as a naïve apolitical person, had picked up a certain amount of techniques in politicking through my experience with Somali politicians, rural and urban. I think that's what I meant, and my experience of trying to have professionally successful relations with the general Somali public. You asked me earlier about incident that had occurred and one incident that I didn't mention was near Hargeisa. I went on a number of occasions to the tomb of Aw Barkhadle Yusuf. I went to try to get material about the history of Aw Barkhadle Yusuf and some idea about the importance of pilgrimage to him. And as you know, if you go there three times, it's equivalent to going to Mecca once, as it is also with Sheikh Huseyn in Southern Ethiopia. I went there three times and, on one of the occasions it must have actually been during the saint's memorial festival. There was a big crowd and, at one point, a man who was obviously in a somewhat ecstatic state appropriately enough, came brandishing a sword and appeared to be about to belabor me with this big, archaic sword. Fortunately for me, however, a number of other people intervened and some local Somali elders got hold of this man and restrained him. That was probably the most physically menacing experience I had.

Obviously I've had other experinces—with being stoned by children and things like that—which was a common experience of foreigners who toured around the bush where they were considered to be pagans (*gal*) and attacked by Somali youths. That often happened to those who traveled in the bush inside Somaliland or Somalia; although this did not happen in southern Somalia where people are quiet, passive, and much less aggressive. I remember being struck how the Rahanwin and Digil, with whom I spent several months on three occasions, where quiet and peaceful and, in comparison with their nomadic countrymen, remarkably pleasant and friendly on first contact. They used, sometimes, the attractive honorific expression "Aw," not only for true Islamic scholars, but also for people toward whom they wished to show some degree of respect. I remember being addressed flatteringly as "Aw Malin" by a number of these southern Somalis in villages where I was camping. It was touching to be fitted into the category of teacher, student teacher, Aw Malin. I never received such a greeting in the north that I can recall. Actually, some Westernized Somalis have been kind enough to refer to me as Malin, but that's a subsequent sophistication. This was a more traditional response.

CG: I remember that the Somalis gave a nickname, not necessarily a flattering nickname, to Reese whom they used to call "Kabba kabba" (someone with a stutter). Are you aware that they ever gave you a nickname or told you of a nickname for yourself?

IL: The nickname that I have heard in the north (there are probably lots that I haven't heard because they're abusive) was "Ferhan," which means cheerful or something like that.

CG: This takes me back to a point that I raised a little while ago. What do you think are the characteristics of a non-Somali that are perhaps important for getting on with Somalis? I often thought that one characteristic that a non-Somali should not have would be to be a taciturn, withdrawn person given the verbal nature of Somali culture and its poetry, and also one would need an interest in humor, which you and I share. You once told me you were interested in puns and the role of puns. Is that another little "open sesame" that you may have had but weren't aware of at the time, but that the Somalis noticed that made your own entry into the culture easier because you saw the lighter side of things? You were able to joke, or able to make puns?

IL: I don't think that northern Somalis are strongly interested in pun-type humor. Or at least, not in my experience. I was disappointed because, obviously, with a restricted Somali vocabulary as I had, there are still various possibilities for making puns, which, in my simple way, I hoped might be of interest or of amusement. But I honestly couldn't say that I could chronicle much success in this activity because I simply didn't find it. The kind of characters that get on with Somalis, I agree that a withdrawn character with a taciturn nature is not likely to get on very well with Somalis.

On the other hand, I think Somalis like people who are quite good at listening. I mean, they want to talk all the time and often they have a lot to say that is extremely interesting from different perspectives. But that requires somebody who is willing to listen, to pay attention, and to be patient, because it's nothing, as we both know, for Somalis to spend hours discoursing in a circular way on some theme, possibly avoiding the kernel that they're really interested in until the punch line comes. If you're temperamentally or professionally prepared to do this, then I think you are at some advantage in dealing with people who greatly value oral performance. I think humor is very important. I agree with you. But unfortunately I didn't find that the pun lines were, in my own limited experience, very successful. I think I discussed this with Goosh, and I don't think he had found any experience of a comparable interest in punning himself. But who knows? I'm really mainly talking about northern Somalis.

CG: Something you mentioned a little while ago struck me. You were saying how peaceful and quiet you found things in southern Somalia....

IL: This is how I found Rahanwin people between the rivers.

CG: ....people in southern Somalia, as opposed to this reputation of turbulence and truculence in the north. Your recollections of the 1950s and even the early 1960s seem to be rather exuberant and joyful in an optimistic, anticipatory time.

IL: Oh yes, definitely.

CG: Then things seemed to change, obviously. Your recollections of Somalia over the last twenty-five years became a very different sort. But ironically, it seems that it's in the north, relatively speaking, where there's less turbulence, less truculence (in terms of the 1980s and 1990s); while it was the south that became the most disturbed, most chaotic, the most violent.

IL: Yes. But it was natural that it would become the most chaotic and the most violent society. It wasn't the Rahanwin and Digil who were the most violent and turbulent. It was the people of nomadic origin, the Hawiye people and some of the Darod groups of the south, who did all these things which are seen to the outside world through the activities of so-called warlords. It is natural that it all happened in Mogadishu, or in the area around Mogadishu, the Benadir Coast, because that formerly was the seat of government, power, and access to resources, as you have pointed out, among others, to external monetary gain and aid of all sorts. The main channel for financial advantage and therefore power, weapons, and everything is the south, especially Mogadishu; whereas the north was mainly a place for exporting livestock, getting money and wealth through livestock. It wasn't a center of political power, except in a limited way in the brief period before the union of Somaliland and Somalia, and in the short history of the Somaliland Republic, which is in many ways exemplary. I think it's a lesson, a monument really, to what Somalis can achieve if they put their minds to it constructively. The same is true to a certain extent in the case of Puntland. Both these examples are remarkable and deserve all our support.

CG: As someone who spent his early research time in the British colonial part of Somalia, do you think the differential colonial legacy is still salient, now forty years after independence?

IL: Yes. I think Somalis will refer to these colonial differences, and attach a lot of importance to them, perhaps the more austere character of British rule compared to the less austere and more flamboyant character of Italian colonial rule, which in many respects was more superficial than the British one, which was more profound although limited in its scope. But I don't know really. There are elements in the two colonial legacies, which can be selectively pointed to and developed and which are of some influence in this sort of background thinking of Westernized Somalis. One has to remember that some major figures in the south had crucial political or administrative experience during the British military administration of Somalia, so there is a certain element of British influence in both areas. Different periods, but in both.

You mentioned Mohamed Abshir who was a police officer in the British police force of Somalia (the Somalia Gendarmerie) after the British military takeover of Somalia, after the defeat of the Italians. So was, of course, Mohamed Siyad Barre. He was actually the same rank, same period, same experience. But they were two incredibly different personalities. I remember Mohamed Abshir telling me that at one point they were asked to write essays on their picture of the ideal police officer and they produced, as you can imagine, totally different pictures.

CG: Can you elaborate on that?

IL: Well, Barre's one was, of course, highly despotic and he stressed the issue of maintaining order by force. Abshir, of course, was saying (well, I don't know if it's true or not), but Abshir's own account was more egalitarian, and with the emphasis on reaching consensus and so on with the public. Those are interesting facets of these two very different personalities, I think.

CG: You wrote this interesting article with a title that was sort of tongue in cheek, "Kim II Sung in Somalia," in which you shrewdly and critically delineated this configuration, this triage, this M.O.D. (see chapter three). Having written that as a strong criticism of Siyad's pattern of government, and given what you say in *Blood and Bone: The Call of Kinship in Somali society* (Red Sea Press, 1994) had you been there and had he listened to your advice, what would you have counseled Siyad as an alternative approach to this kind of trinity?

IL: I think it would just have been, as his own clansmen advised, to have spread the range of involvement in his administration in a less monopolistic fashion. Something simple like that. But he was clearly a despotic leader, dividing and ruling from a small clique power base, employing money, arms, and coercion outside that power base to maintain his rule. Obviously, he could have been a more popular figure if the power base had been widened to effectively include all the major groups in a way that was acceptable and that was not coupled with an authoritarian judicial system that was corrupt. If he had been a more democratic ruler in the style of, let's say, the ruler of Tanzania, things could have been different. He came into power, like so many military leaders, with a lot of public support initially, because people were fed up with the inefficiency as they saw it and the corruption in the previous government. So he had a very good launching pad but, unfortunately, he didn't develop that in a serious fashion.

CG: You don't think that given the strength of the "call of kinship" that, although he was despotic and authoritarian, wasn't he perhaps responding to that "call" himself in that sense?

IL: Well he was, given his despotic blueprint. He was responding to it in his way; in such a way as much as possible to conserve his power or even build it up further with sops to various other groups while relying primarily upon, and giving major benefits to, his own close kin and their clansmen. Any one-man ruler would have been likely to behave in that way in Somalia, because if somebody wasn't behaving in that way he wouldn't have been a one-man ruler. They would have wanted to have some serious power sharing.

CG: When you did the collaborative work with James Mayall on the Menu of Options on decentralized state structures with a group of LSE academics, both of you and the team explored decentralized forms of governance and suggested that such structures are required for progress toward reconstruction. What would you say to the possibility that, in light of political realities, history, and what has happened over the last forty years, the actual endpoint in Somali politics may not be the reconstruction of what had been there before, but that the endpoint itself is a decentralized rearrangement?

IL: Oh yes, indeed, I think that's the most likely scenario. I think probably we were using the phrase "reconstruction" in a general sense to mean restoration of some kind of popularly based civil state. We were not meaning reconstruction, in the sense of the literal rebuilding, of what existed before. I don't think that was at all our thinking. We were trying to make the obvious point, which any political scientist knows well, that a structure that starts off as a series of little autonomous, or semiautonomous units, can easily come together as some kind of federation if it wants to. And, after all, the Somali state, when it existed as a Somali state, was itself an amalgamation of two units. There isn't any structural reason why there should not be some federal organization, whether it is actually a state or whether it is something looser, an economic union, a postal union, or perhaps an airlines naval or fishing union—there are all kinds of possibilities, like the European Union. There are so many possible bases for collaboration between political units, short of forming a single centralized polity, which I don't see at all likely to happen in Somalia in the near future.

I don't see how it can happen. It could only happen, I think, if some external force was interested in recolonizing the country, which, of course, is most unlikely. That is an almost impossible scenario. The other possibility would be if one of the major warlords were to get such an advantage in resources, particularly arms, that he could realistically conquer the whole country and build up a new dynasty. That seems the only other internal possibility. But I think that is extremely unlikely now, fortunately.

CG: We're having this discussion in December 1999 and I've just returned from South Africa. In 1899, at the southern end of the continent, a critical war had broken out, the South African War. Today, it is being celebrated, acknowledged, and rewritten at length in South Africa. Similarly major events were taking place in Somaliland in 1899. But this year there is no acknowledgement, no commemoration, no discussion, no retrospective, no conference, nothing on the development of the Dervish period, or on Sayyid Mohamed Abdille Hassan. Obviously, with national institutions gone, there is no one to take the lead in that. How ironic as the century ends.

IL: Except that as you know very well, Sayyid Mohamed Abdille Hassan is a very controversial figure and it is interesting that, at least as far as I know, in Somalia hardly anybody regards him as a saint, whereas his various adversaries, his various Somali religious adversaries, a number of them, regard him as a devil. Of course, he attacked the cult of saints, so in a way it is consistent with his religious position that he is not regarded as a saint, generally speaking. On the other hand, it says something about the status of his movement in the national context of Somalia, doesn't it?

CG: What would be your assessment of him, now that you know how the twentieth century turned out for Somalis? Where does Sayyid Mohamed fit in as far as you are concerned? Still a protonationalist?

IL: He certainly provided a symbolic figure to which Somalis could refer as someone who heroically defied the might of the colonial powers in the whole area and produced his wonderful poetry, which moved people so strongly. I don't think he had any other concept of the destiny of his country except that of Somali independence. A sort of an isolationist nationalism or protonationalism, as you said a minute ago. You will remember that one of the main British accounts of the Dervish War ended with thoughts of how sad it was that it had all finished without generating a surge of sympathy for the Somalis. The uprising of the Mahdi in the Sudan compared with the uprising of Mohamed Abdille Hassan in Somaliland had very different consequencies. In the British-administered Sudan, a university was started, named after General Gordon (Gordon College), who of course was the British hero killed in the conflict. This became the British-supported University of Khartoum. No comparable, positive commemoration followed in the Somaliland Protectorate when The Sayyid eventually died and his forces evaporated. Various colonial officials have reminisced about that, making that comparison and regretting there wasn't an equivalent input of funds for positive educational purposes in Somaliland. Of course, the circumstances were very different in the two cases. Sudan was an important place at that time in colonial ideas, whereas Somaliland was not.

CG: She was a "Cinderella of empire," and when did the clock strike midnight for Cinderella, to continue the analogy? Was it in October, 1969? Or January 1991? Or was it in the spring of 1978?

IL: I think, unfortunately, it happened in 1969 because as soon as somebody with the character of Siyad Barre came to power, it was almost inevitable that everything that has happened, would happen, don't you think? It was not inevitable that he came to power, but given that he did come to power, and that he had the human characteristics and nature that he had, then more or less everything else followed, with certain other factors playing into it. Obviously, Ethiopia, Kenya, U.S. foreign policy, the Cold War, and so on all played a part. But essentially, it was really a one-man show, a man with a very autocratic model of government that eventually destroyed his country.

CG: I once wrote about it in a positive way, that I'm now slightly embarrassed about, in terms of various projects like sand dune stabilization, literacy, drought relief, and so forth in the 1970s, as a historian who could not anticipate 1980 or 1991. I think everything changed, fell apart, and the die was cast after the Ogaden War. That turned out to be a serious miscalculation.

IL: I agree with you about the Ogaden. But I don't think that was the point at which dictatorial rule began. Dictatorial rule began in 1969, not openly but slowly, and it built up momentum. But it was there then. I don't think it was something that was only invoked in the wake of the Ogaden War, to hold the place together.

CG: when did you begin to sense this yourself?

IL: I think it was quite obvious from the start in 1969. Certainly from the early 1970s. It was clear that there was already a tight political regime, and the Somalis weren't supposed to meet foreigners. It was tight police control, military police control, from shortly after Siyad Barre took power. I think most people imagine that there was a period of gradual decline, or that the whole thing declined much later. I think the seeds of decline were there then. Or at least the seeds of despotic rule were there, and the despotism that produced all this chaos with other external factors playing into it. Unfortunately, many of the warlords unconsciously, sometimes openly, refer to Siyad as a kind of role model. Ironically too, many poor Somalis now feel that they were better off with Siyad there. Because it was relatively orderly at various points in his regime, especially in the beginning.

CG: What would be your advice to an aspiring social anthropologist today who wanted to do research on the Somalis?

IL: The most accessible Somali communities to-day are obviously the refugee communities dotted around the world. Anyone who did any serious, empirically based, in-depth social anthropological research on them would be contributing to our understanding of the adaptability of Somali institutions, as well as of the Somali people, and also to the extent of radical social change taking place among them. This would be very useful and important documentation. That would be the most accessible, but also, as far as I know, the least studied in any depth. I can only think of one or two studies, at least in the United Kingdom, that I'm familiar with. Both are short term, and only one is really much good, in my opinion. The other possibility is to do research on Somali communities in areas of relative tranquility in the Somali region, in Somaliland for instance, possibly in the northeast, in the Puntland State, and perhaps in some Somali regions of Ethiopia.

There has been a lot of incidental research by staff of non governmental organizations and some research on peacemaking and reconciliation. I think the most impressive I have seen is that by Dr. Ahmed Yusuf Farah, the man who wrote the excellent field study of the production of myrrh and frankincense and its gum exports (*The Milk of the Boswellia Forest* E.P.O.S). He has done good work also for the European community and the United Nations, on local-level reconciliation activities where, again, he has made a serious empirical analysis (Chapter Six), not just the usual fly-by-night NGO account, which tends to be extremely superficial. He knew what he was talking about, as a trained Somali social anthropologist with in-depth field experience.

CG: He studied under you?

IL: Yes, I have to say I am partisan, naturally, because he got his Ph.D. in our department.

CG: We mentioned earlier your collection of essays, *Arguments with Ethnography*. What would be your advice to a newcomer to social antrhropology in light of the kind of analysis of ethnography and anthropology that is contained in that book?

IL: One of the most disappointing things to me, in the work by people who present themselves as social scientists interested in Somalia and Somali studies, with some remarkable exceptions is their superficiality and lack of any serious empirical underpinning, with adequate command of the Somali language, but above all, the absence of serious in-depth empirical research. As far as anthropological research is concerned, there is Ahmed Yusuf Farah, whose work is entirely exemplary. He is not somebody who had any ambition to be a well-known theoretical anthropologist. He was essentially a modest man with a field-working ambition to do serious professional research, which he did very well in my opinion. It was a terrible blow to Somali studies when he died in Kenya in 2002.

Then we have two other Somalis who have done impressive work. One of them is A.G. Mirreh whose work is, unfortunately, in German, who wrote an excellent German Ph.D. thesis in the 1970s, based on research in what is now Somaliland. That work updated some of what I've done and examined how changes have occurred relating to further economic commercialization. It is a very good study, although, it's difficult for me because I don't read German with any fluency at all. I wish it was translated into English because, as far as I know, it is the only serious professionally qualified, empirical social antrrhropological research on the northwestern Somali hinterland that I've seen by a Somali in that period. More recently, Marcel Jama, a Somali who trained in France, has done an extremely interesting piece of research for his French Ph.D. on the border region close to Borama. This is a micro political history of two or three different groups and how they've responded to incorporation into states, Ethiopia and Somalia, at different periods, and what they've done since then. That is a very interesting piece of work. Apart from that, I am not aware of any qualified Somali social anthropologists who have worked in the area. Perhaps there are some I don't know about.

CG: Let me ask you a loaded question and put the nitro on the table and you can add the glycerin if you wish. When I spoke to you about coming to do this interview you were candid in saying that you were not impressed by a considerable amount of Somali studies scholarship that has come from American universities, in a number of different fields, over the last twenty years. Could you elaborate on that and tell me what you think is going on, or what is at the root of the lower quality of the research? Exactly what is it that you find, as the doyen of Somali studies, so unacceptable?

IL: What I have personally in mind is the disappointing quality of many publications on Somali themes these days. Language studies are different and it is obviously easier to study the Somali language. You don't have to go to Somalia. You can study linguistics and the structure of Somali wherever there are Somali-speakers. But for the rest, in the social sciences, with the exception of serious historical research by, for instance Said Samatar, Mohamed Haji Mukhtar, Lee Cassanelli, and yourself, there is very little published political history or straightforward history based on direct observation. Quite recently, however, at least one young historian (Jama Mohamed) has begun producing extremely interesting work of high scholarly quality.

We have a lot of superficial little studies by people going and asking this or that, or making a little study in a market, but we do not have extended in-depth studies of how people behave over a period of time, with the student who is writing the account spending a long time in the field and interacting with his informants through the Somali language. (Here an ideal model might be Virginia Luling with her research see below.) An unfortunate idea has also grown up, that if somebody is a Somali who happens to be Western-educated, that in itself makes them an authority on Somali culture and society.

Well, it does with reference to language automatically, obviously, if they speak Somali fluently (and they don't always, of course). But it certainly does not automatically make them an accredited authority on other aspects of social science subjects. For instance, I'm a British citizen. I live in London, but I am certainly not a reliable informant on the British constitution, nor do I know anything particularly about politics, except little bits that I've dabbled in. There are vast areas of British history of which I'm totally ignorant; and I would be a poor informant on most social science subjects if I was encountered by some exotic, foreign anthropologist who wished to use me as an informant. So the notion that, simply because you happen to be a native of a particular culture, that qualifies you as an expert on that culture, is of course nonsense. I think this has to be understood more deeply than is currently assumed in a lot of the writings on Somalia. The mere citation of a Somali source doesn't necessarily convey authority. The citation of a Somali source doesn't convey authority unless the Somali concerned is a serious professional research worker who can speak convincingly by reference to his research base. The problem is the lack of a serious research base outside linguistics, where I am, as I said before, not competent to judge.

Then, of course, there are non-Somali social anthropologists who have produced works of importance and distinction, based on detailed firsthand research with an excellent command of spoken Somali: Virginia Luling on the Geledi sultanate (*Somali Sultanate*, Haan, 2002); and Bernhard Helander whose fieldwork in the Bay region is ethnographically as well as theoretically exciting and whose major book was, alas, published posthumously (*The slaughtered Camel*, Uppsala, Studies in Cultural anthropology, 2003). There is also the interesting work of Jan Haakonsen which includes command of spoken Somali. I cannot think of any comparably significant work by American anthropologists, few of whom in any case carried out extended fieldwork in Somalia. Sadly, such U.S. anthropological interest as there has been in Somalia has coincided with the most negative influences in anthropology, generally postmodernism and what Tom Wolfe calls "rococo Marxism." Unfortunately, these baneful tendencies have, of course, strongly affected all the social sciences, including history, and have all too obviously influenced many of those working in Somali studies.

It is disappointing that the two latest works that are presented by people who call themselves social anthropologists relating to Somalia are, in my opinion, of little value.

CG: Can you say which ones they are?

IL: Yes, of course. Catherine Besteman (*Unraveling Somalia*, Philadelphia, University of Pennsylvania Press, 1999) is one of these people. Not a work of impressive scholarship. It is not enough to produce a bibliography with a lot of names in it. It is necessary to read the material and digest it, as you know very well yourself. It is necessary to be able to control the Italian literature as well as literature in English or French. Very little in German, but some. There are few people who have taken this step. Unfortunately there are a number of books that illustrate the need, the publish or be damned syndrome, to publish in order to advance a person's career professionally but without serious scholarship. I personally have strong reactions to the way in which Somali culture and Somali social institutions can be exploited. As an anthropologist, you see, I regard social anthropology as an intrinsically exploitative activity.

CG: What do you mean by that?

IL: One is using another people's culture for the purpose of one's own research interest, one's own intellectual research interest, for the purpose of one's career, for, often enough, one's whole livelihood, as in my case. I live off the insights and information that I've collected over the years from Somalis in Somalia. I'm very conscious of this issue of exploiting other people's intellectual property.

CG: Whom did you consider your primary audience? Was it non-Somali English speakers? Or was it English-speaking Somalis?

IL: No, it was non-Somali English speakers at first, obviously. But I always hoped it would reach an English-speaking Somali audience as it gradually has done; some of it anyway, which is a source of pleasure. I still regard the anthropological endeavor as intrinsically exploitative. If you haven't got some exotic community to study you can't be an anthropologist. If you want to study your own community, you have to exoticize it in some sense. With historians, it doesn't really matter because with your subject matter, they are dead, the people you study. Or a lot of them, by definition. You are studying the past. And that is also exploitative but you know, it doesn't matter.

CG: The subjectivity and the essential nature of history come alive when we study others. Some African historians say that we realize ourselves most fully when we engage with others who are unlike ourselves. Let us assume that is true for the sake of our exchange. What have you learned from Somalis that has enabled you to learn more about yourself?

IL: You touched on that when you asked me about the question of learning about political activity or learning or sensitizing oneself toward a political dimension of people's interactions. We dealt with that earlier when I think you raised that as a question. You quoted something I had said about losing my political innocence or something like that.

CG: About Somalis being responsible for who you are.

IL: I mean in that one becomes more aware of one's own ethnocentricities by studying other people's ethnocentricities. In a sense, I think that might be one of the basic justifications for teaching social anthropology as a subject at university level:

to make people more aware of their ethnocentric assumptions and the extent to which they have ethnocentric assumptions by confronting other people's ethnocentric assumptions; thereby, coming to realize that the world is a multicultural place, where there are a wide variety of traditions and religions, and that if you want to understand the interactions of the bearers of these different cultures, you have to know a bit about their backgrounds. It is an obviously simplistic point, but I think that might be one of the main justifications for teaching social anthropology as a university subject. In my lectures I used to quote one of the Gulf oil sheikhs saying something along those lines when his daughter studied social anthropology. I rather agree with that.

When I argue that anthropology is exploitive, this is not a position that is well received by my colleagues who think that they are not exploitive people and who regard themselves as being always on the side of the angels, by definition, whoever the angels may be, despite the fact that cosmologies change and angels change. I feel that if one recognizes that one is, in a way, indebted to a foreign culture, as I feel I am for my livelihood, then the least I can do is to try to present that culture accurately and to approach it with appropriate scholarly respect. The kind of standards that apply if you were doing French studies, Italian studies, or German studies should apply also when you are doing Third World studies.

Unfortunately, a lot of people make their careers out of slipshod, superficial work in the Third World, which just becomes a plank in their Ph.D. construction and their career development. I am not saying that wasn't the case with me, but at least I'm aware of that and I have tried to honor and respect the culture and social institutions of the people I'm interested in. It is necessary to treat them with appropriate seriousness, and not to imagine that by spending a few months among them without speaking their language and without seriously understanding them, or the literature that relates to them, one could write something significant about them. That is really my position.

CG: This is odd. It sounds like I am hearing loan Lewis criticize loan Lewis, and Geshekter comes to defend loan Lewis. Are you saying that the way social anthropology was taught, the skills that were developed, and the career that you exemplify is not the way that social anthropology is now encouraged in the United States, in the sense that you concentrated for over forty years on a particular areas of the world, drawing generalizations and other interests from it? Are you suggesting that maybe Somalia is just a kind of ticket on the way to someplace else?

IL: It is for a great many people who produce accounts of it. That would be fine if it was a ticket based on serious, original, in-depth research. This is really a plea for serious, empirically grounded field research in which people spend several years, or over a year and a half at least, in a community where the researcher learns about how the local people really live, through learning the language, learning their culture, and their political culture, as well as culture in a more esthetic sense. The researcher is also required to read the appropriate literature in depth. But those who simply light on Somali culture like a mosquito and try and suck its blood for a bit, and then push off somewhere else, those people, unless they happen to be brilliant, which most of them are not, have, I think, nothing to contribute to scholarship.

CG: It sounds like you have a gloomy and despondent assessment of the current state of Somali studies scholarship, with a few exceptions?

IL: Well I do, and it is not limited to Somali studies. It is reinforced by the so-called postmodernist tendency, which I think is complete nonsense, because it encourages superficiality, ignorance, and the notion that anything goes. I am not interested in the ethnocentric thoughts of some half-baked young person who is trying to make a career in a university. I am interested in the thoughts and ideas that a particular foreign community that I might be studying has. I am not interested in the opinions of some ignorant person from the First World who is simply engaging in superficial, ethnocentric ego trips.

CG: There was a book that I've read reviews of, that seems impressive and I hope you're not going to deflate my balloon on this. It was by Sharon Hutchinson, called (*Nuer Dilemmas: Coping With Money, War and the State*).

IL: I haven't read it I am afraid.

CG: It won the Talbot Prize from the Royal Anthropological Institute.

IL: Yes, I know. I haven't actually read that book.

CG: It kind of situates Evans-Pritchard's work.

IL: I've read some of her articles. In fact, I've been involved in a debate with her on her interpretations of Nuer marriage. I think she is probably very good. There are a number of impressive younger Africanist anthropologists but, unfortunately, the general ethos is very negative and ethnocentric from my point of view. It is interesting how the themes of slavery and race seem to haunt the minds of Americans, which one understands. The extent to which this is exported, ethnocentrically, around the globe is not surprising, but is not conductive to serious, accurate scholarship, which would look at the local conditions and try and appraise them with an open objective eye, without the ethnocentric assumptions of current American society and politics. But as soon as people look for race and slavery everywhere, it's just pointless.
CG: What is Ioan Lewis' favorite book?

IL: In what subject?

CG: In the world.

IL: That is a difficult question to answer because I read a lot of novelists, which I like very much. Obviously, I like classical novels like Conrad's. But I think I would require notice of that question, to tell you the truth. I mean there are so many novelists that I like; my favorite novels tend to be those with a cross-cultural flavor, for example, the works of V.S. Naipaul, Ruth Prawer Jhabvala, Gabriel Garcia Marquez, Kazuo Ishiguro, Vikram Seth, and others. I also enjoy Hilary Mantel and Alison Lurie. There are a number of Canadian novelists I like very much.

CG: Do you like Margaret Lawrence?

IL: Yes, I knew her when she lived in England. She would not be at the top of my list but certainly I do like her. She is one of the more interesting connections with the Somali scene, isn't she? I used to know quite well Barbara Pym, who edited my *Peoples of the Horn of Africa* and *A Pastoral Democracy* and published both.

CG: Any comments on Nuruddin Farah as a novelist?

IL: I'm afraid I find him a baffling novelist and quite disappointing, because I have a rather old-fashioned notion of what a novel is. There should be a clear story line in it and I find his recent writing indecipherable. I don't feel myself at all moved or interested by it.

CG: A number of us have admitted to one another, quite independently, that we've never finished his novels.
IL: I finished one or two of his earlier books; but only the early ones. I know a bit about the way he works because he spent a long time in London. I've seen him sitting writing with a big dictionary beside him, also with a glossary of words. He would think of a straightforward way of saying

something, and then would say "How could I make that more elaborate?" Like Henry James, really, almost. He seems to be interested in complexifying his language. Whereas, as a speaker I think he is very gifted. I've listened to excellent speeches he's given, that I've enjoyed. I've also listened to quite interesting radio broadcasts he has made, but I find his writing very disappointing.

CG: What are your three most significant accomplishments in the field of Somali studies? What is your favorite book, or favorite project, that you've completed on Somalia? Again, without any forewarning.

IL: I Suppose (having just recently reread it) I am fond of my first fieldwork-based book, *A Pastoral Democracy*. Yes, I quite like that, although I think I could rewrite it now in a linguistically slightly different way, perhaps. I liked the poetry book which Goosh and I wrote *An Introduction to Somali Poetry* (Oxford: Oxford University Press, 1964). I suppose that I also like the little book, *Saints and Somalis* (Red Sea Press, 1998), although it is really a collection of essays, written some time ago.

CG: I agree with you. I like the book you wrote with Goosh. Some of us often wondered why the two of you, because you were always twinned with each other and mistaken sometimes as you admit, hadn't done more together or written more things together.

IL: I Suppose it was just a question really of time and opportunity and he was a linguist and I was an anthropologist, pursuing different careers.

CG: Somali society is in the thick of a violent fragmentation and physical and mental exhaustion. Do you see any practical solutions to the predicament?

IL: No, I only see solutions that are built on local experience, that are happening slowly at a local level. I don't see any way in which the situation can be facilitated or remedied globally by some vast external action except, as we said before, by recolonization, which is not going to happen. Obviously, I'm very sad Somalia has disintegrated, like anyone would naturally be very sad. I can see how awful it is for Somalis to turn up and find themselves exiles and asylum seekers in foreign countries. I'm going to court tomorrow about an asylum seeker and their situation is, in many respects, tragic. Although their basic life circumstances as refugees may be not so bad, having lost a country, and that part of their ethnic identity tied up with their country, which they once belonged to, is a tragic thing, and I feel very sorry for these people who have lost everything, not through their own fault after all.

It is difficult to know to what extent we could attribute the chaos in Somalia to many of the individuals who turn up as asylum seekers, unless they happen to be ex-warlords, as some of them are in Britain. Or members of military gangs or parts of the power structure of Siyad Barre, as some of them tend to be. But apart from that, I don't see how one can implicate other ordinary people in the factors that caused Somalia to collapse.

CG: If I asked you what you think were the key factors aside from the despotism and the tyranny of Siyad, would there be institutional factors that you would include as well?

IL: Oh, yes. I think it's extremely difficult to create a centralized state out of Somali political tradition, which is uncentralized. Not just decentralized, but uncentralized, and which isn't only a matter of loyalties to the centre versus to locality; it is a matter of shifting identities the whole time. I mean the Somali system is so flexible, it is very difficult to pursue a coherent political path. And very difficult to have stable political consensus, except at a local level of grouping. That, it seems to me, is the basic kind of problem in the background of Somali political experience. If you compare it, it is true that other African countries with a tradition of political centralization haven't fared much better. But nevertheless, the factors that would have to be somehow overcome, controlled, or accommodated are really formidable in Somalia by any standards.

CG: The paper that I presented in Perth and in Toronto, which I'm fleshing into an extended essay on the meaning of the twentieth century to Somalis, tries to change some basic key dates. I treat 1896 as the starting point for twentieth century Somalia because of Adowa, followed by the treaty of 1897. I try to interpret the past century in terms of the dispersal of power, concentration of power, and redispersal of power, and use that as an overarching theme. The other thing is to globalize a regional history. It is impossible to understand the fate that Somalis experienced without understanding the nature of the Cold War and how it fitted into different....

IL: And the way in which they utilized it.

CG: And manipulated it.

IL: I find irritating the idea that the Somalis were simply victims, who, through all kinds of external pressures, acted as they did, which is current in much of political science writing about Africa.

CG: Your writing clearly states from the beginning the Somali initiative in which Somalis have a tradition of trying to engage people in their own political disputes.

IL: Exactly. I think we are both aware of that and have experienced it. Obviously, the fact that you have global polarization creates an opportunity, which Somalis tried to exploit in various ways with, unfortunately, an overall lack of success in the long term. Perhaps the Somali piracy business is an exception!

Index